D1206264

MUSICAL BACKGROUNDS FOR
ENGLISH LITERATURE

Musical Backgrounds for English Literature: 1580–1650

by

GRETCHEN LUDKE FINNEY

RUTGERS UNIVERSITY PRESS
New Brunswick, New Jersey

Library of Congress Catalogue Number: 61-12407

The articles in this volume which were first published elsewhere are here reprinted or quoted by permission of the original publishers. "A World of Instruments" was published in *E.L.H.: A Journal of English Literary History*, XX (1953), 87-114; "Music: A Book of Knowledge," in *Studies in the Renaissance*, VI (1959), 36-63. The two chapters, "Music and Ecstasy: A Religious Controversy" and "Music and Neoplatonic Love," use material, considerably expanded, from two articles, "Ecstasy and Music in Seventeenth-Century England" and "'Organical Musick' and Ecstasy," published in the *Journal of the History of Ideas*, VIII, Nos. 2 and 3 (1947), 153-186 and 273-292. "Music: The Breath of Life," appeared in the *Centennial Review of Arts and Science*, Spring 1960, 179-205; *Comus: dramma per musica*, in *Studies in Philology*, XXXVII, No. 3 (1940), 482-500; "A Musical Background for 'Lycidas'" in the *Huntington Library Quarterly*, XV, No. 4 (1952), 325-349; "Chorus in *Samson Agonistes*" in *PMLA: Publications of the Modern Language Association of America*, LVIII, No. 3 (1943), 649-664.

This book was manufactured with the assistance of a grant from the Ford Foundation

Made and printed in Great Britain by William Clowes and Sons, Limited, London and Beccles

To Marjorie Hope Nicolson

Contents

Preface

THIS study is concerned only secondarily with techniques of composition or of performing music—with modes or rhythms or meanings of technical terms. It is in no sense a history of music or of musical instruments. The "music" implied in the title, *Musical Backgrounds*, might be called "speculative music," or better—to use baroque terminology —*musica theorica.* This kind of theory had nothing to do with composition of music, *musica poetica* (*poetica* referring to the creation of music). It had nothing to do with musical performance—methods of singing or playing—*musica practica.* Speculative music dealt with the nature of sound, with the position and function of music in the entire system of human knowledge, and with music's usefulness to man. It included, finally, metaphysical speculations on the harmony of the universe, for it was widely taught in the Renaissance that the whole cosmos operates according to musical law.[1]

Musical speculation had effect, without doubt, on musical composition, as Manfred Bukofzer has pointed out,[2] but that relationship will be touched on here in only the most general way. The reflection of these ideas in literature is the primary concern of this study. Techniques of composition and performance also made their contribution to literary expression, but their influence is more easily discernible and has been more often discussed. The speculative aspects of music, as will be shown, provided a background for philosophical ideas and poetic imagery, without which neither can be completely understood or appreciated.

The metaphysical notions involved drew largely upon the theory, attributed to Pythagoras, of a universal harmony or proportion of which sensuously perceived music is but one manifestation. Stars and planets, moving in their spheres, were believed to be ordered harmoniously according to numerical ratios like those in man-made music. Further, there was analogy between macrocosm, the great world, and microcosm, the little world that is man: souls and bodies of men, it was taught, function also according to "harmonical" law. Boethius, whose *De institutione musica* furnished the authoritative theoretical text for more than a thousand years, crystallized this scheme of cosmic musical parallels by designating three kinds of music: *musica mundana,* which might be music of the spheres or concord of elements or seasons; *musica humana,* "which unites the incorporeal activity of the reason with the body"; and *musica instrumentalis,* the music of the voices or instruments man hears. Each level of music resembled the others.[3]

This theory assumed that underlying the changeable qualities in music there is something unchanging and immutable. "The harmony doth still remaine," wrote William Martyn in *Youths Instruction*, "though the notes and tunes and songs be oftentimes changed."[4] As Christian Huygens wrote much later in *The Celestial Worlds Discover'd,* arguing that music on other planets must be the same as ours, "It's the same with Musick as with Geometry, it's every where immutably the same, and always will be so. For all Harmony consists in Concord, and Concord is all the World over fixt according to the same invariable measure and proportion."[5]

The philosopher could admire this basic harmony in any music, be it "popular" music or that heard in church. "Even that vulgar and Tavern-Musicke . . . strikes in me a deep fit of devotion, and a profound contemplation of the First Composer," wrote Sir Thomas Browne.[6]

It followed, then, that if man could understand audible music and the instruments that produced it, he could understand all the music that was not heard, that if the laws of music were immutable, its effects could be determined. The immutable in music drew man's thoughts to God or made him one with all harmony. Guercino's painting of Saint Bruno, lifting his face from cross and prayer book to see a vision of the Madonna, was paralleled in Raphael's "Ecstasy of Saint Cecilia," in which the latter, portable organ in hand, viol at her feet, gazes raptly at a choir of angels. Hence Milton could write in "Il Penseroso" of "pealing Organ" and "full voic'd Quire" that, in "Service high, and Anthems cleer," brought "all Heav'n" before his eyes. Elizabethan writers described the entire universe as an aggregate of sounding musical instruments. They learned lessons about themselves, their society, their world, from the music and the instruments of man. They imagined themselves carried away by music as in an ecstasy, or restored to life by the infused soul of harmony.

Long before these metaphysical notions had waned, however, other theories of the nature of sound and of its effects were gaining ascendance. Puritans attacked the belief in musical ecstasy. Neoplatonists questioned the beauty of music. Musical humanists, especially in Italy, denied that harmonious proportion is determined by natural law and argued that words alone give meaning to music. Scientists reasoned that music is nothing more than material motion, that its effects are purely mechanical.

The different trends overlapped chronologically, each affecting the other. Many a philosopher was put to it to know which to follow and ended in confusion and contradiction. Even when scientific experiment and reasoning had finally won the field and explained away the "mystery" of music, the old belief in its divine virtue persisted, as indeed it does today, for man still feels in music something above and beyond himself that fills a need not satisfied by science.

The imagery that resulted from speculative ideas about music is rich and varied, sometimes purely metaphorical, at other times literal, again revealing half-belief. Metaphorical or not, it is more than mere poetic adornment. By their use of musical imagery writers reveal many secrets—beliefs, prejudices, even personalities. The image is a rule by which one can gauge the changing temper of an age.

Milton is inevitably the major writer who must be considered in any study of Renaissance music in England. Although he lived on into the Restoration period, his poems, even his late ones, reflect interest in earlier metaphysical ideas about music, ideas transformed by genius into the broad meaning of great poetry. He was influenced, too, by ideas of the counter-Renaissance, less by their scientific than by their humanistic aspects, and especially by Italian musical theories and practice, which, it seems to the present writer, were a determining factor in the composition of *Comus* and "Lycidas," and which he acknowledged in the prefatory lines to *Samson Agonistes*.

It may be well at this point to define the geographical and chronological emphasis of this volume. It is concerned primarily with English literature, using the classical and Continental writers less for themselves than as a background for what happened in England. The dates 1580–1650 merely imply the period to which major attention is given. Both the metaphysical and the scientific notions of that period had roots in earlier times; metaphysical speculation persisted throughout the century while scientific theories were becoming established. Many of the references to literary works—to Sir Thomas Elyot's *The Governour*, on the one hand, and to Milton's late poems, on the other—fall before or after this time span. But during these years, when metaphysical ideas still had validity and scientific ones were already gaining momentum, when both music and literature flourished, the old and the new met with dramatic impact.

I wish to express my appreciation to the editors and publishers of the various periodicals in which these essays originally appeared: the Johns Hopkins Press, the Renaissance Society, the *Journal of the History of Ideas* at the College of the City of New York, Michigan State University Press, the University of North Carolina Press, the Trustees of the Henry E. Huntington Library, and the Modern Language Association of America. I wish to thank the many libraries in which I have been able to work—especially the Library of Congress, the New York Public Library, the Bodleian Library at Oxford, the British Museum, and, most of all, the Henry E. Huntington Library, not only for opportunity to use its invaluable collections and for a grant-in-aid, but for the unfailing consideration of its staff. To my husband, Ross Lee Finney, for constant encouragement and advice, I am deeply grateful. It remains to acknowledge my indebtedness to Professor Marjorie Nicolson, without whose inspiration these studies would not have been attempted, and without whose confidence and criticism they could never have been completed.

CHAPTER I

A World of Instruments

THE extent to which the conception of a musical universe pervaded sixteenth- and seventeenth-century thought is nowhere more obvious than in the prevalence of the charming poetic image that pictures the world and everything in it as a musical instrument, an image entirely logical in the light of contemporary conviction. In a universe where "God is a God of harmony," where the elements join in chorus, where microcosmic man is likewise "all o're Harmonie/ Storehouse of all Proportions," where "All things that Are . . . Are Musicall,"[1] whatever physical implement manifests this universal harmony is obviously a musical instrument, both because of the literal meaning of the words and because of consciously intended analogy. The emphasis might be metaphorical, as in Shakespeare's lines:

> And now my tongue's use is to me no more
> Than an unstringed viol or a harp.

It might be uniquely literal, as in Du Bartas:

> Our Tongue's the Bowe, our Teeth the trembling Strings,
> Our hollow Nostrils (with their double vent)
> The hollow Belly of the Instrument.[2]

But the comparison of body or universe to lute or viol was usually elucidation rather than ornament; it explained the concord of the heavens, the relation of soul both to world harmony and to body, the response of people to each other, the functioning of man's physical organs. It brought the divine within human comprehension and glorified the earthly by making it part of a cosmic scheme.

"God made this whole world," wrote John Donne, "in

such an uniformity, such a correspondency, such a concinnity of parts, as that it was an Instrument, perfectly in tune."[3] The spheres were a "nine-stringed heaven," paralleled in the small instrument, man. "The whole world," wrote John Dee, "is, as it were, a lyre . . . and man too, for all is analogous."[4] For Edward Benlowes in *Theophila*, "sweet Religion strings, and tunes, and skrues/The Souls Theorb'."[5] Nature, too, shares in this harmony, for trees supply the instruments man plays: the lute once grew with its "green mother in some shady grove," and

> When Orpheus strook th'inspired Lute,
> The Trees danc'd round, and understood
> By Sympathy the Voice of Wood.

The nightingale "is truly she of al wind-instruments, that carries the silver bel away."[6]

This aggregate of instruments can scarcely be called an orchestra, for the word "orchestra" to the Elizabethan was more closely connected with dance than with instrumental ensemble; Sir John Davies' poem, *Orchestra*, was "A Poeme of Dauncing." "Symphony" referred to effect rather than to means; "th'Angelike symphony" was "perfect concord," vocal as well as instrumental. Even "consort" is not entirely descriptive, for the emphasis of the early seventeenth-century metaphor is usually not on harmonious ensemble or integration; the symphony of this world's music had been broken by "disproportion'd sin." Most often each of man's "organs," each lute, harp, or viol, made its own music, which became one with the music of the universe only when man took his part at last in the more perfect harmony of heaven.

The Elizabethan, in his conception of the universe as an aggregate of sounding instruments, did not lose sight of other imagery by which unity of all life and matter was described —the picturing of the universe as a great chain, each part, from low to high, from earth to heaven, linked to others in predestined order, or as a series of corresponding planes, similar but varying in degree of perfection, or of all creation turning in the rhythmic motion of dance. The harmony of the world *was* the "Golden Chain that unites Heaven and Earth," in the phrase used by Thomas Tryon a century later, in his *Pythagoras, his Mystick Philosophy reviv'd* (1691). More than one music-theorist and philosopher was aware of three kinds of music to correspond to three levels of existence —music of the universe, music of man's soul and body, music of instruments. Motion, dance, and music were inseparable. Yet the literalness of parallel between the body of man, his works, his universe, and the musical instruments that he knew and heard, created an independent imagery that pervaded both poetical and philosophical writing for many years.

I

Such a conception roots obviously in the animistic philosophy of the early Greeks that gave to the universe and everything in it soul, vitality, rhythmic motion; in the Pythagorean and Platonic conceptions of universal harmony and proportion; and in the resulting relationship of microcosm to macrocosm.[7] All life's relationships were absorbed into this theory of harmony; the small world was an image of the great, man's music a copy of the universal, his instruments a suggestion of heaven's. All order, motion, unity were explained in terms of the musical theory and the instruments that men knew.

Through actual experiment with musical strings Pythagoras or his followers discovered the theory, still accepted, of the relation of pitch to the length of the string. On the basis of this relationship of distance to pitch, not only musical but planetary intervals were explained. The spheres thus became a cosmic lyre, the music of which Pythagoras was purported to have heard and which he is said to have imitated in the musical instrument called a "heptachord." Its seven strings were thought to parallel the number of the spheres and to reveal to man the music that only few could hear.[8]

Although Aristotle denied the existence of the music of the

spheres, many philosophers through the centuries affirmed it. Plutarch did not completely agree with those who held the theory that the planets compose a macrocosmic stringed instrument—with those "who fancy the earth to be in the lowest string of the harp"—but he did defend the only slightly less literal theory that distances and speeds of spheres and stars have proportions like those of musical instruments.[9] "Heaven is the archetype of musical instruments," wrote the Hellenistic Hebrew philosopher, Philo. Among the Romans, Cicero and Quintilian echoed the idea, and Censorinus joined them with "Dorylaus has written that the universe is the musical instrument of God."[10]

Having postulated a macrocosmic instrument, a world-lyre, modeled on the instruments he knew, the philosopher then saw everything in the universe as exhibiting similar musical characteristics. Man's world, his body, his natural environment, were also like musical instruments and could produce a harmony similar both to that of the universe and to that of heard music. Plotinus, having explained that the stars "are like the strings of a lyre which, being struck in tune, sing a melody in some natural scale," then imagined the world of man responding to the heavens in the same way that a musical instrument sounds when another, similarly tuned, is struck.[11] Harmony in a state, wrote Cicero in his *Republic*, is like that of "harps and flutes."[12]

Man's body, too, was compared to a musical instrument, and considerable argument ensued as to whether soul is harmony produced by the tuning up of the natural body (as Aristoxenus was credited with saying) or whether soul is like a musician who plays upon body. If the soul is a harmony of the elements of the body, argued the Pythagorean philosopher, Simmias, in Plato's *Phaedo*, then "it is clear that when the body is too much relaxed or is too tightly strung by diseases or other ills, the soul must of necessity perish, no matter how divine it is."[13] Such a conclusion was, of course, unacceptable. Plotinus, arguing the same issue later, thought the soul more like the musician "who produces the accord upon the strings" than like the subsequent music.[14] However it was interpreted, the image was used for centuries to explain in one way or another the relation of soul to body.

Inclusion of inanimate nature in this musical scheme was inherent in the Pythagorean philosophy of universal harmony. Plutarch explained that by virtue of harmony and number in the universe, "The slightest and meanest of insensible substances, even stocks and stones, the rinds of trees, and sometimes even the rennets of beasts by various mixtures, compositions, and temperatures, may . . . be wrought and hollowed to send forth pleasing musical sounds."[15]

To see musical instruments in trees and beasts, however, needed no philosophy. The earliest drums and horns were less man-made than provided by nature; the pipe, the "vocall" reed, simply grew; a stiff blade of grass had only to be blown upon by man or wind to make sound; gourd or hollow tree trunk became a drum. The animal world provided essential parts of instruments; the horn of a sheep might become a musical horn, his skin or gut a string or drumhead.

Patristic writers absorbed from the Greeks the conception of a universal harmony that was shared by man. St. Gregory of Nyssa likened the melody of the universe to that of stringed instrument: "Just as an instrument of various strings when struck produces concordance, so does the universe produce harmonious melody."[16] Clement of Alexandria was both more comprehensive and more explicit, for to him the universe was a "many-voiced instrument." Man is a pipe "by reason of the breath of God," and Christ, too, since man was made in His image. But man-made instruments, which were associated with pagan worship, "those lifeless instruments of lyre and harp," did not share in the cosmic glory. However, while the condemnation of musical instruments denied their Pythagorean significance and virtue, this very denial gave impetus to the conception of man as musical instrument, for man must himself be the organ of God's praise. Man's body, his institutions, his tenets, his laws, were God-created instruments. How superior, wrote Clement, is the new song of Christ to that of Orpheus:

He who sprang from David . . . scorned those lifeless instruments of lyre and harp. By the power of the Holy Spirit He arranged in harmonious order this great world, yes, and the little world of man too, body and soul together; and on this many-voiced instrument of the universe He makes music to God, and sings to the human instrument. "For thou art my harp and my pipe and my temple"—my harp by reason of the music, my pipe by reason of the breath of the Spirit, my temple by reason of the Word. . . . The Lord fashioned man a beautiful, breathing instrument, after His own image; and assuredly He himself is an all-harmonious instrument of God, melodious and holy.[17]

The musical instruments recommended in the Old Testament were interpreted by patristic writers and by later churchmen, too, merely as symbols. They might symbolize Christian virtues and faith: the trumpet stood for "the efficacy of the Word of God; the tympanon . . . the destruction of lust; cymbals the eager soul enamored of Christ."[18] To worship God with the ten-stringed psaltery ("in psalterio decachordo") meant to worship Him through faith in the Ten Commandments. But, as often happens, symbol and object came to be identified. Since the psaltery was a symbol of the Ten Commandments, the Commandments had ten strings. Organized laws and tenets became musical instruments. "Witness the decachord of the Ten Commandments," cried the Roman statesman-monastic, Cassiodorus, in defense of music.[19] The instruments of the Old Testament stood also for the parts of man's body, for the tongue or heart, which were symbols in turn for devout personal worship of God. And again the two sets of symbols became identified: instrument signified tongue; the tongue was thereby an instrument. Clement wrote,

"Praise Him on the Psaltery"; for the tongue is the psaltery of the Lord. "And praise Him on the lyre." By the lyre is meant the mouth struck by the Spirit, as it were by a plectrum. . . . "Praise Him on the chords (strings) and organ." Our body He calls an organ, and its nerves are the strings, by which it has received harmonious tension, and when struck by the Spirit, it gives forth human voices.[20]

Clement could reason in Pythagorean vein—"By the power of the Holy Spirit He arranged in harmonious order this great world, yes, and the little world of man . . . on this many-voiced instrument of the universe He makes music to God, and sings to the human instrument"—or he might reason symbolically, looking toward New Testament canon—" 'Praise Him on the Psaltery'; for the tongue is the psaltery of the Lord." Man might be an instrument because he was a little world, and thus shared with harp or cithara the great world's harmony, or because he had his own God-given natural organs. But both processes led to the same imagery, an imagery conspicuous in the Elizabethan view of the universe.

Arabic writers of the ninth and tenth centuries, in their application of cosmic musical parallels to therapeutics, helped also to literalize the association of man with musical instruments. The spheres, themselves, according to the Pythagorean philosophy developed by the *Ikhwān al-Safā*, produce musical sounds, but metallic rather than of strings or sirens' voices: "Some of them (the spheres and stars) touch, knock, and rub one another, and resound just as iron and bronze resound." Earthly instruments bridge macrocosm and microcosm, for they "convey to the soul through the sense of hearing, the harmonious sounds which are created by the motions and contacts of the heavenly spheres."[21]

Going back not alone to the Greeks—to Pythagoras, Plato, and the Galenic system of elements—but to the occult philosophies of the East—Byzantine, Syrian, Chinese—the Arab writers saw in the four strings of their musical instrument, the *'ūd,* a microcosmic representation on one level of the four quarters of the zodiac and of the four elements of the universe, and on another of the four elements, the four temperaments, and the four humors of the human body. There was a further parallel with the four faculties of the soul. The treble string corresponded to fire or yellow bile. It was hot and dry and corresponded also to summer. The second string, in descending order, represented air or blood and was humid and hot like spring. The third, representing earth, paralleled in black bile, was dry and cold like autumn. The bass, water or phlegm or winter, was cold and moist. Flower perfumes were also included in the scheme, the treble string related to musk or jasmine, the next lower to violet or marjoram, the next to rose or aloes, the bass to narcissus and water lily. The seventeenth-century Arab writer, al-Makkarī, reported that in the ninth century in Spain a fifth string was added to the *'ūd* to represent the soul and that the strings were dyed to correspond to the colors of the humors. Since the soul coexisted with the blood, the fifth string was placed in the middle.[22] It followed in Arabic reasoning that the body could be manipulated musically as could an artificial instrument, and these theories had an effect on the later use of music as medicine. But the idea of the elements of the universe and of man as strings of an instrument also influenced the Elizabethan "world picture."

Christian writers of following centuries accepted these theories along with the speculative thinking of the early Greeks, and the re-examination during the Renaissance of past thought gave new life to old ideas. Neoplatonism and occult philosophy united with Christian mysticism to contribute to a revivification of the idea of a universal harmony expressed through and by means of everything on earth and in the heavens.[23] The *Occult Philosophy* of Cornelius Agrippa (1531) made specific application of occult theories to music. The planets sound musical notes, he wrote. The four strings of instruments are paralleled in the four elements, the four humors, the four parts of the soul—sense, imagination, reason, intellect. The music scholar, Zarlino, saw a similar analogy.[24]

Such interpretation depended on seeing similarities between physical or numerical characteristics of the heavens, of man, and of tangible instruments. It depended, too, on a close relationship of "speculative" and "practical" music, on the possibility of discussing divine harmony in terms of the harp, the harp in terms of universal music. With a growing skepticism toward theories of the ancients, with simplification of music theory for the growing group of musical amateurs, and for many other reasons, the breach between "speculative" and "practical," always present, widened. But during those years when the past still held men's imaginations and forward-looking science had not yet silenced the heavens and made all life mechanical, there appeared again and again in philosophy and in poetry the conception of the universe as harmony, of man, his institutions, and his works, as musical instruments.

II

The Elizabethan inherited these musical ideas from the past, but he supported them with the evidence of his own observation. Inasmuch as man breathes or is filled with the breath of God, he was likened to a wind instrument; inasmuch as he is bound by cords and tendons, fibers and nerves, that give life and motion and that respond to stimulus, to stress and feeling, he or the parts of his body were likened to lute or viol. The stringed instrument suggested sensitivity, responsiveness, intimacy of control in man, orderliness and proportion in everything, but the suggestion was one of containment, limited size and sound, degree and distance that could be measured and understood. The universe was imaged in a single string or in a lute. The wind instrument, on the other hand, especially the organ, was more suggestive of unconfined and pervasive harmoniousness, of the mysterious relationship of performer to instrument—of soul to body, God to universe.[25]

Elizabethan writing is filled with imagery of musical strings. Shakespeare, as all readers are aware, frequently compared tongue, heartstrings, senses, to strings of an instrument. His metaphors usually involved broken strings or instruments out of tune or badly played. He wrote in *Richard II*:

> His tongue is now a stringless instrument;
> Words, life, and all, old Lancaster hath spent.

In *Henry VIII* he punned on both "fret" and "string": without frets, neither notes nor heartstrings are in tune. Norfolk remarks of the King, "He is vex'd at something," to which Surrey replies:

> I would't were something that would fret the string,
> The master-cord on's heart!

Shakespeare played on the popular conception of the heart as instrument in *Richard III*, and also on the phonetic similarity of "harp" and "heart." Ideas are like strings of an instrument, but strings of an instrument are like heartstrings. "Harp not on that string, madam," warns the King, to which the Queen replies, "Harp on it still shall I till heart-strings break."[26]

Pericles, contrasting love and lust, describes the senses emblematically as strings of a viol when he speaks of Antiochus' daughter:

> You are a fair viol, and your sense the strings,
> Who, finger'd to make man his lawful music,
> Would draw heaven down and all the gods, to hearken;
> But being play'd upon before your time,
> Hell only danceth at so harsh a chime.

Health of the body, like the harmony of musical instrument, depended upon the tension and in-tuneness of its strings, the senses, as Cordelia implies when, gazing at her maddened father, she exclaims:

> O you kind gods,
> Cure this great breach in his abused nature!
> The untun'd and jarring senses, O, wind up
> Of this child-changed father!

And when finally "the strings of life/Began to crack," life had its ending.[27]

Soul, mind, disposition were described by many writers as stringed instruments which had to be tuned before they could make perfect music.

> For to glorify God is an action that cannot proceed but from a disposition of nature that is altered and changed. The

instrument must be set in tune before it can yield this excellent music, to glorify God as the angels do; that is, all the powers of the soul must be set in order with grace by the Spirit of God.[28]

Before the soul could join in heaven's choir, it had to be pitched to a higher level:

Rowze thee, my soule; and dreine thee from the dregs
Of vulgar thoughts: Skrue up the heightned pegs
Of thy Sublime Theorboe foure notes higher,
And higher yet; that so the shrill-mouth'd Quire
Of swift-wing'd Seraphims may come and joyne,
And make thy Consort more than halfe divine.[29]

There could have been no higher compliment than that paid by Sir John Davies to Astraea on "the Organs of her Minde":

By instruments her powers appeare
Exceedingly well tun'd and cleare:
This lute is still in measure,
Holds still in tune, even like a spheare,
And yeelds the world sweet pleasure.[30]

For Davies, the soul is most often the musician who plays on the body's instruments. Refining the image of sensuousness, of concrete literalness, almost of musical reality, he makes of it an allegory to explain the relation of soul to body, the true *musica humana*:

Thus the soule tunes the bodie's instrument;
These harmonies she makes with life and sense;
The organs fit are by the body lent,
But th'actions flow from the Soule's influence.

Functions of the rational nature, of "wit and will," however, are in the hands of the angels:

Her harmonies are sweet, and full of skill,
When on the Bodie's instrument she playes;
But the proportions of the wit and will,
These sweete accords, are even the angel's layes.

Faults in the music, then, are those of instrument, not of musician:

These imperfections then we must impute,
Not to the agent but the instrument.[31]

Our world and its society are also stringed instruments, and here again there was more emphasis on discord than on harmony. The instrument was first put out of tune by Adam who

. . . being chief of all the strings
Of this large Lute, o'r-retched, quickly brings
All out of tune.[32]

John Donne imagined the broken string of this once-perfect lute replaced by the Messiah: "We may say the trebles, the highest strings were disordered first; the best understandings, Angels and Men, put this instrument out of tune. God rectified all again, by putting in a new string . . . the seed of the woman, the *Messias.*"[33]

By breaking established order, "modern" man, too, might spoil the world's music. When George Herbert, in "Doomsday," saw old order giving way to new he expressed his dismay in imagery of instruments:

Man is out of order hurl'd
Parcel'd out to all the world.
Lord, Thy broken consort raise,
And the musick shall be praise.[34]

Robert Fludd, in Pythagorean tradition, imaged the whole of creation in the extent of a single string that reached from earth, through the elements, to the planets above, the hand of God reaching from a cloud to tune it.[35] But traditionally the universe made an instrument of many strings, as it did for William Drummond, who described "this great All" with charming imagery as a lute, the body the heavens, the elements the strings played upon by the hand of God:

God, binding with his tendons this great All,
Did make a lute which had all parts it given;
This lute's round belly was the azur'd heaven,
The rose those lights which he did there instal;
The basses were the earth and ocean;

The treble shrill the air; the other strings
The unlike bodies were of mixed things;
And then his hand to break sweet notes began.[36]

III

As the Elizabethan found in cords and tendons a suggestion of the strings of the viol, he saw in the breathing apparatus, the bodily organ, a suggestion of wind sounding through flute or recorder, instruments also called "organs." Do we not all have windpipes that sound perhaps "as the maiden's organ, shrill and sound," or a "big manly voice,/ Turning again toward childish treble," that "pipes/And whistles"?[37] The whole body, in fact, was thought to be permeated by airlike spirits, by which soul acted upon body, and which were carried not through a single pipe, but through the multitude of pipes and channels making up the human mechanism. Soul itself, or divine Spirit, according to Genesis, is the breath of God, for God "formed man of dust of the ground, and breathed into his nostrils the breath of life; and man became a living soul." "Thou art . . . my pipe by reason of the breath of the Spirit . . . a beautiful, breathing instrument." Furthermore, the "all-quickning Spirit of God" breathes through the whole organ of the universe, mounting "every Pipe of the Melodious Frame."

The many meanings of the word "organ" were not ignored by a century with a metaphysical turn of mind, and this multiplicity of meanings, frequently superimposed, further encouraged the comparison of both man and nature to musical instruments. From the Latin *organum*, it indicated both "instrument" in the general sense of tool or implement and musical instrument, either pipe or large organ,[38] and also an instrument of the senses, a bodily organ. Figuratively it meant that by or through which one speaks. "Organ" as synonymous with "instrument," that with which one works, frequently carried the immediate suggestion of musical instrument, but not necessarily of any specific kind of instrument, as in Sir John Beaumont:

Some play, some sing: while I, whose onely skill,
Is to direct the organ of my quill,
That from my hand it may not runne in vaine,
But keepe true time with my commanding braine.[39]

"Organ" is both bodily organ and musical instrument in a general sense in: "The Nightingale is the litle Orpheus of the woods . . . that hath for Lyre the litle Clarigal or Organ of his throat."[40] For Du Bartas the serpent tempting Eve was the "organe du Diable," translated by Sylvester "Satan's instrument," an instrument compared to fiddle or lute:

. . . an old, rude, rotten, tune-less Kit,
If famous Dowland daign to finger it,
Makes sweeter Musick then the choicest Lute
In the gross handling of a clownish Brute.[41]

But most often "organ" implied a wind instrument, a symbol of the operation of air in vocal organ, of spirits in the body, of the breath of God in all that He created.

The natural instrument of the voice was traditionally a wind instrument—pipe, trumpet, or organ—as in Shakespeare's *Coriolanus*:

My throat of war be turn'd
Which choir'd with my drum, into a pipe
Small as an eunuch's—

or in *King John*:

I am the cygnet to this pale faint swan,
Who chants a doleful hymn to his own death,
And from the organ-pipe of frailty sings
His soul and body to their lasting rest.[42]

The clown in *Othello*, in one of the few intentionally humorous references of the kind, recognizes more lowly organs as wind instruments in his conversation with the musicians:

CLOWN: Are these, I pray you, wind-instruments?
FIRST MUS: Ay, marry, are they, sir.
CLOWN: O, thereby hangs a tail.

FIRST MUS: Whereby hangs a tale, sir?
CLOWN: Marry, sir, by many a wind-instrument that I know.[43]

In *Hamlet* the entire man is a "little organ," an organ of a single pipe, the recorder. Hamlet (indulging in typically Elizabethan bawdry) urges Guildenstern to try his hand at playing:

> 'Tis as easy as lying. Govern these ventages with your finger and thumb, give it breath with your mouth, and it will discourse most excellent music.

When Guildenstern protests his ignorance, Hamlet has won his point: what he has demonstrated by the "discourse" of musical instrument, he applies to the "music" of man:

> Why, look you now, how unworthy a thing you make of me! You would play upon me, you would seem to know my stops, you would pluck out the heart of my mystery, you would sound me from my lowest note to the top of my compass; and there is much music, excellent voice, in this little organ, yet cannot you make it [speak. 'Sblood,] do you think I am easier to be play'd on than a pipe?

He might well have continued with his own earlier praise of Horatio:

> . . . and blest are those
> Whose blood and judgement are so well commingled
> That they are not a pipe for Fortune's finger
> To sound what stop she please.[44]

Shakespeare's interest in musical sound was in the techniques of playing instruments, enriching "our knowledge with two things at once, with the truth and with the similitude."[45] These metaphors were used most often to explain man's behavior and his relationships with other people. Donne, on the other hand, used "organ" in a more general sense with philosophical meaning rather than sensuous effect. He was concerned primarily with the direct relation of God to man, with man as the mouthpiece of God's infused wisdom and harmoniousness, with the relation of small world to great. The prophets of "The Litanie" were the "Church's Organs," speaking by virtue of divine afflatus. In "Upon the translation of the Psalmes by Sir Philip Sydney, and the Countesse of Pembroke his Sister," the poet is imaged as an organ filled with the blessed Spirit, the instrument spoken through:

> A Brother and a Sister, made by thee
> The Organ, where thou art the Harmony.

The earth and its government are likewise organs. In "A Funerall Elegie," the ruler of the state (that Shee who is universal goodness—Elizabeth Drury, Queen Elizabeth, the Goddess Astraea, the spirit of love—whichever is implied) tunes and sets and animates this organ as spirits animate and control the human body and as air in a musical instrument gives life and sound. Without wonder, love, spirits, breath, inspiration, there can be no music:

> . . . The world containes
> Princes for armes, and Counsellors for braines,
> Lawyers for tongues, Divines for hearts, and more,
> The Rich for stomackes, and for backes, the Poore;
> The Officers for hands, Merchants for feet,
> By which, remote and distant Countries meet.
> But those fine spirits which do tune, and set
> This Organ, are those peeces which beget
> Wonder and love; and these were shee; and shee
> Being spent, the world must needs decrepit bee.

The cosmic parallel is completed in "Obsequies to the Lord Harrington," when the soul, infused breath of the small organ, joins at last the soul of God's great organ of the universe:

> Fair soule, which wast, not onely, as all soules bee,
> Then when thou wast infused, harmony,
> But did'st continue so; and now dost beare
> A part in Gods great organ, this whole Spheare.[46]

Robert Fludd pictured "this whole spheare" as a flute—the seven planets the seven vents—one sounded by the breath of God as the other by man.[47] The great pipe organ, however, had more cosmic implications. "Wherefore well sayd Dorilaus the Philosopher, That the World is Gods Organe," wrote the sixteenth-century scholar, Ornithoparcus, in a triumphant climax to his statement of Boethius' three musical categories.[48] His own and the next century repeated and echoed him. Du Bartas used the image, with suggestion both auditory and visual as well as ideological, to describe creation: God's breathing into the frame of the universe is like the blast of air in a vast organ. Sylvester translated it thus:

> Where, as (by Art) one selfly blast breath'd out
> From panting bellows, passeth all-about
> Wind-Instruments; enters by th'under Clavers
> Which with the Keys, the Organ-Master quavers,
> Fils all the Bulk, and severally the same
> Mounts every Pipe of the Melodious Frame;
> At once reviving lofty Cymbals voice,
> Flutes sweetest ayre, and Regals shrillest noise:
> Even so th'all-quickning Spirit of God above
> The Heav'ns harmonious whirling wheels doth move.[49]

"That deep and dreadful organ-pipe" heard in the thunder of *The Tempest* was part of a cosmic instrument that symbolized for many the harmony of the universe:

> Thus God framed this great Organ of the world, he tuned it . . . that it might be fitted and prepared for the finger of God Himself, and at the presence of his powerful touch might sound forth the praise of its Creatour in a most sweet and harmonious manner.[50]

IV

As the musical spheres were replaced by infinite and silent space and the elements by "chymicals," as the conception of universal harmony gave way to that of music as acoustically measured wave lengths, the whole microcosmic-macrocosmic system of harmony broke down. It was no longer possible to parallel the music of the spheres, of man, and of instruments. Rationalism in its various manifestations, science with its empirical method, aesthetics, all undermined the Pythagorean philosophy: "The new Philosophy calls all in doubt," said Donne, in "The First Anniversary." The old world was alive and intelligent, orderly because it had soul of its own; the new world was a machine. The soul no longer played upon the body's instruments, nor did the universe operate because God continually filled it with His breath.

In the years after 1650, the musical imagery familiar to the Elizabethan all but disappeared. It may be found occasionally in poetry, more as trope than as truth, in the late poems of Marvell and Cowley or in the poetry of Thomas Traherne. Dryden, in "To the Memory of Mr. Oldham," compared the soul to a lyre:

> For sure our souls were neare allied, and thine
> Cast in the same poetick mold with mine.
> One common note on either lyre did strike.

But when he wrote his poem to St. Cecilia, the universe, though framed by harmony, was no prototype of the earthly instrument that was the inspiration of the poem. As he said in his *Apology for Heroic Poetry and Poetic Licence*, he could be "pleased with the image, without being cozened by the fiction."[51]

The image recurred, however, in the final few years of the century, in arguments over the value of the organ in church services, the image being used both by defense and opposition. The latter saw man as a natural instrument superior to the artificial; the former found in man a natural sympathy and correspondence with the instruments he played. Reformers quoted freely from Clement or Isidore:

> Praise him with strings, and the Organ, For he calls the body the Organ, and the Nerves of it its Strings, which being plaid upon by the Spirit sends forth humane sounds.[52]

For the defender of church music, on the other hand, these very nerves made men receptive to the organ in church:

As we are fenc'd about with Nerves, we find our selves ready strung, and most of us tun'd for this Heavenly Entertainment: By a kind of Sympathy sometimes we tremble.[53]

The dissenter might cry: "Is this a time to lavish a great deal of Treasure upon Inanimate Organs, when as the animate ones, I mean, the Poor, are ready to famish for want of their Daily-bread?" to hear in rebuttal that man's breath and that of artificial instruments are akin, that men may "mount up to Heaven on the alone wings of their own breath" or be "advantag'd in their ascent thither by the breath of Musical Instruments."[54] But there is no intention of literalness. Man is not a string of a great lute, nor is he, as an "organ," ultimately a part of God's great organ above. The image is useful, but not part of a world view.

Writers of the early eighteenth century found the image of little serious interest. Alexander Pope, it is true, still wrote of Cowley that he "strung/His living harp"; he still likened the "well-mix'd state" to an instrument in tune; but he had no desire to be "stunned . . . with the music of the spheres." "The great chain . . . that draws all to agree" is not musical.[55] Addison's readers were presumably highly amused by his fun with an old painting that suggested the similarity of men to instruments—an idea that seemed to Addison novel and quaint. Playing with this idea, Addison reveals perhaps unintentionally the similarity of temper that actually does exist, even though the philosophical background is not understood:

For my own part, I must confess, I was a drum for many years; nay, and a very noisy one, till having polished myself a little in good company, I threw as much of the trumpet into my conversation as was possible for a man of an impetuous temper, by which mixture of different musics, I look upon myself, during the course of many years, to have resembled a tabor and pipe. I have since very much endeavoured at the sweetness of the lute; but in spite of all my resolutions, I must confess with great confusion, that I find myself daily degenerating into a bagpipe.[56]

Swift could apparently think of no more absurd situation than the courtiers in Laputa playing musical instruments in imitation of the music of the spheres, the final absurdity being a state dinner of "two Ducks, trussed up into the Form of Fiddles; Sausages and Puddings resembling Flutes and Haut-boys, and a Breast of Veal in the Shape of a Harp."[57]

In the present age, men can "trumpet" their views without being musicians, nor are official "organs" or physical ones commonly thought of as musical instruments. Yet the old musical association persists in an unconsciously metaphorical vocabulary. When one says that he is "keyed up" or "unstrung," "in (or out) of tune" with his time, he echoes, though faintly, the Elizabethans, for whom image was so perfectly suited to abstract idea that metaphor and belief very nearly became one.

CHAPTER II

Music: A Book of Knowledge

THE Elizabethan universe sounded with music of instruments that were imaged in lute and organ. The parallel provided a charming figure of speech, but it did much more than that. It suggested a usefulness in music from which man hoped to profit. If the instruments of the universe, of the state, of the soul and body of man, are like man-made instruments and if they sound a music imaged in that which may be heard, surely it should be possible to learn about one from the other, to discover the secrets of inaudible music from that of instruments. This knowledge to be gained from music did not demand emotional involvement or susceptibility. It did not depend on an infused gift or divine power. It was knowledge naturally acquired by observation and reasoning, and to be acquired not because it might affect the soul or move the affections, but because it satisfied the desire to know. It also satisfied the need of practical men to find a use for whatever God had given.

Renaissance man was as eager as any twentieth-century scientist to understand the universe and himself, the center of that universe, but he sought that knowledge in a different way. He relied heavily upon the Word of God. He accepted with little question the words of wise men of the past—Plato, Aristotle, Cicero, Boethius, St. Augustine. He was fascinated by the mysterious hieroglyphics and drawings left by the Chaldeans and Egyptians, untranslatable in his time but thought to be an esoteric language which might reveal hidden secrets of the universe. But his most accessible book was the "universal and publick Manuscript" of nature,[1] that great volume written in the language of God, sometimes in "Hieroglyphicall Characters" difficult to decipher, again in figures and "letters" easily understood by any one who would take time to observe them. Sir Walter Ralegh stated the view of his time in unforgettable prose:

> But by his owne word, and by this visible world, is God perceived of men, which is also the understood language of the Almightie, vouchsafed to all his creatures, whose Hieroglyphicall Characters, are the unnumbred Starres, the Sunne and Moone, written on these large volumes of the firmament: written also on the earth and the Seas, by the letters of all those living creatures, and plants, which inhabit and reside therein.[2]

In "Stars Voluminous" man read his own fate. In the world around him he saw demonstrated principles of government or of moral law which he himself should heed. Robert Anton imagined the "busie Bees" distilling "sweet maximes" for man's use, singing "in Hieroglyphicks" to "teach a King,/ The politicks of state."[3] It is from the book of nature, from the "churlish chiding of the winter's wind," that the duke in *As You Like It* learns, as does Lear, the shallowness of "painted pomp," the essential being of man. "And this our life," he muses, "Exempt from public haunt,"

> Finds tongues in trees, books in the running brooks,
> Sermons in stones.[4]

John Donne in Neoplatonic tradition in "The Extasie" described the body as a book from which the soul can learn the mysteries of love:

> Loves mysteries in soules doe grow,
> But yet the body is his booke.

Music, too, was "more than meets the ear." Music revealed God and nature and the working of their laws. It was a book of knowledge, which made known through the ear the harmony that existed in heaven, in the universe, and in the body and soul of man, all the kinds of music that had other names —beauty, peace, love, virtue, health. Music was proportion and concord, and wherever there were concord and proportion there was music. "Sounds that charm our ears,/Are but one Dressing that rich Science wears,"[5] but one manifestation of all the harmonies that are created by God, "le grande Maistre de la musique."[6] It afforded more than pleasure to the ear, more than emotional experience or mysterious elevation. It offered to the intellect knowledge of truth beyond that perceived by the senses. "It is," wrote Sir Thomas Browne, "an Hieroglyphical and shadowed lesson of the whole World, and creatures of God; such a melody to the ear, as the whole World, well understood, would afford the understanding."[7] The idea came from God, the "first Composer"; it was embodied in notes by an inspired human composer, who, by "profound and hidden power," as William Byrd put it, was able to express "some celestial harmony";[8] its language was universal, "like that miraculous tongue of th'Apostles . . . alike knowne to all the sundry nations of the world."[9]

The value of this book of music was denied by the materialist, the rationalist, the more crabbed moralist, the church reformer who, like William Perkins, condemned "consort in musicke in divine service," on the grounds that it fed the ears without "edifying the minde,"[10] or, like John Cotton, denied that the "voyce of Instruments" was "significant and edifying by signification."[11] Others, while granting that ancient music might have had value to man, believed with Ludovick Bryskett that the "corrupted musike which is most used now a dayes" carried "with it nothing but sensuall delight to the eare, without working any good to the mind at all."[12]

Music had sturdy defense, however, from non-reformist churchmen who saw in it an image of heaven and from moralists who found in it parables applicable to the life of man. It had use, too, for artists, architects, alchemists, astronomers, who made practical application of the underlying principles of order demonstrated in mathematical-musical relationships. One might read in the "large volumes of the firmament" the design of God, or see in the circling stars or seasons a revelation of His harmoniousness; one might find "books in the running brooks"; but music held its place, too, as a science and an art both speculative and practical and was, as Mersenne wrote in his *Traité de l'harmonie universelle* (1627), a "virtue" from the understanding of which man may be led to an understanding of all truth. One may find in music, he wrote, the "rapport" that sounds, consonances, and other intervals have with the rhythm and metric feet of verse; with colors, smells, geometrical figures; with virtues and vices; with the qualities of the elements, the heavens, and many other things. There is nothing in nature, he concluded, that cannot be related to the consonances of music as well by experience as by reason.[13]

These ideas had their origins, needless to say, in the past, especially in the well-known Platonic and Pythagorean theories of music as an image of world harmony and in the Greek doctrine of *ethos*, as they came down through St. Augustine, Boethius, Ficino, and many others. But they were revived in the Renaissance with extraordinary enthusiasm and credence, first on the Continent and then in England, where, especially from 1580 to 1640, by which latter date the great scientific manifestoes were beginning to appear, music was regarded as one of the volumes of the sensory world given by God not only to delight but to instruct.

I

The first section of the book of music consisted largely of emblematic pictures and thus most nearly resembled the books of emblems so popular in the sixteenth and seventeenth centuries—usually made up of pictures or devices with hidden symbolical significance, accompanied by short verbal interpretations—which were vehicles for abstract concepts or moral lessons. Their aim was, in Horatian tradition, to give pleasure as well as to be useful, to feed both mind and eye.[14]

Some emblems, especially those related to occult philosophies, were intentionally esoteric, designed to convey ideas only to the initiated. As Elias Ashmole put it in his alchemical work *Theatrum chemicum Britannicum* (1652), paraphrasing the words of Christ to his disciples, "Unto you it is given to know the Mysteries of the Kingdome of God; but to others in Parables, that seeing they might not see, and hearing they might not understand."[15] Such emblems were related to the pictorial symbols of the Chaldeans and Egyptians, called *sacrae notae*,[16] or to their "marks and characters," traced back to Adam, Noah, or Moses, "under which all the precepts of their wisdome were contained."[17] Others were less abstruse, and yet "wittie" and "cunning," "somethinge obscure to be perceived at the first, whereby, when with further consideration it is understood, it maie the greater delighte the behoulder."[18] Still others were exceedingly simple, intended as an aid to "the weaknes of common understandings."[19] And so were presented religious truths, maxims of government, morals for everyday life.

Not all emblems were in emblem books. An emblem was so called whether "embrodered in garmentes, graven in stone, enchased in golde, wrought in Arras."[20] Mosaics were emblems revealing "what Rome, Greece, Palestine, ere said."[21] The armorial device, that outward sign of the gentleman, was a kind of emblem, for, as George Puttenham explained in *The Arte of English Poesie* (1589), it combined "ocular representation" with "wittie sentence or secrete conceit."[22] The painter of the Renaissance employed an iconography to be interpreted by whoever wished to study it. "And, indeed," asked Francis Quarles, in the preface to his *Emblemes* (1635), "what are the Heavens, the Earth, nay every Creature, [but] Hierogliphicks and Emblemes of His [God's] Glory?"

How then is music an emblem? In one sense music is an auditory image illustrating and completing the words of a song to which it is lovingly "coupled." Or one might say that the notes and signs written on a page, where "note" is understood to mean, as Campion explained, "*signum pro signato*, the signe for the thing signified,"[23] are like the *sacrae notae* of the Egyptians, that they are characters and symbols representing sounds, which can be read and interpreted by the skilled musician. These signs, in themselves, often had significance that did not depend on sound. The medieval theorist Jean de Muris regarded quadrilateral notation as "arbitrarily representative of numbered sound measured by time."[24] Thomas Ravenscroft, in *A Briefe Discourse*, designated the "Round Circle . . . O" as the symbol of "the perfection of Time (as growing out of Circular motion," suggestive as in past centuries of all perfection.[25] Other special devices were more obvious to eye than to ear, with an appeal that had more meaning then than it would today, since music was not written for an audience but for the performer, who could enjoy visual as well as auditory significance. John Farmer's volume of forty canons, each with two imitative voice parts written upon "one playnsong," was "seen" as emblematic device:

1. Who so delights in Musickes skill
   and thereof judges right,
   May here perceive a straunge devise
   most plainly in his sight.

2. Two parts in one uppon a ground
   in number fortie wayes,
   A thing most rare surpassing farre
   most songsters now a dayes.[26]

Yet music was sound, too, what Andrew Marvell described as a "Mosaique of the Air,"[27] not for eye but for ear. Its auditory pictures comprised a great volume which was studied and variously interpreted for a hundred years by poets, divines, moralists, and musicians themselves. It was a volume of hieroglyphics for the initiated, of "portraitures" for less intellectual "readers," of parables both pleasing and moral, a volume that it was man's privilege and man's duty to study. Through the ear he saw with the eye of the mind, and thus, as John Donne explained out of St. Augustine, "Every sense is called sight."[28] The "pealing Organ" and "full voic'd Quire" of "Il Penseroso" could, through the *ear*, bring all heaven before the *eyes*.

In its most literal interpretation, music was a fleeting echo of the everlasting harmony that surely sounds in heaven, or of the singing of the angels, music both actual and symbolic. It "resembleth in a certaine manner the voices and harmonie of heaven," wrote Thomas Wright.[29] Thomas Adams, preaching in the 1620's with reference to the first chapter of the Epistle to the Romans, in which St. Paul condemns the heathen because they do not learn the invisible things of God from His visible works, recounted the laudable example of a preacher who, by using the book of music, avoided similar censure, and who, at the conclusion of a concert, exclaimed, "What music may we think there is in heaven!"[30] It was an introduction to the harmony in which man hoped some time to share. Sir Philip Sidney's biographer, Fulke Greville, related that Sidney, on his deathbed, called for music, "to fashion and enfranchise his heavenly soul into that everlasting harmony of angels, whereof these concords were a kinde of terrestriall echo." "And in this . . . orb of contemplation," concluded Greville, "he blessedly went on, within a circular motion, to the end of all flesh."[31]

On a more symbolic level music was an image of all concord and unity, whether in heaven or on earth. It was through "divine sounds" of music that Milton imagined the "undisturbed Song of pure concent" above.[32] But it made comprehensible as well all agreement, wherever it was found. Humphrey Sydenham, in a resounding sermon entitled "The Wel-Tuned Cymball," saw in church music not only a resemblance to "Halleluiahs above, the Quire and unitie which is in Heaven," but an "Embleme of unity in the church":

> And as it is a representation of that Unitie above, so is it of concord and charitie here below, when under a consonance of voyce, we find shadowed a conjunction of minds, and under a diversitie of notes, meeting in one Song a multiplicitie of Converts in one devotion, so that the whole Church is not onely one tongue, but one heart.

"I cannot but justle," he concluded, "with those spirits of contradiction, which are so farre from allowing Harmony, an Embleme of unity in the Church, that they make it their chiefe engin of warre and discord."[33] Notes "linkt and wedded togeither" seemed "lively Hierogliphicks of the harmony of mariage."[34] It was with recognition of music as an emblem of concord that William Byrd, whose metaphysical bent is so often revealed, dedicated his *Psalmes, Songs, and Sonnets* in 1611 to his patron with "the desire . . . to present your Lordship with a fit Embleme to your minde . . . which is a Harmony of many excellent Vertues."

Not everyone attempted rational analysis of music's emblematic meaning. For many, music remained one of the "Mysteries," as it did for George Wither. "I am perswaded, that in the Quires and Musicke, used in the Christian Churches," he wrote in *A Preparation to the Psalter* (1619), "there be great Mysteries; and that they have in them . . . proper representations of somewhat in that triumphant assembly to which we all aspire."[35] In his book of emblems he emphasized again the "Mysticke" implications of music:

> It, also may in Mysticke-sense, imply
> What Musicke, in our-selves, ought still to be:
> And, that our jarring-lives to certifie,
> We should in Voice, in Hand, and Heart, agree.[36]

But because music was a model of all harmony, many speculative philosophers sought in it either a more exact understanding of the factors common to all concord or, more frequently, confirmation of explanations inherited from the past. There were various ways of analyzing the essentials of harmonious order, no one of necessity excluding the others. One theory, as will be seen later, was that all harmony depended on numerical proportions. Other notions were less "scientific" and less concerned with specialized musical procedures.

Harmony in general, it was often said on ancient authority, depended on the reconciliation of opposites.[37] It resulted from the uniting of things or qualities that were by nature different or discordant. There were some things that were so antipathetic by nature that they could never be made to agree, but remained discordant always. There could never be harmony, it was believed, between the wolf and the sheep. Even after death this hatred persisted, so that notes sounded on strings made of sheep gut were discordant with those sounded on strings of wolf gut. "Be the musitian never so cunning in his skil, yet can he not reconcile them to an unity & concord of sounds."[38] But wherever opposites were reconciled there was harmony.

This concord derived from essential difference was evident in the sundry motions of celestial bodies; among the four elements, where fire and water, earth and air had contrary qualities; among the differing segments of a state made up of rich and poor, old and young, high and low; in the union of man and woman in matrimony; in the reconciliation of "discording and repugnant affections unto Reason."[39] "All things that moove within this generall globe," wrote La Primaudaye, "are maintained by agreeing discords."[40] Nowhere was this agreement more clearly demonstrated than in music, where opposites of high and low, loud and soft, slow and fast, concordant intervals and intervals by nature discordant were blended into a whole that was completely harmonious. "How doth Musicke amaze us," exclaimed Henry Peacham, "when . . . of discords she maketh the sweetest Harmony?"[41]

What then were the essential characteristics of this order in diversity, in music and hence in all harmony? In answering this question, composers' techniques for ordering sound were largely ignored by the lay philosopher, who relied either upon observation of aspects of music that had general application or upon opinions of the ancients. To many, "degree" was the essential quality. Steps of the scale, it was said, were established by nature. In four-part writing, each part was harmoniously contributive only when it remained within a prescribed and limited voice range, neither too high nor too low. Each string of a musical instrument functioned satisfactorily only when it was kept at an established pitch. Excess or change of relative position marred the harmony.

This analysis gave support to those who argued for maintaining the distinctions of social rank. Perfect harmony, wrote Sir Thomas Elyot, arises from "an ordre of astates and degrees," all things in their place, "higher or lower, accordynge to the soveraintie of theyr natures." It was for this reason, he believed, that music could give the student knowledge valuable in public affairs. The tutor then

> shall commende the perfecte understandinge of musike, declaringe howe necessary it is for the better attaynynge the knowledge of a publike weale: whiche, as I before have saide, is made of an ordre of astates and degrees, and, by reason thereof, conteineth in it a perfect harmony. . . . In this fourme may a wise and circumspecte tutor adapte the pleasant science of musike to a necessary and laudable purpose.[42]

The breaking of "degree" in heaven, in the state, in any group working together for a common end, brought ruin, as Shakespeare noted in *Troilus and Cressida*:

> . . . O, when degree is shak'd,
> Which is the ladder to all high designs,
> Then enterprise is sick! . . .
> . . . .
> Take but degree away, untune that string,
> And, hark, what discord follows![43]

Other writers, however, emphasized not the necessity of contraries in harmony, but the importance of interdependence of tones, each contributing its share to the whole, no one part standing out above the other. Francesco Patrizi, whose treatise on government was translated in 1576 as *A Moral Methode of Civile Policie*, having stated his opinion that "musicke doubtlesse is profitable unto a cyvyll person," argued that it is equality, not degree, that makes concord: it is "Equality amongst Cytyzens" that "causeth concord, without the whych, civyll societye is seene to be neyther firme nor stable at al."[44] The composer Robert Jones, illustrating the common opinion that "there is Musicke in all things," emphasized in the dedication of his *Ultimum Vale or the Third Booke of Ayres* (1608) the need for mutual service both in state and in music: "Politie or the subject thereof, a Commonwealth, is but a well tunde Song where all partes doe agree, and meete together, with full consent and harmony one serving other, and every one themselves in the same labour."[45]

Concord, on whatever it might depend, was not always maintained. Shakespeare and many others observed that one false member in a group, one string of an instrument out of tune, made the whole harmony discordant. As one lax string spoils the music of an instrument, wrote John Case in his *Apologia musices* (1588), or one lax nerve in the body causes paralysis and tremors, so one false member in a state brings confusion and danger. It is for this reason, he argued, that knowledge of music has use in politics for the preserving of unity.[46] In all society, wrote Samuel Rowley, this law is evident:

> Yet mong'st these many strings, be one untun'd
> Or jarreth low, or higher than his course,
> Not keeping steddie meane among'st the rest,
> Corrupts them all, so doth bad men the best.[47]

What course does one follow, then, in rectifying the wrong? Does one pluck out the string and destroy it, or does one strive to put it in tune? John Ferne demanded, in Machiavellian spirit, that it be destroyed. One discordant man in a commonwealth may cause sedition, he wrote in his *Blazon of Gentrie*: "If there be but one in a whole common wealth, yet is he able to disturbe the quiet concord & agreement of many thousands of good subjects, even as one string . . . is able to confound the harmony of many other well tuned strings." This evil member must be rooted out "by force of strength . . . which cannot be better brought to passe, then by the severing of his head from the shoulders."[48] John Davies of Hereford, guided no doubt by Plato's *Laws*, expressed the other opinion. Do not tear out the discordant elements ("So bee't they breake not bounds of Charitie"). Have patience; instruction is better than correction. Thus instruments are treated; so must people be controlled:

> Instruction sooner then Correction drawes
> Such Discords to a perfect Unity,

That yeelds a sweete Soule-pleasing harmony:
For, when a Violl's strings doe not concent,
We doe not rend them straight, but leisurely
With patience put in tune the Instrument;
So must it be in case of Government.[49]

John Donne, preaching on "God's Justice," used similar argument: "God is a God of harmony, and consent, and in a musicall instrument, if some strings be out of tune, we do not presently breake all the strings, but reduce and tune those, which are out of tune."[50]

From the book of music Renaissance man learned many things about those "sweet Societies that sing" in Paradise and about their lesser copies here below.

II

The second part of the book of music was related to the first. It had the same cosmic implications; it, too, contributed to an understanding of concord. But the chief emphasis here was on music not as emblem, but as mathematics. It contained number symbols, numerical ratios and formulae, which represented to men the mathematical ordering of the universe.[51]

Pythagoreans discovered that a string half as long as another but at the same tension and of the same thickness sounded an octave higher, making the interval called diapason, that one two-thirds as long sounded a fifth or diapente, that one three-fourths as long sounded a fourth or diatesseron. An octave was thus represented by the ratio 1 : 2, the fifth by 2 : 3, the fourth by 3 : 4. Tones were thus measured in space. This discovery was thought to reveal all the harmoniousness that existed in the universe.

Plato in his *Timaeus* explained the concordant creation of the universe as being based on an arithmetical sequence of numbers from 1 to 27, the squares of these numbers and their cubes built geometrically into pyramids, numbers "which embrace the secret rhythm in macrocosm and microcosm alike. For the ratios between these numbers contain not only all the musical consonances, but also the inaudible music of the heavens and the structure of the human soul."[52]

These early theories of measurement had scientific implications, for they explained qualitative differences in terms of mathematical measurement. But it is easy to see how the *Timaeus*, especially, could have led to what E. A. Burtt has described as the "mystical manipulation of numbers, or aesthetic contemplation of geometrical fancies,"[53] and how naturally the basic argument could accrete occult notions, as it did in the hands of later Platonists, alchemists, astrologers, and magicians, who believed that by means of the magical power of numbers they could control spirits or elements, read the stars, or comprehend secrets of life and death.

The basic Pythagorean ideas were repeated by many classical and Neoplatonic writers, from Aristotle to Macrobius, to be absorbed into the philosophy of the early Christians, who found support for it in the apocryphal Book of Wisdom: God "hast ordered all thinges in measure, nombre & weight."[54] According to these theories, to understand God or the universe or man himself, it was necessary to understand numbers and their relationships. Numbers were nowhere more available for study than in music, which was based entirely on numerical relationships, in the spatial measurement of intervals and their various proportions, or in metrical measurement in time, which made comprehensible the measurements of all that was intangible or invisible. Arithmetic, geometry, astronomy, and music, wrote St. Augustine, are all sciences of number through which "the mind is raised from the consideration of changeable numbers in inferior things to unchangeable numbers in unchangeable truth itself." And to the earlier concept of spatial ordering, as has been pointed out, Augustine added that of order in time, which applied equally to music and to poetry, both based on temporal measurement of number.[55] For Boethius, too, music was one of the four mathematical disciplines, in which he found the pattern both of world harmony (*musica mundana*) and of music in man, the relation of body and soul (*musica humana*).[56]

Isidore of Seville's treatise on music in the seventh-century *Etymologiae* followed Pythagorean tradition in its relating of musical ratios to those of the universe, and an anonymous theoretical *Scholia enchiriadis* (*c.* 900) again described the four mathematical sciences ("to speak with Boethius") as dealing with truth that could give an understanding of everything created by God: "For these four disciplines are not arts of human invention, but considerable investigations of divine works; and by most marvelous reasons they lead ingenious minds to understand the creatures of the world."[57]

These theories persisted throughout the late Middle Ages, in spite of the domination of Aristotelian logic, both in their original form and combined with notions both occult and "practical" introduced through Arabian writings. Roger Bacon in a chapter on mathematics argued, on Augustine's authority, that by study of numbers in music man learns the "invisible things of God." Following the opinion of Arabian doctors, he insisted that the physician must be instructed in the proportions of music.[58] Robert of York, in his *Correctorium alchimae* (*c.* 1348), suggested that both the elements with which the alchemist worked and the projecting rays of the planets, which the astrologer believed dominated the lives of men, might be arranged according to musical proportions.[59]

As a result of a mystical interpretation of Christian Pythagoreanism, it was widely believed that the three notes of the triad revealed the divine Three-in-One of God, that the harmonious sounding together of four parts in music illustrated the harmony of the four elements or the four humors, that the seven steps of the scale, returning at the close to the original tone of the octave, represented the perfect circling of the spheres, the seven spirits about the throne of God, or the seven days of creation. Musicians themselves recognized this function of music. Bukofzer has pointed out evidence in medieval music of a conscious attempt to translate symbolic number into musical notation.[60]

With the revival of Neo-Pythagorean and Neoplatonic ideas in the fifteenth and sixteenth centuries, philosophers, both scientific and metaphysical, first in Italy and then north of the Alps, turned with renewed enthusiasm to mathematics as a key to all knowledge. On it Copernicus based his reasoning in astronomy, Pico della Mirandola his theology, Dürer his aesthetic principles. The "Universal mathematics of nature" was still believed—by occult philosopher, musician, artist—to be revealed in music. Harmony also, wrote Cornelius Agrippa, consists of numbers and is the image of all things.[61] Gioseffo Zarlino, in his *Istitutioni harmoniche* (1558), granted to musical ratios the authority of natural law. They form the basis of everything, he wrote, of the heavens, the four elements, the soul and body of man. Arithmetic, geometry, architecture depend upon musical harmony. The physician must know music if he is to combine medicines, judge the pulse beat, or understand prenatal development, which progresses according to intervals of fourth, fifth, and octave.[62]

Musical proportions were given practical application by many Renaissance architects and painters, who (partly on the authority of Vitruvius) turned to music for the secret of ideal beauty. "The same numbers, by means of which the Agreement of Sounds affects our Ears with Delight, are the very same which please our Eyes and our Minds," wrote the architect Alberti, in 1450. "We shall therefore borrow all our Rules from the Musicians, who are the greatest Masters of this Sort of Numbers." He analyzed music in terms of the numerical relationship of intervals (1 : 2, 2 : 3, 3 : 4) which he applied to the proportions of open areas and of buildings.[63] Palladio, more than a hundred years later, still insisted, in his *Quattro libri dell' architettura*, that music was the *sine qua non* of an artist's education. Giovanni Lomazzo's *Trattato dell' arte della pittura* (1584) applied musical measurements to portraiture.

These Pythagorean theories were given recognition in England when their influence on the Continent was waning and a more empirical approach to measurement was about to appear. To many writers in various fields, however, they gave to music an added dignity and usefulness. "How valuable a thing music is," wrote Richard Mulcaster, in prefatory verses to Tallis and Byrd's *Cantiones sacrae* (1575), "is shown by those who teach that numbers constitute the foundation of everything which has form, and that music is made up of these."[64] "By the artificialnesse of the number & proportions," wrote Stephen Batman, "it delighteth reason it selfe."[65] It was for skill in "measuring" and "numbering" that John Ferne granted to the musician the standing of a "gentleman" worthy to bear a coat of arms.[66]

Numbers in music were regarded both as mystic symbol and as mathematical rule. The three parts in music were still considered a revelation of God. Thomas Robinson, in the dedication of *The Schoole of Musicke: wherein is taught, the perfect method, of true fingering of the Lute* (1603), was explicit:

> for Musicke is none other then a perfect harmonie, whose divinite is seene in the perfectnesse of his proportions, as, his unison showeth the unitie, from whence all other... springeth, next his unitie, his third... representeth the perfect, & most holie Trinitie: his fift... representeth the perfection of that most perfect number of five, which made the perfect atonement, betweene God, and man; His eight (which as it is, but as his unison,) representeth his Alpha and Omega: & as what is above his eigth, is but as a repetition, as from his unison, as it were a new beginning; so it sheweth our returne from whence we came.

The notes of the octave, because they include "all manner of harmony, Diatessaron, Diapente, Diapason," represent all perfection, wrote William Ingpen.[67] Charles Butler saw in the "perpetual order of the notes in the gam-ut as of the moonths in the yeere" a circular figure "which hath no end."[68]

Metaphysical interpretation of number as revealed in music was basic to occult philosophies in England. John Dee, the scholar in occultism, in his preface to Euclid's *Elements of Geometry*, recommended music, as had St. Augustine, as a key to all number. "From audible sound, we ought to ascende, to the examination: which numbers are Harmonious, and which not," he wrote, and from there proceed to heavenly harmony or that of "our Spirituall part."[69] William Ingpen, in an ardent restatement of the *Occult Philosophy* of Agrippa, considered skill in the art of numbering essential to all knowledge of the secrets of the universe and of man. Man cannot be a "secret-ary" of the Holy Ghost, he wrote, he cannot use the "book" of nature, without knowledge of numbers (arithmetical, geometrical, and supernatural), and he constantly implied, as well, those to be found in music, the "Imitatrix of the starres, of the soule and body of man."[70]

This conception was not restricted to occult philosophy, however. On the Continent, the astronomer Kepler, whose thinking, as E. A. Burtt has pointed out, "was genuinely empirical in the modern sense of the term," found no conflict between the metaphysical and the scientific. He was convinced that the mathematical harmony in celestial order must be analogous to musical harmony, and in his *Harmonices mundi* (1619) he attempted to express planetary motions in musical notation.[71] A few years later, in 1627, Mersenne, in a comment on Tycho Brahe written in scientific context, stated his opinion that the musician can give the reasons for distances between the planets and can thus be called seer and interpreter.[72]

The more practical application of Pythagorean proportion to architecture and painting was well known in England. Lomazzo's work was translated in 1598 and Franciscus Junius' history of ancient painting, which argued similarly, in 1638.[73] Notations made by Inigo Jones in his copies of Plato's *Republic* and of Plutarch's *Morals* indicate that he knew this theory of musical mathematics applied to art, and judging from Ben Jonson's jibes at "Iniquo Vitruvius" in his masque, *Love's Welcome*, Jones subscribed to it.[74] "Time, and Measure, are the Father, and Mother of Musique," wrote Jonson, "and your Coronell Vitruvius knowes a little."[75] Sir Henry Wotton in *The Elements of Architecture* (1624) depended, in his advice for the measurements of doors and windows, on the authority of Alberti, who had learned "from the Schoole of Pythagoras" that harmony in sight is related to harmony in sound. These proportions depend mainly, wrote Wotton, on the octave, the fifth, and the fourth, which apply as well to architecture as to music. He admitted that this speculation might not appeal to "vulgar Artizans." "Yet wee must remember," he wrote, "that Vitruvius himselfe doth determine many things in his profession by Musicall grounds."[76]

Edmund Bolton, in *The Elements of Armories* (1610), theorized on the practical use of musical principles in designing armorial devices, for "the pleasing and wondrous varieties" possible in a coat of arms depend on secrets of concords which make them "not onely (as to the unlearned) an entertainment of the eye, but a food, and musicke to the minde." "As single notes are no concords, nor proportions in Musicke," he wrote, "so single colours have no Armoriall harmonie." The interval of the second demonstrates that too close juxtaposition of figures is discordant, for the "number Two having nothing betweene cannot be said to have any distance, muche lesse proportion . . . cannot decently posesse the whole Field . . . [and] is, by necessary sequel, a discord."[77]

The significance of music's temporal measurement was not ignored. The rhythm of the human pulse was still thought, as in the past, to resemble that of music. "Each Chords tun'd pulse" reveals the "mystick soul" of music; man's pulse reveals harmoniousness of mental or physical condition, as Hamlet testifies when he says: "My pulse, as yours, doth temperately keep time,/And makes as healthful music."[78] The physician then might still learn from musical rhythms, as Roger Bacon and Zarlino had advised, how to measure the pulse. On the Continent Mersenne and the great encyclopedist Athanasius Kircher both reflected a persistent recognition of the use of musical number in medical practice. Mersenne (at a time when he was already leaning toward the new scientific approach to musical sound) commented in his *Harmonie universelle* (1636) on the utility of music for physicians, and Kircher transcribed, in notes of varying time value, rhythm, and pitch, fifteen kinds of pulse rhythm, knowledge of which could assist in both the diagnosis and the cure of disease.[79]

Practicing physicians in England, however, apparently did not look upon this theory with as much favor. Thomas Campion, who as poet described the Creator as the "Author of number, that hath all the world in Harmonie framed," who as musician repeated, in his book on counterpoint, the notion that the four voice or instrumental parts in music "are said to resemble the foure Elements," was, as physician, obviously skeptical of the value of music in judging pulse; he wrote that he himself, the ancients notwithstanding, did not dare attempt "such far-fetcht Doctrine."[80] But even though exact correlation of bodily and musical rhythm might not have been admitted, the association was often made, and still is today, as is evident in recent studies in music therapy.[81]

The most legitimate use of temporal measurement of music was made by the Elizabethan poet. The poet was indeed a musician and thought of himself as such. George Puttenham was stating a commonplace when he wrote that the poet "by his measures and concordes of sundry proportions doth counterfait the harmonicall tunes of the vocall and instrumentall Musickes." These proportions depend in both arts on "the Mathematicall sciences." The whole world is made according to number and measure, Puttenham continued, and on them poetry too must be based.[82] In this idea, Campion concurred: "The world is made by Simmetry and proportion, and is in that respect compared to Musick, and Musick to Poetry." He too had in mind mathematical quantities similar in the two arts, even though syllables in poetry and notes in music depend not merely on count but on duration in time:

> When we speake of a Poeme written in number, we consider not only the distinct number of the sillables, but also their value, which is contained in the length or shortnes of their sound. As in Musick we do not say a straine of so many notes, but so many sem'briefes. . . .

Campion turned to music both to illustrate and to prove his

argument for the need of "rests" in verse to perfect "number": "For we find in musick that oftentimes the straines of a song cannot be reduct to true number without some rests prefixt in the beginning and middle, as also at the close if need requires."[83]

Any study of the effect of music on metrical structures, on mathematical balance of verse, on prolongation of vowel sounds must be inconclusive. It would be a mistake to press too far the application of Pythagorean number theory to poetry. But when Samuel Daniel wrote that "English verse then hath number, measure, and harmonie in the best proportion of Musicke,"[84] "number" and "measure" and at times "proportion" meant, to some degree at least, mathematical measurement which was the same in the arts and in the universe.

It is obvious that in the late sixteenth and early seventeenth centuries in England, belief in the metaphysical aspect of Pythagoreanism was on the wane. It was accepted most seriously in occult philosophy, the resurgence of which (culminating in the 1650's and 60's) was contrary to the scientific trend of the time. Yet the old idea that numerical ordering of the universe was revealed in music persisted and added essential elements to the fabric of Renaissance thought. This mathematical book of music was not yet entirely obsolete.

III

The last part of the book of music contained, not imitations of heaven or the universe, not images of eternal qualities of concord or perfection, but reflections and emblems of human frailty and mutability. There was, as always in this metaphysically inclined age, cosmic reference—for man, the "little world," shared characteristics with the great one—but the chief concern here was with human existence. Man saw in music, as in a mirror, his own life. He enjoyed the pleasures of recognition, but he searched, too, for those lessons that could prove the validity of ancient claims that music has moral value, that it is "profitable for the seeking out of that which is good and honest."[85]

Music, like the life of man, represented ordering within time. It had beginning, middle, and end (another trinity). It had climax, contrast, measure, and proportion. Music was believed to image human feelings, "affections" being revealed in pitch, rhythm, and inflection similar to those of speech, differing in degree, not in kind.[86] In these parallels men took an often melancholy pleasure, convinced that they could learn from them lessons applicable to the ordering of their own behavior.

Music demonstrated more poignantly than any other art the inevitability of death, which comes just as man has reached his "highest pitch," when life is sweetest. The Elizabethan poet dwelt much on the "sweetness" of life and of music. In Samuel Rowley's play, *When you see me, You know me*, the prince comments thus on the music of Dr. Tye:

> . . . methinks in this sound I proove a compleat age,
> As Musicke, So is man govern'd by stops,
> . . . .
> . . . and when he hath attain'd,
> His high and loftie pitch, breathed his sharpest and most
> Shrillest ayre, yet at length tis gone,
> And fals downe flat to his couclusion [*sic*].

Yet there was always more music, a new life, "Another sweetnesse, and harmonious sound,/A milder straine, another kind agreement."[87] George Herbert, in melancholy vein, saw in music a symbol of all mortality, of the death of all "sweets," when he wrote "Vertue":

> Sweet spring, full of sweet dayes and roses,
> A box where sweets compacted lie;
> My musick shows ye have your closes,
> And all must die.

For the dying John of Gaunt in *Richard II* music is not, as for Sidney, an emblem of eternity but of the passing of life, which is sweetest at the close:

The setting sun, and music at the close,
As the last taste of sweets, is sweetest last,
Writ in remembrance more than things long past.[88]

King Richard himself regrets not having learned from music the lesson that only tragedy can result from anticipating time's natural progress or from attempting to rise above a destined role. Shakespeare, who was more perceptive of musical subtleties than were many more pedantic philosophers, recognized the fact that "time" has many implications. *Tempus* in music meant more than mere passing of events. It indicated measured time that was given order and proportion. But *tempus* was also akin to *temperare*, "to temper," to adjust harmoniously. To temper a string of an instrument meant to put it in tune, to give it proportion in pitch. Richard, who has exceeded the authority of divine law, who has seized property not rightly his, has thus broken the right order of events, has taken "from Time/His charters and his customary rights," has not let "tomorrow then ensue today." Yet it is only "by fair sequence and succession" that he is a true king. This same Richard, facing death, sees in music a parallel to his own life:

. . . How sour sweet music is,
When time is broke and no proportion kept!
So is it in the music of men's lives.

Musical "time," he understands now, is more than minutes counted off by a clock. Its significance depends on proportion, and proportion involves also tempering, an ordering of "state" or pitch, a string in tune:

And here have I the daintiness of ear
To check time broke in a disorder'd string;
But for the concord of my state and time
Had not an ear to hear my true time broke.
I wasted time, and now doth Time waste me;
For now hath Time made me his numb'ring clock.[89]

And in the end he, also a "disorder'd string," must be destroyed.

Music represented also the changing emotional experiences of man. It "resembleth the changes of mens lives, and the conversions of manners," wrote Ingpen.[90] In these comparisons music gave comforting demonstration of the value of unhappiness, for it seemed axiomatic that in music, as in all arts and "sciences," discord (here difference unreconciled, and hence unpleasantness) served to make ensuing concord more sweet. Francis Bacon, who was unwilling to "presume by the contemplation of nature to attain to the mysteries of God," still saw in music illustration of the value of discord in the life of man. "A science be constituted," he wrote,

> which may be a receptacle for all such axioms as are not peculiar to any of the particular sciences, but belong to several of them in common. . . . For example . . . "A discord ending immediately in a concord sets off the harmony," is a rule in Music. The same holds in Ethics and in the affections.[91]

This "rule" whose image was in music the emblem writer applied to relationships between brethren, friends, and lovers. Henry Peacham, in *Minerva Britanna* (1612), used a music manuscript to illustrate the juxtaposition of concord and discord, explaining that "the first Discord here taken is from the eleventh to the tenth," the second from the major second to the unison. In this image he saw the sweetness of concord after a quarrel.[92] So it is between lovers, wrote George Wither under an emblem of love:

> Nay, ev'n those Discords, which occasion'd are,
> Will make your Musicke, much the sweeter, farre,
> And, such a mooving Diapason strike,
> As none but Love, can ever play the like.[93]

Writers who reflected on musical and human fallibility were aware that all music was produced by an instrument (whether voice or viol) and that its perfection depended both on the condition of the instrument and on a performer's skill. Whether performed "by Voyces, or Instruments," warned William Byrd, "the best Song that ever was made will seeme harsh and unpleasant" if it is not "well expressed."[94] The music of a man's life also depended on instrument and musician, on physical elements (body or senses), and on their government by his own reason, by other people, or by God.

On this parallel emblem writers and others platitudinized often and at length. Henry Hawkins, in his *Partheneia Sacra* (1633), argued the necessity of intelligent performance of the reason, whether the instrument be harp or "Faculties of the Soule." What was true for one must be true for the other:

> And Man is a Harp; the Powers and Faculties of the Soule, the strings; the Reason, the Harper. . . . If Reason then playes wel his part, which makes the honest man, Oh what a harmonie there is in al, & especially where the tongue and hart agree togeather? . . . Is it so in the Harp, & not in the Organ of the voyce?[95]

Be the skill of the musician what it might, however, it was obvious that an instrument out of tune gave no pleasure to either performer or listener. With an untempered body the soul itself could be perverted, "even as a musitian misseth of true musick, when his harp is out of tune." "The soule therefore must be carefull of the body, and make it a fit instrument for her selfe . . . slackening, and sometimes winding up, according as necessity requires."[96]

Henry Peacham, moralizing upon the emblematic harp lying alone in the wilderness, imagined man tuned directly by the hand of God, "from discord drawne, to sweetest unitie." John Donne, in a "Hymne to God my God, in my sicknesse," tuned his own thoughts to God, knowing that no instrument can take part in an ensemble with which it is not in tune:

> Since I am coming to that Holy roome,
> Where, with thy Quire of Saints for evermore,
> I shall be made thy Musique; As I come
> I tune the Instrument here at the dore,
> And what I must doe then, thinke here before.[97]

In instrumental music man found more homely lessons as well. He learned that diligence pays, in personal life as in government. As a "Lute . . . caste aside," because it "lack'de bothe stringes, and frettes," "being tun'de" could sound so harmoniously that "trees their toppes did bende," so it is with man, argued Geoffrey Whitney in *A Choice of Emblemes*:

> Even so, the man on whome dothe Nature froune,
> Whereby, he lives dispis'd of everie wighte,
> Industrie yet, maie bringe him to renoume [*sic*].
> And diligence, maie make the crooked righte.[98]

Constant tuning of strings, however, constant use of bow and instrument, may retard success. There must be moderation even in striving; man, as well as instrument, must have rest and relaxation. The muse, wrote John Davies of Hereford, cannot "be ever on her Wings":

> Wee Bowes unbend, and slack the Viols Strings?
> That usèd so, wee them may longer use.[99]

John Donne illustrated the maxim that too much practice does not make perfect:

> . . . Release your strings
> Musicians, and dancers take some truce
> With these your pleasing labours, for great use
> As much wearinesse as perfection brings.[100]

Yet, as Timon of Athens remarks cynically, a friend, like an instrument, is of no value if not used at all, for friends "were the most needless creatures living should we ne'er have use for 'em, and would most resemble sweet instruments hung up in cases that keep their sounds to themselves."[101] Timon is confident, apparently, of his own ability to "use" his friends, to play upon them. He is to this extent a musician, as Guildenstern in *Hamlet* is not. To play on either artificial or human instrument, as Hamlet demonstrates from music, demands skill and understanding.

Not everyone found in music a guide to conduct, a way to "that which is good and honest." Fulke Greville condemned poetry and music alike because they make no impression "Really either to enrich the Wit,/Or, which is lesse, to mend our states by it."[102] In many an emblem book lute and viol were symbols, not of a man of "tempred judgement," but of vanity, instability, "wit's sour delights."[103] It was frequently observed that skill in tuning an instrument was rarely transferred to tuning of manners. The most ill-regulated dispositions, it was contended, were those of musicians "who onelye study to have their stringes in tune, never framing their manners to order," who "by their Discord make that Art uneven,/Whose Concord should expresse that Peace in Heaven."[104] In time, moreover, the concept of a book of music went out of fashion. The "new Philosophy" brought it, too, "in doubt"; more rational theories of sound were to strip music of metaphysical association and moral implication.

As old books were put away, new ones were opened. These new books of science pictured a different universe, based on different mathematical formulae. The order of the "numbering clock" replaced the rhythm of music. Having cast aside the volumes of the past, philosophers were forced to start again to understand their universe and themselves, by means of volumes fascinating but still mysterious and obscure, understood only gradually, and then by the trained scientist or philosopher. Many a bewildered man found himself, as did Joseph Glanvill, gazing at a dark and mysterious universe, with "the plainest things . . . obscure," as much a stranger to himself "as to the inhabitants of America."[105] The knowledge of God through His works, that "bright leme of a torche or candel" given by God to all "the blynde inhabitantes of this worlde,"[106] was no longer visible. But while it had shone, it had given our ancestors a sense of understanding of themselves and a contact with universe and heaven that modern man may envy.

CHAPTER III

Music and Ecstasy: A Religious Controversy

MUSIC was a book of knowledge, but it had other uses as well. Like poetry (which was also a kind of music), it not only taught, but gave pleasure and moved the emotions. Indeed, from ancient times men had believed that music could alter man's whole being, that because it imaged all harmony, because the soul, too, was harmony, music could restore the divine nature of the soul and even draw it from the body.

Of all the ideas about music that the seventeenth century inherited from the classics, none was more persistent than the belief that music had power to elevate and refine the soul to ecstasy or rapture. The conception was woven into the poetry of Shakespeare, Milton, and many lesser men. But the idea was not only a poetic one; it became a basic factor in seventeenth-century arguments over the use of instrumental music in church. The poet, moved by song, might feel his "ravish't soul . . . in heav'nly extasie" transcend "the starres"; the divine, elevated by church music, might imagine the soul carried by "Tune" and "Ditty" into ecstasies that "cleave and sunder it from the body."[1] But there were other religious men who insisted that ascent to God demanded more thoughtful and more arduous endeavor than listening to choir or organ, who denied the divinity of harmony. Here arose one of the many controversies of a controversial age.

To say that music causes ecstasy, that it ravishes, or separates soul from body, invites explication. The soul was thought to be a real thing, a substance like fire or air. It was infused at birth and left the body at death with man's last breath. It was said, by some, to resemble air, by others to bear resemblance to water, fire, light, or breath.[2] Aristotle had localized its functions in the heart, Plato in the brain; the Neoplatonists supposed it to penetrate the entire body. Sometimes soul was described as being really three souls—rational soul residing in the head, sensitive soul in the heart, natural soul in the lower part of the body.[3] A majority of writers, however, imagined one soul with different functions.

Always it maintained contact with the body (willingly or not) by means of "spirits," airy vapors which shared in both physical and divine qualities. The interrelationship of soul and body was the subject of innumerable treatises, medical and philosophical; the conflict between them was the theme of many a moral drama. Aristotelians were inclined to insist that soul was not infused into body but was the "form" of body, that it depended on body for its being and had no independent existence. The Platonists, on the other hand, thought it an infused portion of the harmonious world soul, which it "subconsciously" remembered and to which it always wished to return. But since its original purity was often contaminated by the bodily senses, it could regain its unity with the divine only by withdrawal from them.

Whether this separation of soul from body could be complete, except in death, was again a matter of question, as were the means by which it could be attained. Philosophers themselves were not always explicit in their opinions, although many men throughout the ages considered ecstasy a possible phenomenon. Plato believed that complete ecstasy could not be achieved in life. Plotinus, however, writing in the third century, apparently thought that it could, and he described a "mystic trance" in which the soul might be lifted to one-ness with the Supreme.[4] St. Thomas Aquinas described the abstraction from sense attained by contemplation of God: "Therefore the mind that sees the divine substance must be totally divorced from the bodily senses, either by death or by some rapture."[5] The striving of the medieval mystic for union with God was premised on the possibility of ecstatic experience, a ravishment that might induce merely "a sudden and agreeable elevation of soul," but which might in some ideal moment effect spiritual union with God. Against false ecstasy inspired by the devil, the devout must ever be on guard.[6]

The Renaissance philosopher, Marsilio Ficino, distinguished between the actual leaving of the body by the soul and an inner rapture, in which the soul separated itself from the body by withdrawing into itself within the body, a state which might be induced by sleep or solitude. "This separation of the Soul," writes Kristeller, "which is by no means a mere metaphor, is conceived in its highest degree as a ravishment or rapture (*abstractio*) out of the body." But, according to Ficino, "bodies are most eagerly attached to their souls, and are separated from them with the greatest reluctance." Complete separation could, he thought, rarely be attained; only the philosopher, through the highest contemplation, might achieve this end. There were, however, various degrees of elevation, as the soul refined itself through contemplation of the earthly manifestations of God.[7]

Godfrey Goodman, later Bishop of Gloucester, described this state in *The Fall of Man* (1616): "Yet it is not unknowne to Philosophie, that there is an extasis of the soule, wherein she is carried in a trance . . . while the body lies dead like a carkasse, without breath, sense, motion, or nourishment, onely as a pledge to assure us of the soules returne."[8] Soul leaves the body in apoplexies, in epilepsies, and in ecstasies, wrote Joseph Glanvill in *Some Philosophical Considerations touching the Being of Witches and Witchcraft* (1667), and he suggested this flight of soul as a possible explanation for the remote activities of witches.[9]

Other thinkers denied the possibility of ecstasy, even in death. Milton, for one (at least in his middle years), leaned, it has been suspected, toward Mortalism. The separate existence of the soul, he wrote, is "at variance both with nature and reason."[10] The immortal part of man, according to many, was something above soul, something called "Spirit," a divine spark of God (not to be confused with medically defined "spirits," to be encountered later). But the notion persisted that ecstasy was possible and that it could be induced by music.

Under the impact of science, as of Puritan rationalism, the old idea that music could separate soul from body gradually lost much of its original force; yet it endured throughout the seventeenth century not only as a figure of speech, but also as a provocative theory which, if not always literally interpreted, was seriously defended and vigorously attacked.

This idea revealed itself in two different forms, the first of which was evident primarily in writings and sermons on church music, though it appeared in poetry also; the second was echoed chiefly in lighter, Neoplatonically inspired verse. Both manifestations derived from ancient sources, often from the same source, but they followed different trains of thought. This chapter will confine itself to the more serious approach, that which formed the basis of sixteenth- and seventeenth-century religious controversy.

II

The conception that attributed to music power to elevate the soul had variety in origin. Sometimes ancient ideas were paraphrased with a fair degree of exactness; again they were combined with utter disregard of original intention. It is not always possible to disentangle the web that provides background for this belief. Writers about religious music drew mainly on two (perhaps one should say three) sources: the traditional use of music to excite to prophecy, and Platonic or Pythagorean theories of a world harmony to which soul is irresistibly drawn. But inextricably connected with attraction of soul to original harmony was a third theory, that of Platonic love as it was developed by Plato and Plotinus, which should probably be considered as a separate influence. Not by natural instinct alone, it was said, but by contemplation of basic principles of universal harmony or beauty, man could rise by gradual steps to union with the divine.

The use of music to excite worshiper or priest to an ecstatic state in which he was thought to be at one with a god or to have prophetic vision was commonly associated with early Thracian or Phrygian religious rites and with the cults of Cybele and Dionysus, which had entered Greece from the Orient. In these rites the participant was inspired by music and by dance to a religious frenzy in which he was possessed by the god or carried beyond himself. The aulos, a reed pipe, was considered most efficacious for this purpose, especially when used for the melodies of the Phrygian musician Olympus. The tunes, in themselves, invariably had this effect, says Alcibiades in Plato's *Symposium*, "so that if anyone, whether a fine flute-player or paltry flute-girl, can but flute his tunes, they have no equal for exciting a ravishment."[11] Aristotle, too, wrote of the power exercised "by the melodies of Olympus" to inspire enthusiasm,[12] an enthusiasm associated with prophecy by Cicero in his work on divination. This kind of prophecy Cicero defined as "natural" divination, in which the diviner does not proceed by "reason" or "deduction," but "under the influence of mental excitement" induced by external influences, among which he included music:

> Those then, whose souls, spurning their bodies, take wings and fly abroad—inflamed and aroused by a sort of passion—these men, I say, certainly see the things which they foretell in their prophecies. Such souls do not cling to the body and are kindled by many different influences. . . . For example some are aroused by certain vocal tones, as by Phrygian songs.[13]

"The Priests of Cybele," wrote a late seventeeth-century churchman, in defense of organ music, "advanced their Enthusiasm by the use of Cymbals: so did the Bacchae in the Rites of Bacchus, who for the time were transported besides themselves . . . They brought themselves to that Condition among other means, by this also of Instrumental Musick."[14]

A chief explanation of seventeenth-century credulity lies

undoubtedly in accounts of similar experiences in the Old Testament. When Elisha reluctantly consented to prophesy, he said, "But now bring me a minstrel." The account continues: "And it came to pass, when the minstrel played, that the hand of the Lord came upon him" (II Kings 3:15). According to Samuel's words to Saul (I Samuel 10:5): "And it shall come to pass, when thou art come thither to the city, that thou shalt meet a company of prophets coming down from the high place with a psaltery, and a tabret, and a pipe, and a harp, before them; and they shall prophesy." Scripture added to classical account the validity necessary for sincere believers in the word of God. Du Bartas, in the sixteenth century, described Christian prophecy in terms of pagan possession, the prophet's rapt soul replaced by divine spirit. In Sylvester's translation:

> So, at the sound of the sweet-warbling brasse,
> The Prophet rapting his soule's soule a space,
> Refines himself, and in his phantasie
> Graves deep the seal of sacred Prophecie.[15]

Use of music in mystic rites contributed vastly to the influential Greek "Doctrine of *Ethos*," which gave music an unparalleled function in the molding of character. In general, music was thought to affect the mind in three ways: it could stimulate to action; it could strengthen (and conversely undermine) the will; or (this third function is the concern of the present study) it could excite the listener to the point where he rose above and beyond himself, to a state of ecstasy, usually the function of the Phrygian mode. Plato's *Republic* and Aristotle's *Politics* firmly established this ancient doctrine. According to Aristotle, rhythm and melody supply imitations of human "affections"—sobriety, sadness, or enthusiasm—which bring about a change in the soul of the listener:

> Even in the nature of the mere melodies there are differences, so that people when hearing them are affected differently . . . [they] listen to some in a mournful and restrained state, for instance the mode called Mixolydian, and to others in a

softer state of mind . . . the Dorian mode alone of tunes seems to act, while the Phrygian makes men enthusiastic.[16]

Richard Hooker in 1597 translated this passage with fair accuracy, but in place of "the Phrygian makes men enthusiastic," with its suggestion of excitement and frenzy, he wrote: "There is also that carrieth as it were into ecstasies, filling the mind with an heavenly joy and for the time in a manner severing it from the body."[17] This translation of pagan "enthusiasm" into "heavenly joy" reveals the second, even more influential, explanation of musical effects.

Seventeenth-century claims for musically inspired ecstasy mainly repeated the Platonic notion that the soul of man and the soul of the universe are similarly harmonious and that the harmony of music reveals to man the divine harmony in which his soul shares, a notion to which the orgiastic use of music was not entirely unrelated. For this reason, it was believed, the "motion" of music could restore the soul of man —even without his taking thought—to its original state and recall it to the divine.

Although Plato, in the *Phaedo*, denied the theory, attributed to Aristoxenus, that the soul is a harmony resulting from tuning of the body, he did, nonetheless, in the *Timaeus*, define soul as harmony in another sense. God, through reason, he wrote, brought the matter of chaos into mathematical harmony and proportion, and after that the world soul, setting it in a circular motion that is characteristic also of the soul of man, which pre-existed as a part of world soul. Music, too, an imitation of divine harmony, has circular motion which can alter that of the soul, seemingly without operation of intellect or will:

Music too, in so far as it uses audible sound, was bestowed for the sake of harmony. And harmony, which has motions akin to the revolutions of the Soul within us, was given by the Muses . . . not as an aid to irrational pleasure, as is now supposed, but as an auxiliary to the inner revolution of the Soul, when it has lost its harmony, to assist in restoring it to order and concord with itself.[18]

The soul may thus become one with the greater harmony from which it sprang.

Cicero, in his "Dream of Scipio," defined musical creation of the universe and of the spheres in terms of proportioned intervals and tones and concluded that "Learned men, by imitating this harmony on stringed instruments and in song, have gained for themselves a return to this [higher] region."[19] This passage Macrobius interpreted in the light of the *Timaeus*: "Plato reports, as we have previously stated, that the divine Creator of the Soul, after weaving it from unequal numbers, filled the intervals between them with sesquialters, sesquitertians, superoctaves, and semitones." These tones, he continued, "had to be harmonious, for they were innate in the Soul which impelled the universe to motion." This same world soul, moreover, provides all creatures with life; "consequently it is natural for everything that breathes to be captivated by music since the heavenly soul that animates the universe sprang from music." Macrobius then added the idea of the soul's recognition of its origins. Even barbarous people, he said, are moved by music, "for the soul carries with it into the body a memory of the music which it knew in the sky."[20] As John Case put it, in his *Praise of Musicke* (1586):

> For as the Platonicks and Pythagorians think al soules of men, are at the recordation of that celestial Musicke, whereof they were partakers in heaven, before they entred into their bodies so wonderfully delighted, that no man can be found so harde harted which is not exceedingly allured with the sweetnes thereof.[21]

Closely related to this philosophy of the natural attraction of the soul to all harmony was the philosophy of Platonic love, which described gradual ascent through contemplation of earthly beauty—a theory of which Macrobius was obviously aware. In the *Phaedrus*, Plato described the process by which the soul, recollecting those things that it "once beheld, when it journeyed with God," lifts "its vision above the things which we now say exist" to rise into real being.

There, as in the *Symposium*, he wrote of the kind of ecstatic madness inspired by love of earthly beauty, of the lover "who, when he sees beauty on earth, remembering the true beauty, feels his wings growing and longs to stretch them for an upward flight."[22] Only the philosopher, however, has this winged soul, and in neither work did Plato include music as a means of ascent, providing wings for the soul, as Crashaw did later, when he called "Complaining Pipes, and prattling Strings" his "Soul's most certain Wings," or as did George Herbert, who spoke of rising with the wings of music, which knows "the way to heaven's doore."[23] It is the philosopher or the lover of visual beauty or of virtue who, according to Plato, may have a vision of the divine.

Plotinus, however, gave to actual melodies and rhythms, as Plato had not, a function in this ascent. According to Plotinus, the aim of man must be to raise his soul to the "Primal-Principle" by contemplation of the inner essence of that principle. The first step in that ascent is seen in the musician, who through love of the beauty in "melodies and rhythms" progresses from love of form to love of ideal form, form apart from matter: "Harmonies unheard in sound create the harmonies we hear and wake the soul to the consciousness of beauty, showing it the one essence in another kind." The lover and the philosopher mark the next progressive steps in the struggle, until finally the soul, "resting, rapt, in the vision and possession of so lofty a loveliness," rises above earthly cares and becomes one with the "Supernals."[24]

The uses of the two terms "harmony" and "beauty" are not without significance. What constitutes beauty and whether or not harmony and beauty are identical both in nature and effects are questions underlying centuries of aesthetic reasoning, from ancient times to the Renaissance and beyond, questions that plague the modern scholar who attempts to understand Renaissance attitudes toward music. The subject was discussed at length by Renaissance Neoplatonists in connection with the causes of the ecstatic experience of love, and from their explanations of this experience sprang an imagery that described music's drawing the soul out of the ear. This erotic aspect of Neoplatonism will be avoided in this chapter, however, just as it was avoided by seventeenth-century churchmen.

Even in the pre-Christian era, there had developed philosophies that bore germs of reaction against the conception of music as an inducement to ecstasy. Cicero, in *De finibus*, aligned himself with Epicurus in his decision that "music and geometry, arithmetic, and astronomy" are "merely childish amusement."[25] Philodemus of Gadara (first century B.C.) argued that music has no influence on the movements of the soul, that only words and actions have moral value.[26] Skeptics, like Sextus Empiricus in the third century (as Lactantius later), declared that music is completely distracting and an inducement to debauchery. "That the universe is ordered according to harmony," wrote Sextus Empiricus, "is shown to be false by a variety of proofs."[27]

III

Both attitudes toward music—acknowledgment of its divinity and denial of it—appeared in the writings of the Church Fathers. Rationalism and asceticism predominated, a tradition surviving, with some fluctuation in emphasis, until it provided Calvin with a musical creed, which was in turn taken up by the seventeenth-century Puritan. The early Christian disapproved in principle of all pagan religious practices. The mysteries were utterly condemned, and, with almost no exception, the musical instruments associated with them. A passage (attributed to Justin Martyr) which became dear to the Puritan centuries later, differentiated between Christian and pagan worship on the basis of the infidel's use of inanimate instruments.[28] Leave the pipe and flute, said Clement of Alexandria, to those inclined to idolatry: "We must be on our guard against whatever pleasure titillates eye and ear."[29]

Singing of psalms and of similar divine songs, the early Christian writers accepted, granting the value of music to make the soul more receptive to the word or to sweeten religion for the young in faith. St. Basil, in his homilies on the Psalms,[30] St. John Chrysostom, in the exposition on Psalm XLI,[31] defended it thus. This defense was, on the whole, for music accompanied by words, not for instrumental music. The church leader feared the enticements of musical sound and often qualified his recommendations of it with warning of its dangers. Not instruments, but the Word of God, has power over the soul, stated Justin, and Jerome echoed him.[32]

Nonetheless, the concept of cosmic harmony found its way into Christian writings and with it an irrepressible belief in the power of its sensible manifestation. Many early Christian writers explained creation of the world in Pythagorean terms. Clement, in spite of his fear of music, wrote, allegorically, that God by heavenly song "composed the entire creation into melodious order": "By the power of the Holy Spirit He arranged in harmonious order this great world, yes, and the little world of man too, body and soul together."[33] St. Gregory of Nyssa described a universe based on musical proportion and, like Clement, found parallel in the microcosm. With this universal harmony, sensibly perceived music was allied.[34] St. Chrysostom stated definitely, in the exposition on Psalm XLI, that melody in itself gives to the singer a great joy, and he continued by explaining, in a passage easily adapted to defense of musical sound itself, that nothing is so effective as modulated melody and divine song to awaken the soul, strengthen its wings, free it from the shackles of the world, and deliver it from those of the body.[35]

Even St. Augustine's fear of the distraction of musical sound furnished, by its very indecision, an argument for the defenders of instrumental music. He was writing of psalm-singing, of airs together with the words "by virtue of which they receive life," and he confessed himself "to have grievously offended" when he was "more moved with the voice than with the ditty," but he pointed out, nevertheless, that there is a secret association of our souls with the sound of the voice, a secret power which was to explain for the seventeenth-century churchman the ecstatic effects of music: "I perceive withal, how that the several affections of our spirit, have their proper moods answerable to their variety in the voice and singing, and by some secret association therewith they be stirred up."[36] St. Augustine's *De musica* is itself an indication of his devotion to music. The effects of music, he declared in that work, if not ecstatic, were at least elevating for one who considered the cosmic implications of "numbers."[37]

In terms of music the late medieval mystic, under Plotinian influence, attempted to describe the cosmic rhythm of the universe and his own union with God. "There are three kinds of music," wrote Hugh of St. Victor, " the music of the worlds, the music of humanity, the music of instruments. . . . Of the music of humanity, one is of the body, another of the soul, another in the connexion that is between them."[38] Richard Rolle "was acutely aware of this music of the soul, discerning in it a correspondence with the measured harmonies of the spiritual universe."[39] It is reported that Denis the Carthusian "was instantly transported [by the melody of the organ] into a prolonged ecstasy."[40]

In the late fifteenth and early sixteenth centuries, Renaissance Neoplatonists, especially Ficino and Pico della Mirandola, again brought the idea of ecstasy "into Vogue." It was essential to their philosophy of love, since their ultimate aim was ecstatic union with divine beauty by means of its reflection in earthly form, as Plato and Plotinus had taught. The place of music in this scheme was often debated, as will be seen in the next chapter, for auditory "harmony" and visual "beauty," it was argued, had not necessarily the same effect. Still, there is no question that the early Neoplatonists were responsible for the ubiquity in the following century of the notion that through the senses, through ear as well as eye, man's soul could be drawn from his body.

Their influence is clear in secular musical imagery. By the late sixteenth and early seventeenth centuries, however, the theory of Platonic love had been so debased that religious writers seem consciously to have avoided reference to it. They might turn momentarily to mid-sixteenth-century theorists who had diverted the Ficinian stream into safer channels—to the writings of members of the Pléiade, who saw in music an epitome of all harmony and who attempted to restore to music its ancient effects, and especially to Pontus de Tyard, who described music as an image of all harmony, which could as such regulate the motions of the soul.[41] Usually, however, men who argued that music in church could elevate the soul were content with the authority of ancient writers—with that of Plato, Macrobius, the Church Fathers, or Scripture.

IV

The two conflicting views on the value of music in religious worship reflected in patristic writing persisted into the seventeenth century. There were those who claimed that instrumental music could draw the soul to God, that it "carries such extasies, and Raptures with it, as elevate the Soul . . . into a higher Region." Others objected and replied that "the Musick and Melody of an Organ may put a pleasing Motion upon the Blood and Spirits. . . . But what is this to the stirring up of Pious and Religious thoughts in the Mind?" "Musical harmony whether by instrument or by voice," decreed Richard Hooker, may carry one "into ecstasies, filling the mind with an heavenly joy and for the time in a manner severing it from the body." John Cotton answered that such efficacy could result only if "holy songs" accompanied the "playing on Instruments."

Whether or not anyone believed that music could literally separate soul from body, an entirely possible phenomenon in the opinion of certain seventeenth-century philosophers, is not of primary concern. There was caution on this point. Claims that music could create ecstasy were usually modified by such phrases as "for the time," "in a manner," "as it were," or "almost." What *is* important is that the idea of music's power to elevate the soul to God was carried on into the seventeenth century, and that it was at that time explained in terms of ecstasy as it had been in the past; more than this, it became a question for controversy.

Broadly speaking, it may be stated that on one side were ranged those of more conservative or Catholic views who "let the pealing Organ blow,/To the full voic'd Quire below," and on the other, the more Puritan group who objected to the use of all instrumental music in church service, while permitting "vocal melody to remain." This is not to say that all conservative churchmen believed in the mystical power of music, or that all those protesting denied it. But on the whole, the defense of musical sound came from the more Catholic church groups who defended all church ceremony, and the attacks upon it came from the Puritan elements, whether within or without the Church of Engand, who supported, as against ceremony, the value of Scripture and the sermon.[42]

Basically the two parties were arguing for and against the fundamental premise that music has power to elevate the human soul to God. The one, believing, as did Hooker, in that power, found arguments among those ancient writers considered above, adding to the classics the authority of the Old Testament. It found support also in those Church Fathers who had absorbed Pythagorean and Platonic philosophy. The reformer followed the basic tradition of the patristic writers in his emphasis upon spiritual worship, and frequently quoted Justin Martyr on the use of instruments. Clement, Basil, St. Thomas, he said, had also condemned them. But for the most part, having before him a specific problem unknown to the early church, he relied on the Gospels.

The focal point of the whole matter was whether or not instrumental music was legitimate in divine service, since almost all congregations permitted at least psalm-singing in church. There were, to be sure, some extremists who permitted no kind of music, as is shown by such works in its defense as Nathaniel Homes's *Gospel Musick* (1644) and John Cotton's *Singing of Psalmes a Gospel-Ordinance* (1647). The Apostle James had said, "Is any among you afflicted? let him pray. Is any merry? let him sing psalms" (James 5:13). But St. Paul had implied that singing should be silent, with the heart only: "And be not drunk with wine, wherein is excess; but be filled with the Spirit; Speaking to yourselves in psalms and hymns and spiritual songs, singing and making melody in your heart to the Lord" (Eph. 5:18–19). There were few objections, however, to the singing of psalms if they were sung "in a plain tune, easy both to be sung of those which have no art in singing, and understood of those which because they cannot read cannot sing with the rest of the church."[43] Whitgift declared in his early controversy with Thomas Cartwright, "Singing I am sure you do not disallow, being used in all reformed churches, and an art allowed in scriptures, and used in praising of God by David."[44] Henry Ainsworth, in his *Counterpoyson* (1642), said irritably, "And when they write agayn, let them not bring proofs for things that we deney not; as that Davids Psalmes may be sung in the church."[45] "Concerning . . . Vocal Church-Musick, such as they the enemies to instrumental music have made to themselves," wrote Joseph Brookbank in 1660, "that is received without quarrel, by them of more sound Principles."[46] The abrogation of singing was an extreme position even among reformers.

The basic difference, then, on the subject of church music concerned the use of instruments in church. The objections most commonly made by the opposition were these: it was popish, and it was not commanded in the Gospels. Thomas Cartwright objected to the use of organs, "which beside the popish abuse reneweth Judaism."[47] "Singing with Instruments, was typicall, and so a ceremoniall worship," wrote John Cotton in 1647, "yet now in the growne age of the heires of the New Testament, such externall pompous solemnities are ceased."[48] "And because the Holy God rejects all he does not command in his Worship," explained Cotton Mather later, "he now therefore in effect says unto us, *I will not hear the melody of thy organs.*"[49]

These arguments, while they implied a denial of the value of musical harmony, were not in their inception based on any philosophy of aesthetics or on any reasoning about music as such. In fact, the Puritan seems to have had none of the traditional "Puritan" eagerness to argue on this particular subject. The question of musical sound was apparently disposed of for him by scriptural omission. But when one of the reforming faction did take the trouble to go beyond his basic objections in answering the contentions for the efficacy of musical sound to elevate the soul, his only answer could be a denial of that power, and in that denial he was forced to take a definite rational stand on a question which concerned actual music.

The argument for the defense was based chiefly on the assertion that the effects of music are "natural," that they derive from a "vertue" "naturally in Musicke," from a "native puissance and efficacy," from a "naturall correspondence" between our diviner parts and harmony. These effects depended not on supernatural power or magic, not on beauty or on knowledge, but on the nature of the soul and the corresponding nature of what is heard.

Every student of Renaissance thought realizes with what diversity of meaning the word "nature" was used. In these discussions of music it meant, first of all, the "essential property" of soul and of music. It assumed an immutable characteristic that makes soul or music what it is. The soul of man and of the world is "by nature" harmony, it was believed, a notion that had come down from the Pythagoreans, from Plato's *Timaeus*, from Cicero's "Dream of Scipio" and the commentary on it by Macrobius. But the same musical proportions were thought to be the basis of music that is heard, so that music itself has "by nature" an identical harmony.

"Nature" was also a governing principle, a creative force that worked inevitably in certain ways according to established laws. Laws of nature were comparable to, but more stable than, human laws. One of them was the "law of sympathy" by which like is attracted to like, by which objects are drawn to what they need for subsistence, by which things react sympathetically to other things that are like them. Thomas Wright in his enumeration of the ways in which music may move the passions—by an act of God, by motion of the spirits, and by sympathy—explained this law of nature. There is "a certain sympathie, correspondence, or proportion betwixt our soules and musick," he wrote, and "no other cause can be yeelded." He added:

> Who can give any other reason, why the loadstone draweth yron, but a sympathie of nature? Why the Needle, toucht but with such a stone, should never leave looking towards the North Pole? . . . a lyon will eat no hay, nor a bull beefe . . . if a man should beat his braine to find out the reason, no better can be given, than sympathie of nature.[50]

The mutual sounding of two similarly tuned stringed instruments seemed to prove this law.[51] For this reason it was thought "natural," as Macrobius had said, that the soul, which is harmony, should love music, which is also harmony. Because of this correspondence, it was only "natural" that the soul (granted that it had retained a vestige of its original purity) should be attracted to music, just as it was inevitable that a discordant soul or evil spirit should flee from it, as the evil spirit in Saul fled from the sound of David's harp.

Yet the workings of nature were not always understandable. The power of music might be secret and mysterious even while it was natural. Music could, by natural means—by "natural magic"—engender divine "vertues" in our minds—"vertue" meaning, not "moral excellence" or "integrity of character," but "an active quality or power," energy, strength, potency.

The Puritan and the rationalist in general denied this natural "virtue" in music to touch the soul and thus denied both the harmoniousness of the soul and an immutable quality in music. The effects of music, they said, are of a very different sort. Any miraculous effects it may seem to have do not derive from the music itself, but from God's use of it for some special occasion. In so arguing, they split off the natural from the supernatural. Grace was exalted above nature.

V

The debate in England over the power of musical sound to elevate the soul to God did not actually begin with Richard Hooker, but his eminence made it into the widespread controversy that it became. Whitgift and Cartwright had sparred over the subject in their exchange of tracts between 1572 and 1577. Cartwright's objections were purely dogmatic: he condemned "organs and curious singing" merely because they were "proper for popish dens." Whitgift's reply, in Stoic tradition, was less a defense than a passing rebuke: "Those things that be indifferent are not repugnant to the word of God."[52]

A more vivacious and elaborate argument, one in which the idea of ecstasy was introduced, was that of John Case in *The Praise of Musicke*, where he argued that music is useful not only in "civill matters" but also "in the congregation and Church of God." He had no hesitation in using pagan authority to prove his point. The soul, having originated in celestial harmony, is both allured and elevated by the divine influence of music. It is for this reason, he wrote, that "the ancient Philosophers" supposed "an hidden divine vertue . . . naturally to be ingenerated in our minds." "Musick with the concinnitie of her sound, and the excellency of harmony doth as it were knit & joyne us unto God."

In the end, he turned from pagan philosophers to the authority of St. Augustine and the more theologically acceptable opinion that God, having given music to man, should be worshiped with his own gift. It was this giving, receiving, and returning of gifts that constituted for the Stoics the significance of the three Graces. Even here, however, he admitted the power of music to divide soul from body:

> Hee, which hath made us, and the world, and preserveth both us and it, should be worshipped and honored with that thing which is most excellent in man, dividing as it were his soule from his body, and lifting up his cogitations above himselfe. And S. Austen saith of himselfe, That the voices, of

the singers, did pierce into his eares . . . & that thence was inflamed in him an affection of godliness.[53]

The more often quoted statement (still quoted in New England in 1764)[54] was that of Richard Hooker in *Of The Laws of Ecclesiastical Polity.* He gave less overt acknowledgment to the Platonists. He avoided the theological heresy of preexistence of soul as part of world soul by reversing, as did so many of his contemporaries, the Platonic argument. He did not say that because the soul is harmony it is allured by the harmony of music, but rather that because the soul is allured by music "some have been thereby induced to think that the soul itself by nature is or hath in it harmony." He leaned heavily on Aristotle's theory of music as an imitation of "affections." But his conclusions were in the Platonic tradition as it had come down through Pontus de Tyard, whom he freely quoted. The fact that he returned, at the close, to the power of music to "temper" rather than to "ravish" (to restore "the inner revolution of the soul . . . to assist in restoring it to order and concord with itself," as Plato had written in the *Timaeus* and Tyard in the *Solitaire Second*) does not annul his other suggestions: the harmony of sounds, even without benefit of God's word accompanying them, has a "native puissance and efficacy":

> Touching musical harmony whether by instrument or by voice, it being but of high and low in sounds a due proportionable disposition, such notwithstanding is the force thereof, and so pleasing effects it hath in that very part of man which is most divine, that some have been thereby induced to think that the soul itself by nature is or hath in it harmony . . . there is also that carrieth as it were into ecstasies, filling the mind with an heavenly joy and for the time in a manner severing it from the body. So that although we lay altogether aside the consideration of ditty or matter, the very harmony of sounds being framed in due sort and carried from the ear to the spiritual faculties of our souls, is by a native puissance and efficacy greatly available to bring to a perfect temper whatsoever is there troubled. . . . They which, under pretence of the Law ceremonial abrogated, require the abrogation of

> instrumental music, approving nevertheless the use of vocal melody to remain, must shew some reason wherefore the one should be thought a legal ceremony and not the other.[55]

Once so influential an authority as Richard Hooker had stated not only that church music was legitimate, but that music itself, by its very nature, possessed power to elevate the soul of man, those who required "the abrogation of instrumental music, approving nevertheless the use of vocal melody to remain," found themselves in an anomalous position; they must indeed "shew some reason wherefore the one should be thought a legal ceremony and not the other."

George Wither repeated ideas of Case and of Hooker, without their attempts at rationalization, leaving a place, thereby, for the possible operation of God's "grace" in music. Nonetheless, he wrote, as had his predecessors, of a "vertue naturally in Musicke," a "secret power" to "dispose the soule unto heavenly meditations," and to "raise the spirits to that excessive height, as the soule is almost ravished, and in an extasie":

> Nor is Musicke . . . onely powerful; as, to dispossesse us of evill affections, and such like: but it hath also divine raptures, that allure and dispose the soule unto heavenly meditations, and to the high supernaturall apprehension of spiritual things. . . . Yea, the inarticulate sounds have, in themselves, I know not what secret power, to move the very affections of mens soules. . . . Some raise the spirits to that excessive height, as the soule is almost ravished, and in an extasie.[56]

Charles Butler, the philologist, having claimed in his preface the authority of St. John Chrysostom and of St. Augustine, discussed the problem in *The Principles of Musik in Singing and Setting: with the two-fold Use thereof, Ecclesiasticall and Civil* (1636), but his explanations were in terms of musical modes, which by that time had been largely abandoned. The Lydian and Phrygian modes, he wrote, are both conducive to ecstasy. The Lydian which is used (Butler here departs, certainly, from ancient tradition) for "those solemn Hymns and other sacred Church-songs, called *Moteta, à motu*

. . . moove[s] the harts of the hearers, striking into them a devout and reverent regard of him for whose praiz they are made." Through "heavenly harmoni," it ravishes "the minde with a kinde of ecstasi, lifting it up from the regarde of earthly things, unto the desire of celestiall joyz . . . which it dooeth lively resemble." The Phrygian, he described, as had the ancients, as being more exciting: "The Phrygian moode dooeth distract and ravish the minde, and dooeth as it were set it besides it self: having the same force among the Moodes, that the Pipe or Fife hath among Instruments."[57]

Humphrey Sydenham in 1637 continued the argument in phrases clearly reminiscent of the "unparalell'd Mr. Hooker" and added a glimpse, too, of his adversaries in this debate on the nature and power of musical sound:

> If they could but wipe off a little those wilfull scales which hang upon their eyes, they could not but see the admirable vertues and effects which melody hath wrought even in that part of man which is most sacred; Insomuch, that both Philosophers and Divines have jump'd in one fancie, that the Soule is not onely naturally harmonicall, but Harmony it selfe.

For those who were "dyving after reasons" why music should "so strangely set passions aloft," he repeated without acknowledgment theories listed by Thomas Wright in *The Passions of the Minde* (1604). The first concerned "Sympathia, a naturall correspondence . . . between our diviner parts and harmony," and to this he added St. Augustine's conclusion that there is "a secret association" between song and "affections" of our spirits. The second proposal, sometimes admitted by the opposition, was that the effects come not from music itself: "God by his Ordinarie naturall providence produceth them." In putting forward a third, he began with Wright's description of the material effect of music on the spirits, but the implications of this explanation Sydenham apparently did not understand, and he veered illogically into a paraphrase of Hooker which is totally unrelated:

> So that although we lay altogether aside the consideration of Ditty or Matter, the very murmure of sounds rightly modu-

> lated and carried through the porches of our eares to those spirituall roomes within, is by a native vigour more than ordinarily powerfull, both to move and moderate all affections; and therefore Saint Augustine would have this custome of Symphony kept up in the Church.

But Sydenham then retreated, much indeed as St. Augustine himself would have done, and as did Wright in fact, and admitted that the senses do not apprehend the essence of things, which is a task for our intellectual powers alone; that over-complicated music "leaves the spirituall faculties untouch'd"; and that the ideal lies in "a sober mediocritie and grave mixture of Tune with Ditty." It is this combination, he said, that "rocks the very soule, carries it into extasies, and for a time seemes to cleave and sunder it from the body."[58]

The silence of the Commonwealth years was broken in 1660 by Joseph Brookbank, who paid tribute to the "Pious, learned and most elegant Mr. Sydenham" and continued his argument: "Sweetness of harmonical sounds, insinuates it self into the soul of man, prepares the affections for the service of God, lifts up the heart towards heaven, delights the mind, kindles Devotion, inflames desire, and ravisheth the spirit with celestial joy."[59]

Dr. Hickman, "Chaplain in Ordinary to his Majesty," who preached an oratorical sermon on St. Cecilia's Day, 1695, set no limit to the power of musical sound over the soul:

> 'Tis this that fits us, not only for the Operations of Reason, but is an Inlet also to Divine Visions, and Revelations. It carries such extasies, and Raptures, with it, as elevate the Soul of man into a higher Region, teach him Seraphical Flights, and give him a clearer Insight into the things above.[60]

Both from the classics and from the Old Testament, these seventeenth-century defenders of church music argued that this mysterious art by a "native puissance and efficacy," by a "vertue naturally in Musicke," could ravish "the spirit with celestial joy." It could "dispose the soule unto heavenly meditations, and to the high supernaturall apprehension of spiritual things." It "ravisheth the minde with a kinde of ecstasi."

VI

The opponents of church music, on the contrary, categorically denied the spiritual value of musical sound. It appealed to the senses, they said, to the ear, and not to the mind. It did not in its nature induce spiritual thoughts. Not by musical sound did the prophets come into contact with the divine. If there was any power in David's song, such power lay in the words sung to the music; it was still more probable that the evil spirit in Saul was exorcised not by David, but by the interposition of God. Scholars no longer believe that the Puritan disparaged the practice of music outside of church or objected to its use as recreation, but his opinion of the "secret power" of music to elevate the soul was at variance with that of many other people.

The Puritan's statement of his opinion is refreshingly succinct. William Perkins added to a list of detestable popish practices "consort in musicke in divine service, feeding the eares, not edifying the minde."[61] This was the common cry, as may be seen in a tract printed in 1643—*The Holy Harmony: Or, a Plea for the abolishing of Organs and other Musicke out of Protestant Churches of Great Britain.* " 'Tis hard for the vulgar sort to know the Psalme which is clearly lost by the Organs, and the Quire," the author expounded. "Well may they admire the art of the Musician, but not edify themselves." The bedchamber is a fitter place for the pack of minstrels than the house of God. Souls cannot be "raised from their slumbers of sin . . . while they suffer themselves to be transported with the raving rapture of their foolish jollities."[62]

John Cotton made it clear that efficacy lay either in the idea of the words, or else in the special blessing of God at the time, a blessing above art or nature. Certainly no mere sound of instruments gave music its seeming power, music which in itself possessed no rational appeal, without which it was of no worth:

> Singing of Psalmes is accompanied and blessed of God (by his grace) with many gracious effects, above nature or art.

> . . . It was not the sound of Davids Harpe that could have this power, either over the evill spirit, or over the sinfull passions of Saul himselfe, if the sound of the Harpe had not been quickned and enlived, as it were by a spiritual song, and by the Spirit of God breathing therein. . . . In I Sam. 10.5,6, they could not be said (as there they be) to have prophecied with Harpes and Violls, unlesse they had sung holy songs, together with their playing on Instruments. For Prophecy is an utterance onely of the word of God, and of the things of God contained in it; which Instruments without voyce cannot doe.

He rejoiced at the state of divine service among dissenters: "Nor is any voyce now to be heard in the Church of Christ, but such as is significant and edifying by signification, (I Cor. 14.10, 11, 26) which the voyce of Instruments is not."[63]

In *A Reverse to Mr. Oliver's Sermon of Spiritual Worship*, preached in 1660, Matthew Poole was, on the whole, conciliatory in his attitude, defending himself against "Calumnies which have been cast upon me," among which was "that I wish'd their fingers might rot that played upon the Organs, whereas I only declared my dislike of Organs in our Churches." Nevertheless, he, too, denied that music leads the worshiper to God:

> I appeal to the experience of any ingenuous person, whether curiosity of voice, or musical sounds in Churches, doth not tickle the fancy with a carnal delight, and engage a man's ear and most diligent attention upon those sensible motions and audible sounds, and therefore must necessarily in great measure recal him from spiritual communion with God.

The end of worship, on the contrary, is "the elevation of the Soul to God," which pleasures of sense cannot effect.[64]

James Peirce, prolonging the argument into the early years of the next century in *A Vindication of the Dissenters*, was equally skeptical of the power of music to excite "spiritual affections." It pleases, but any further effects must depend on grace or on a natural virtue that his opponents have not proved:

> That there is a great force in music, and that it wonderfully pleases men, is certain. Nor are we so unmusical as to deny

it. But the question is: Whether it . . . can, by its own virtue, excite devout and spiritual affections in us? . . . And unless our Adversaries can prove, that our minds are carry'd toward spiritual and heavenly things, by some hidden virtue, that nature has planted in these musical instruments, or by certain divine grace accompanying them, as God's own institutions; they really say nothing to the purpose.[65]

That these statements were not merely random thrusts, but were consciously intended as counterblows, may be seen in a series of pamphlets written at the close of the century which brought into sharp focus the whole question of the nature of music. The immediate controversy was occasioned by the installation of an organ at Tiverton in Devon in 1696, and involved John Newte, who preached the sermon in praise of organs on that occasion, the anonymous author of *A Letter to a Friend in the Country,* who took exception to Newte's remarks, and Henry Dodwell, who came to Newte's defense. A conspicuous point of difference among the disputants was the "native efficacy" of music to affect the soul.

In his sermon on *The Lawfulness and Use of Organs in the Christian Church,* Newte quoted freely from Richard Hooker's famous passage (although he omitted the part on ecstasy):

Touching Musical Harmony, (says he) whether by Instrument or by Voice, it being but of High and Low in Sounds a due proportionable Disposition, such notwithstanding is the Force thereof, and so pleasing Effects it hath, in that very Part of Man which is most Divine, that some have been thereby induced to think, That the Soul it self by Nature is, or hath in it Harmony.

Newte insisted that, so far as the prophets were concerned, instrumental music alone was "able to stir up the inspired Principles of their Souls." His conclusion was that music "by the Subtlety of its Nature, and the insinuating Sweetness of its Sound, will strike deeper into the Heads of some, than the closest Reason possibly can into their Hearts." He referred to the judgment of "some Eminent Divines who have separated from us, as particularly Mr. Baxter," who had defended church music and by whose judgment he hoped "to balance any thing can be said, by any of the Separation, to the contrary."[66]

The author of the *Letter* answered Mr. Newte with equal vigor. Music's effects, he said, are the result of the "Extraordinary concerns of God":

> I confess, if God please to make use of this kind of Musick as an Instrument to produce some great, and notable effects, it shall be attended with success; But then those effects are not so much to be ascribed to Musick, as to the Extraordinary concerns of God therewithall.

Instrumental music is "no Rational Act":

> Singing of Psalms with the Voice . . . is a Rational act, and expresseth in a Melodious Manner the Conceptions of the Mind. But Instrumental Musick is only Ceremonial, for it is no Rational Act, neither does it Articulately express the Affections, and Serious Conceptions of the Soul.

He insisted that the effect of music is at most physiological:

> I grant that the Musick and Melody of an Organ may put a pleasing Motion upon the Blood and Spirits, may, perhaps, cause the Blood to glide along the Veins and Arteries with somewhat more briskness. But what is this to the stirring up of Pious and Religious thoughts in the Mind?

As Baxter, the nonconformist, furnished an argument for the defender of church music, the anonymous author continued, Jeremy Taylor, the loyal churchman, did as much for the opposition, with his decision that instruments "are not . . . fitted for edification." Finally, as for Newte's argument that it is the "nature of this musical instrument the organ to excite and raise men's affections," what, asked the author with some pertinence, did he mean by "nature"?[67]

At this point, Henry Dodwell came to Newte's defense with a pamphlet to which Newte himself wrote a preface. Newte, calling the *Letter* a repetition of "an old base and scandalous objection, against the innocent Rites and Ceremonies of the Church of Engand," again paraphrased Hooker, even including the passage on ecstasy which he had previously omitted: "For Musick may be such, and of that Efficacy, as to carry the Mind as it were into Extasies, filling it with heavenly Joy for the Time, and in a manner severing it from the Body (as says our judicious Mr. Hooker)." He reiterated his opinion about the Old Testament prophets, remarking that "Instrumental Musick, alone, is there made use of, as a means to awaken their inspired Souls, &c." And he insisted again on the unchanging "nature" of music: "The Nature of the thing is always the same; if it had that Efficacy under the Law, to quicken and excite Mens Affections in Devotion, as 'tis certain it had . . . it has not altered its Nature since."[68] The power of music, therefore, is no secondary manifestation of Deity; such power is inherent in music itself.

In the body of his tract Dodwell for the most part emphasized Newte's arguments: the nature of a thing is always the same; the power of music is no different today from what it was in the remote past; that power is inherent in the very nature of music. But he added the testimony of pagan religions:

> I know our Adversaries are more willing to impute this Usefulness of Instrumental Musick, rather to the extraordinary Interposition of God, seconding his own Institution. But why should they think it derogatory to the Providence of God, that he should make use of the Power, himself has given to the Natures of Things? Or why should they deny the Experience of so many Heathens, who . . . receiv'd the same Practice of Instrumental Musick on account of the Devotion they pretended to feel rais'd in themselves by it, in their several false Religions. This could be imputable to nothing but the Natures of the things themselves. . . . The Priests of Cybele, the Galli, advanc'd their Enthusiasm by the use of Cymbals: So did the Bacchae in the Rites of Bacchus, who for the time were transported besides themselves, and knew not what they did, so absolutely they were under the power of

> that emotion of Mind which they believe Prophetick. They brought themselves to that Condition among other means, by this also of Instrumental Musick.[69]

On the one hand, then, the supporter of church music—usually of the conservative church party—insisted that music is in its nature divine, that it is, as he so often said, "a gift of God." For his arguments, he went back to old ideas of the power of music to separate soul from body, to elevate the soul to a closer contact with God. On the other hand, the objector—usually the reformer—argued that music is not necessarily good, and that whatever power it may have is due either to the words that accompany it or to the special interposition of God. Music, he usually granted, has certain physical effects on blood or spirits; it may cure melancholy; it delights the ear; but it does not edify. Only the eloquence of the inspired word can do that.

While the defender of ceremony, loving church music as he did, often paused for at least a moment's tribute to its power in his pamphlets and tracts, it was characteristic of the dissenter that he was not passionately interested in the subject. The Lord "now therefore in effect says unto us, *I will not hear the melody of thy organs.*" That was enough for many a Puritan. His mind was on higher things—on vital questions of sacrament or church government. Yet when he did pause to counter the Anglican arguments for the "pealing Organ," he went the whole way, insisting that any power of music was exercised upon the lower rather than the higher man, upon senses not reason. He denied the ecstasy and rapture which for centuries had been associated with music; his soul was not ravished by "sweet sounds" nor did organ and voice dissolve him into ecstasies and bring all heaven before his eyes. Thus he not only denied the power and efficacy of instrumental music, but in so doing denied the birthright of his century—the long Platonic musical tradition which had become one with the tradition of the prophetic books of the Old Testament.

Many forces other than Puritanism were, of course, active

in undermining belief in the natural power of music to free or to elevate the soul. Studies in physiology and acoustics explained away both the law of sympathy and the divine origin of harmonic proportion. The new scientist had no time for religious "enthusiasm." Yet for the churchman of the seventeenth century this was no minor conflict, nor would it be today if there were attempts to banish all music from the churches on the ground that it is no more than sensuous entertainment.

CHAPTER IV

Music and Neoplatonic Love

WHEN churchmen claimed that music could, by its very nature, lift the harmonious soul and carry it as it were into ecstasies, the origins of their ideas were clearly in writings of the ancients. When Chapman, however, described how his whole being was converted into spirit by the alchemy of music, as it might have been by the alchemy of love, or when James Howell wrote in a letter to a "Noble Lady" that her music "so enchanted me . . . that my soul was ready to come out of my ears," their thought was obviously moulded by influences beyond those of Pythagoras and Macrobius.[1] This association of music with love demands a different frame of reference. Here it is necessary to turn to the philosophy of the Renaissance Neoplatonists, whose ideas the churchmen who argued for music's elevating power so completely avoided.

During the Renaissance, any subject connected with Platonism was swept into the current of Neoplatonic love philosophy, in which all relationships, cosmic or human, aesthetic or ethical, were explained in terms of love. Many ideas about music were subjected to this influence, especially those concerned with ecstasy, which was an essential factor in union of lovers with each other or with the divine.

I

Love, a Musician is profest
And, of all Musicke is the best.[2]

Love had many meanings, then as now, and with almost all of them music, from ancient times, had been closely associated.[3] It must suffice here to attempt a study of the place of music, equivocal and widely debated, in the love philosophy of Renaissance Neoplatonists, and the effect of these opinions on later musical imagery and evaluation. According to this philosophy, not music but Love (whether imaged as Eros or as the Spirit of God Himself—the two were not always clearly distinguished) gave order and unity and life to an animated universe:

> Love chaines the earth and heaven,
> Turnes the Spheares, guides the yeares in endless peace.
> The flourie earth through his power
> Receiv's her due encrease.[4]

The God of Love, wrote Spenser in "An Hymne of Heavenly Love," moved in all things and made them "pregnant still with powrefull grace." The earthly counterpart of Love governed man, giving him life and fertility and attracting him to others of his kind. By "sympathy," a manifestation of love, all things were kept in their proper place as by a magnetic force. By love, not by music, man was led from earthly image to divine perfection; by love soul left body as in an ecstasy.

Between these two theories—the one that love governs the universe, the other that music regulates all things—there is not necessarily any conflict. In an abstract sense love *is* music, for love is harmony and harmony is music. Amity in the universe, in the moving of the spheres, in the reconciliation of elements, wrote the oft-quoted Spanish Neoplatonist, Leo Hebraeus, may be called "a harmony, music or concord."[5] Even when love was both condition and feeling, the two terms, "love" and "music," were used interchangeably. "The love of the King and his subjects, the Father and his childe, the Lord and his Slave . . . this is right Musicke," wrote Stephen Gosson. The passionate love of Othello and Desdemona is music, which Iago threatens to destroy when he says, "I'll set down the pegs that make this music."[6] It is scarcely necessary to call attention to the translation of "making love" into "making music" that provided the basis for so much familiar and bawdy metaphor in Elizabethan drama.[7]

Love and music were identified on still another basis, not because love and music meant the same thing or were the same thing, but because music was one of various manifestations of love. Love was imagined to be felt as flame, savored as sweetness, heard as music. The medieval mystic Richard Rolle, in his *Incendium amoris* (translated as *The Fire of Love or Melody of Love*), described an experience in which the heat of love was followed by a sensation of sweetness, and this by a "celestial melody . . . heard by him with the outward as well as with the inward ear," a harmony that was an expression both of his own passion and of the love that was in heaven. The speech of circling Love in Dante's "Paradiso" was heard as melody.[8] George Herbert joined the music of his love of God with that of lute (in a key learned from the "stretched sinews" of the crucified Christ):

> His stretched sinews taught all strings what key
> Is best to celebrate this most high day.
>
> Consort both heart and lute, and twist a song
> Pleasant and long.

So did Crashaw, whose love harmonized with sound of "Lutes & Harps" to become one with the "unbounded All-imbracing Song" above. Love will "flow forth, like a rich perfume," sings Euphemus in Ben Jonson's *Loves Triumph*,

> . . . or some sweeter sound
> Of melting musique, that shall not consume
> Within the eare, but run the mazes round.[9]

The identities of love and music merged in still another way. Both were characterized by circular motion, and the motion set up by one could change into the motion of the other. The motion of sound, Plato had written in the *Timaeus*, is circular, akin to the circular motion of men's souls and to the motion of the spheres. Sound was described for centuries—first probably by Zeno, later by Boethius and by innumerable other scholars, poets, and philosophers—by analogy with a stone dropped into water, making a series of concentric circles, the image of perfection, for "perfect motions are all circular":

> As when a stone, troubling the quiet waters,
> Prints in the angry stream a wrinkle round,
> Which soon another and another scatters,
> Till all the lake with circles now is crown'd:
> All so the aire struck with some violence nigh,
> Begets a world of circles in the skie;
> All which infected move with sounding qualitie.[10]

As readers of Donne know well, love, too, makes circles that resemble the motion of the spheres:

> If, as in water stir'd more circles bee
> Produc'd by one, love such additions take,
> Those like so many spheares, but one heaven make,
> For, they are all concentrique unto thee.[11]

Circular motion, imaged in dance, is both love and harmony in Sir John Davies' *Orchestra*:

> Dauncing, the child of Musicke and of Love;
> Dauncing it selfe, both love and harmony.

George Chapman, in *Ovids Banquet of Sence*, imagined the circular motion of music converted into love when he wished that Corynna's singing could be spread

> . . . as far as Phoebus sees
> Through earths dull vaines; that shee like heaven might move,
> In ceaseless Musick, and be fill'd with love.

And this image he reversed when he described a conversion of love's kiss into music. The circling motions of the spheres and of a kiss are alike, and both make music to which the lover (like a musical instrument) responds by sympathy:

> The motion of the Heavens that did beget
> The golden age, and by whose harmonie
> Heaven is preservd, in mee on worke is set,
> All instruments of deepest melodie
> Set sweet in my desires to my loves liking

> With this sweete kisse in mee theyr tunes apply,
> As if the best Musitians hands were striking:
> This kisse in mee hath endlesse Musicke closed,
> Like Phoebus Lute, on Nisus Towrs imposed.
>
> And as a Pible cast into a Spring,
> Wee see a sort of trembling cirkle rise . . .
> So this perpetuall-motion-making kisse.[12]

As controlling forces in the universe, music and love might be two aspects of one reality, similar ways of explaining cosmic dynamics. If love made the world harmonious, if music brought amity, each was projecting or infusing its own nature, which was both love and music. If love of God, by its motion, swayed the world of man "in perfect Diapason," it was because love is music and music love. But from another point of view they were quite different. During long centuries when the little world of man was considered a copy of the great one, and when the great world was interpreted in terms of human experience, it was impossible not to think of eternal love and music as resembling their earthly counterparts of human love and the music that may be heard, which are two very different and distinct phenomena. Since human love is an emotion and music an aural sensation, one an inner experience, the other an external event, they are obviously two different things, and the distinction between them was carried over from the personal and concrete to the metaphysical and abstract level.

Music, while it might be defined as the reconciliation of opposites and thus similar to love, was more often described, by those writers who imagined it the basis of the universe—by Plato in the *Timaeus*, by Macrobius in the commentary on the "Dream of Scipio," by the Renaissance architects and painters—as a rational principle expressed in mathematical proportion like that of audible music.[13] Love, on the other hand, as an active creative force, or as a spirit pervading the universe, was thought by Neoplatonic writers, and many others as well (it was an idea older than Aristotle), to resemble human love, which was not at all like rational mathematics.[14] God, the Creator, was motivated by "infinit Love," and was "stirred up by his owne wil" to bring order into the world. The angels "for Love wherle about the superiour Spheares in continuall motion." The elements "have for their Love that invisible appetite . . . to attain their determinate endes."[15] All nature experiences a feeling of love:

> Ask the female palm how she
>   First did woo her husband's love
> And the magnet, ask how he
>   Doth th'obsequious iron move;
> Waters, plants, and stones know this:
> That they love; not what Love is.

"Yea plants, yea stones detest,/And love," wrote Donne.[16]

Music itself was made harmonious by love, and artists must investigate, wrote Ficino, "what ratios love . . . what other ratios." "They find the least affection [*amorem*] between the first and second steps in the scale and between the first and seventh. They find a rather strong affinity [*amorem vehementiorem*] between the first and third . . . but the strongest [*vementissimum*] between the first and eighth." From this love "smoothness and sweetness of harmony derive."[17] Thomas Morley quoted Plato in *A Plaine and Easie Introduction to Practicall Musicke* (1597), agreeing that "Musick . . . is a science of love matters occupied in harmonie and rhythmos."[18]

This concept colors much Elizabethan musical imagery. Shakespeare, writing in Sonnet 8 of "the true concord of well-tuned sounds,/By unions married," continued:

> Mark how one string, sweet husband to another,
> Strikes each in each by mutual ordering,
> Resembling sire and child and happy mother,
> Who all in one, one pleasing note do sing.

Andrew Marvell, in "Musick's Empire," imagined a musical marriage:

> Each [sound] sought a consort in that lovely place;
> And Virgin Trebles wed the manly Base.
> From whence the Progeny of numbers new
> Into harmonious Colonies withdrew.[19]

Words and notes were "lovingly" coupled together; voice and verse "wed" their "divine sounds." And this union paralleled the love of real people, for, as may be seen in *The Passionate Pilgrim*:

> If music and sweet poetry agree,
> As they must needs, the sister and the brother,
> Then must the love be great 'twixt thee and me,
> Because thou lov'st the one, and I the other.[20]

This music created by love is no longer described as a controlling force in the universe, or as an image of cosmic order. Music is merely one of love's creations, and one of the less consequential. It is united and sweetened by love, not ordered according to mathematical proportion. "Love is the teacher and Master of all the arts," wrote Ficino, quoting Plato.[21] Inspiration of love must govern all artists, not knowledge of a universal mathematics that was imagined to be reflected in music. In its ideal interpretation, such a philosophy could inspire the aesthetics of a Michelangelo; in its lowest, it fostered the seeds of anti-rationalism "inherent in any philosophic system which emphasized the role of love."[22] But even in its original Platonic-Ficinian intention, this idea implied a subordination of music to love. *Amor musicam docet*: love teaches music. The old proverb was a favorite in emblem books well into the seventeenth century.[23] "Love becomes music" was altered to "without love there can be no music." If love is, then, Master of the arts, music must be the servant of love, as it became in time the slave of poetry. This is perhaps drawing too fine a distinction, for poets said, often enough, that music is divine. Members of the cult of love did, nonetheless, tend to dissociate heard music from the cosmic scheme, to ignore the divinity of its mathematics, and to evaluate it in terms of its relation to love.

Orthodox Neoplatonists excluded music altogether from the philosophical formula. Others, less strict, and less concerned with divine love than with human, admitted that it might serve a function in increasing love. A completely unorthodox group fancied music the desired object of love, even of a passionate love, which could, in its intensity, elevate soul above body. All felt a compulsion to judge music in terms of love, and by so doing they brought into question its divinity. Neoplatonism, which had contributed so much to the revival of Platonic and Pythagorean ideas about music, contributed also to their decline.

II

Love's Appetite
Did Beauty first Excite.[24]

How then may music serve love? Love, wrote the Neoplatonists, is desire for beauty. The innate creative impulse characteristic of love desires to produce beauty, but it desires always to return to divine beauty, God Himself, who is both love and beauty. This return to God, this kind of ecstasy, is accomplished, they said, through love of the reflection of divine beauty in earthly objects, a love that can lead by gradual steps to union with the original image. Several questions then arose. What is beauty? Does music possess beauty? If it does, can man, by love of beauty in music, elevate his soul to God?

This age-old question of the nature of beauty, which has never been satisfactorily answered, plagued many a Renaissance philosopher and artist, whether Platonist or not. Does it consist in "magnitude and arrangement," as Aristotle dictated, or is it, as it was for Plotinus, a more intangible and elusive quality, a more "remote principle" beyond mere human skill?[25] Most Neoplatonists concluded that beauty is incorporeal, a divine light shining through man-made objects.

Does music, then, which is based on proportion, possess a beauty that can inspire elevating love? Plotinus decided that it does:

> Beauty addresses itself chiefly to sight, but there is a beauty for the hearing too, as in certain combinations of words and in all kinds of music, for melodies and cadences are beautiful;

4+

> and minds that lift themselves above the realm of sense to a higher order are aware of beauty in the conduct of life, in actions, in character, in the pursuits of the intellect.[26]

In Avicenna's influential treatise on love, Plotinian doctrine was re-stated: the soul always loves that which is beautiful and harmonious in composition and construction; for example, the soul loves harmonious sounds and cadences, which have affinity with the highest harmony and beauty.[27] Plato, on the other hand, in spite of his use of music to image cosmic order, named only "personal beauty" as providing the "rungs of a ladder" leading man aloft.[28]

The writings of Ficino, at the end of the fifteenth century, reflect the ambiguity of music's position. In his commentary on Plato's *Symposium*, he wrote that through love, "the creator and preserver of all natural things," everything is given orderliness, and "the attractiveness of this Orderliness is Beauty."[29] In his initial statement he included music. "This charm is three-fold," he wrote. It may be found "in the harmony of several virtues," in the harmony of color and line, and in "the best harmony of several tones." Beauty is the "illuminating light of God," a light that shines through what God has created, through "the souls of men, the shapes of bodies, and sounds." The pleasing quality in all three summons and attracts the soul "through reason, sight, or hearing." It moves and delights the observers, and "in delighting them, it carries them away, and in so doing, inflames them with burning love."[30] When Ficino explained the process by which love is aroused and by which it is refined, however, he wrote, not of audible beauty, but of visible.

In Ficino's treatise on love, the way in which beauty causes love and draws soul from body is described by different speakers on several different levels—as an involuntary magnetism, as a perceptive process, and as a physical experience. The Sixth Speech tells how a ray of beauty is sent from the beautiful object through the eyes and into the soul of the beholders, and how it draws the soul from the body, "like a fish on a hook," by a magnetic attraction which fills the soul with "glowing love." The same speaker explains, in a later chapter, the process of perception, in which the beautiful image is reflected in the "spirits" and is converted by the mind into a more spiritual form.[31] The word "spirits" is used here in a medical sense, to mean "a certain very thin vapor, created through the heat of the heart from the purest part of the blood." The spirits were the "median" between soul and body; by means of spirits, soul controlled body and all sense impressions reached the soul. They could even leave the body and return again. Having issued from bodily apertures, in tears, or on the breath, but especially from the eye, with the light that was imagined to shine from it, they might then enter the eye or ear or pores of another person and pass from the sense organ to other parts of the body, to carry qualities of the sender.

Ficino sometimes wrote of the spirits going out of the sense organ to receive the sense image, but in the *De amore* he described the image of beauty entering the eye. Because the soul is "present to the spirit in every part, [it] easily sees the images of bodies shining in it as though in a mirror," and "while it sees these images, it conceives in itself," through imagination or phantasy (as by a kind of spiritual impregnation), "images like them, but much purer," and through these images "the eyes of the soul are wakened to behold the Universal Ideas of things."[32]

The Seventh Speech discusses the bewitchment of physical love, which occurs when spirits issuing from the eye of one person penetrate the eyes of another and pass directly into the heart, disregarded, apparently, by phantasy and reason. This penetration of the arrows of love (a "conceit . . . already traditional in the twelfth century"[33]), poets, for centuries, had never wearied of describing. Ficino, however, unlike many other writers both before and after, did not make this penetration a preliminary to intellectual love. These penetrating spirits, he wrote, infect the blood of the receiver. But in condensing on the wall of the heart they become again the blood of the sender and long to return to their home. At the same time the heart from which they came longs to have what it has lost. There follows then a yearning for physical union that is not love but a disease, for which music is not cause but cure.[34]

Ficino's final decision, it must be assumed, was that music does not inspire the kind of love that he had in mind. In spite of his initial statements to the contrary in the *De amore*, he concluded finally, even there, that "all love begins with sight."[35] In a letter to Pellegrino de Gl'Agli (although he paid tribute to the image of divine harmony in music), he said that only beauty seen with the eyes creates that ardent desire of the soul for all beauty that is called love. With the ears man may perceive divine harmony, and he may then wish to return to it, but to create this kind of longing, voices and strings are of little value, for poetry alone appeals to the mind.[36]

In his famous analyses of musical effects, he did not specifically relate music to love. Yet these writings did influence thought about music's power to induce physical love and to produce other effects, as will be seen in later chapters. One statement, in a letter to Antonio Canisiano, is in medical context and describes not the effect of sound alone, but of music with words, which, having been formed by imagination, mind, and passion of the heart, enter the ear and penetrate the imagination, mind, and heart of the listener:

> Since song and sound arise from the cogitation of the mind, the impetus of the phantasy, and the feeling of the heart, and, together with the air they have broken up and tempered, strike the aerial spirit of the hearer, which is the junction of the soul and body, they easily move the phantasy, affect the heart and penetrate into the deep recesses of the mind.

Another, in his commentary on Plato's *Timaeus*, accounts more especially for the effect of musical sound itself. It penetrates the ear by means of air, as spirits penetrate the eye in the "disease" of love, and moves the spirits of the listener. It stirs emotions and affects the mind; it gives exquisite pleasure, as man is flooded and possessed by sweet, flowing sound:

> Musical sound . . . conveys as if animated, the emotions and thoughts of the singer's of player's soul to the listener's souls . . . by the movement of the air [it] moves the body; by purified air it excites the aerial spirit which is the bond of body and soul: by motion it affects the senses and at the same time the soul: by meaning it works on the mind: finally, by the very movement of the subtile air it penetrates strongly: by its contemperation it flows smoothly: by the conformity of its quality it floods us with a wonderful pleasure: by its nature, both spiritual and material, it at once seizes, and claims as its own, man in his entirety.

For these reasons, he continued, Alexander was moved from one violent emotion to another, as legend relates.[37]

Music, as Ficino analyzed it, does not lead to elevation or to divine love. The very fact that sound affects primarily the spirits and that reaction to it is passive rather than active, the very suddenness of the event, all make its effects closer to physical than to intellectual love. Still, there is in both passages an explanation of the transfer of emotion from singer to listener that was widely considered (not on Ficino's authority alone) a means of "infection"; and the second contains a suggestion of amorous penetration and possession that later writers, Chapman especially, recognized and developed, not as serious philosophy, certainly, but as charming imagery.

There were motives both rational and doctrinal for omitting music from the category of beauty that inspires love for itself or for its divine counterpart. Reaction to music is obviously different from reaction to people: love of the one scarcely resembles passionate love of the other. The immediate and involuntary response to music—always a marvel—excluded it from the experience of ideal love, which involved contemplation of beauty. Traditionally there was a great variety of kinds of music, each arousing a different emotion. The Greek doctrine of *ethos* was based on this assumption. Moreover, from ancient times, music had been associated with air, beauty with the higher element of fire or with light, both of which radiated from the sun, which shed its beams to give warmth and life and divine power. This light gave "grace" without which beauty did not exist, gave that something beyond mere proportion that lodged in the soul, from whence it shone through the features, but especially through the light of the eyes, to kindle love in the heart of the beholder. From the time of Plato it had been believed that love enters only by the eye. In Provençal love poetry, in the verses of the *stilnovisti*, in Petrarch (who exerted a compelling influence during the Renaissance), this idea persisted. There was doubt that a blind man could fall in love. "How comes it to pass," asked Robert Burton, as had Andreas Capellanus long before, "that a blind man loves, that never saw?"[38] Any aural inspiration of love was by speech, not melody. "For speech is nothing (sure)," Sylvester translated out of Du Bartas, "But th'unseen soules resounding portrature."[39]

The more Neoplatonic philosophy focused, as it inevitably did, on love of man for woman, rather than on an ideal love of virtue or of God or of abstract beauty, the more confused the position of music became. If music did possess beauty, if, for this reason or for others, it did inspire love, toward what was this love directed? This analysis of music is only one thread in a complex strand of thought. Many writers had no interest in Neoplatonic love; they liked or disliked, praised or condemned music, free of love philosophies. In general, however, there was in the Renaissance a self-consciousness in the application of the words "love" and "beauty" to music that is not shared today, and music's relation to love was often debated.

III

For where is any author in the world
Teaches such beauty as a woman's eye?[40]

Pico della Mirandola, the spokesman for the orthodox Neoplatonic love tradition, clearly excluded music from the truly beautiful. "Beauty in the largest sence," he wrote, is "the same with Harmony," but "Beauty in a restrict acception relates to a proportionable concord in visible things, as Harmony in audible. The desire of this Beauty is Love; arising onely from one knowing faculty, the Sight." Beauty in a restricted sense is more than proportion; it is a "certain quality which cannot be exprest by any term better than Gracefulness, shining in all that is fair," and pre-eminently in the human body. It is this beauty alone that inspires love —which is, ideally, a separation of soul from body in desire to unite with God.[41]

This distinction went beyond mere semantics: it denied the divine in music, as it brought into question the divine "glow" in all man-made art. Innumerable treatises on love throughout the sixteenth century, following Pico's doctrine, continued to ignore music, as did those of Lorenzo de' Medici, Benedetto Varchi, Flaminio Nobili, Torquato Tasso, and a score more. Symphorien Champier included "voice" as a cause of love, but did not relate it to music. Mario Equicola uttered only that stereotyped recital of music's virtues to be found in innumerable writings from the time of Boethius through the seventeenth century.[42]

Count Annibale Romei, in *The Courtiers Academie*, and Tommaso Buoni, in his *Problemes of Beauty*, gave further reasons for this omission. Romei's chief speaker, Signior Francesco Patritio, presents the usual definition of beauty, which makes it depend both on proportion and on the shining light of God, which glows through color.[43] When a companion objects that he has omitted various other kinds of beauty, including music, his answer is that "onely proportion in bodies, according to Platoes minde, is called Beauty," that the corresponding attribute in music is harmony, in humors, health, and that the terms should not be confused. He continues then with the reasoning that music is the work not of nature, but of art: "Beautie of bodies is absolutely a work of Nature, shining of it self, without the help or adoperation of Art: But harmonie is not wholy a worke of Nature" either in composition or in performance. Beauty derives from God; music is the work of man. Man himself, not music, is made in God's image.[44]

Buoni, answering the question, "Why is beauty especially apprehended by the sight?" hazarded a similar opinion:

> Perhaps because Beauty is a certaine divine splendour which is shewed unto us in thinges naturall, and that doth most participate of the divine Nature, which is least earthly, and such is the eye (among other senses) in apprehending thinges. . . . Or Perhaps because the eye is, as it were the cleare looking glasse of the soule, in which are descried all the affections of the minde.[45]

The most truly Platonic English poet, Edmund Spenser, did not mention audible music in his *Fowre Hymnes* to love and beauty. Beauty is to be found pre-eminently in the human form. It is a "love-kindling light," infused in varying degree in "all things faire," shining through proportion and color.[46] For John Donne, too, as for Cicero and Augustine, beauty was color and proportion: "Beauties best" is proportion, but beauty has a "second Element,/Colour and lustre," which again implies light. "Nature and grace doe all, and nothing Art."[47] Music played no part in his Neoplatonic love poems, and even elsewhere, although he used a musical imagery to project abstract concepts, his references to the effects of audible music were conspicuously few.

Music, in this orthodox tradition, gives joy; like poetry, it arouses admiration or wonder or amazement, but not love. Sir Philip Sidney put the matter succinctly in *Astrophel and Stella*, in verses that begin,

> O You that heare this voice,
> O you that see this face,
> Say whether of the choice,
> Deserves the better place.

Reason and Common Sense agree that

> Love more affected seemes
> To Beauties lovely light,
> And Wonder more esteemes
> Of Musicks wondrous might.[48]

Music breathes "foorth Wonders Winde,/Which mounts, above it selfe, the heaviest minde," wrote John Davies of Hereford, but he did not include music in his enthusiastic definition of the beauty that causes love, for

> . . . the pleasures which we doe receave
> From Nature's works have much more force then those
> That we from Artificiall things conceave.[49]

A study of why music was assumed to rouse these "passions" (for admiration and wonder were considered passions[50]) leads into a field of aesthetics, a very important one, that cannot be explored here. It is necessary to return to the place of music in the philosophy of love. Music had had too long an association with love—from the time of the *Homeric Hymns* and the legends of Arion's amorous dolphins—to be easily discarded. And Ovid's *Art of Love* could hardly be ignored. "A persuasive thing is song," he had written. "Let women learn to sing; with many voice instead of face has been their procuress."[51]

IV

> She heard his eloquent Tongue, and charming Lyre,
> Whose artful Sounds did violent Love inspire.[52]

The belief that music has beauty that inspires an elevating love, as that notion had come down from Plotinus to Ficino, did not entirely disappear. Leo Hebraeus, writing in the early sixteenth century, supported this view, insisting that there is beauty in music as well as in the human form. Music, too, he argued, possesses a spiritual grace which moves not only to delight, but to love.[53] The Italian Neoplatonists, Pietro Bembo and Giuseppe Betussi, also defended the idea of auditory perception of beauty. In England, the opening song of Ben Jonson's masque, *Love's Welcome*, names all the senses, even smell and taste, as ways by which love may lift the soul "To knowledge of that pure intelligence,/Wherein the Soule hath rest, and residence."[54]

By the late sixteenth and early seventeenth centuries, however, the original seriousness was rarely apparent. More typical is Shakespeare's amused skepticism, revealed when Titania, in *A Midsummer Night's Dream*, gazing at the ludicrous Bottom, recalls Ficino's three sources of love-inspiring beauty—music, shape, and virtue—in a highly humorous context and with no suggestion of spiritual refinement:

> Mine ear is much enamour'd of thy note;
> So is mine eye enthralled to thy shape;
> And thy fair virtue's force, perforce, doth move me,
> On the first view to say, to swear, I love thee.[55]

Furthermore, the fact remains that most serious Neoplatonists excluded music from the realm of beauty.

Even though it was usually agreed, however, that music does not have beauty, the notion that it causes or increases love persisted, less in a carefully formulated philosophy than in poetic imagery. It appeared in a variety of hybrid forms that resulted from compromise between, or combination of, Neoplatonism and popular musical traditions. Its roots were in ancient ideas of the power of harmony, in legend, in the works of Ovid, but they drew nourishment, too, from the writings of Ficino, and most of all from that famous Neoplatonic book, Castiglione's *The Courtier*. Music, whether it has beauty or not, it was said, can cause, or at least encourage, love, both for other people and for music itself.

The act of singing (of performance on an instrument to a lesser degree) was in itself a means not only of expressing feeling but of literally projecting it—a notion the implications of which will be further examined in later chapters. As Ficino had written, sound and song, since they come from the mind, imagination, and heart of the singer, carry ideas and emotions to the soul of the listener. Platonists say, Mersenne reported in 1636, that sound carries the ideas and affection of the singer to the depths of the spirits of the listener. Song is "a very echo to the seat/Where Love is thron'd," and thus "love begets love," as the old proverb stated.[56]

Music could also infuse its own love, for music itself was thought to contain love, in a literal sense. Music might not have beauty, but it did have harmony, and harmony, according to Platonic tradition, is the creation of love. As concord or consent, harmony *is* love. The love in music was more than an abstraction; it was often described as a real thing. This opinion was encouraged by the personification of love as Cupid or Eros, and by the idea that love is a pervasive spirit, but it was in keeping, also, with the persistent medieval conception of qualities as realities. Like heat and cold, love might be a "distinct substance." As Huizinga puts it, "beauty, tenderness, whiteness, being realities, are also entities." Thus music, since it possesses concord, which is a form of love, projects love. "Musicks Love" could be breathed "Through pores of senseles trees, as it could make them move," wrote Sir Philip Sidney.[57]

Music that entered the soul of the listener, since it carried love with it, could engender the state or the emotion of love, love which could be directed wherever inclination tended, but which, in erotic poetry, was commonly directed toward the performer of the music. Music could literally breathe into the listener not only the contagious love of the singer, but its own. Poetic imagery often implies both events. "Transform'd to ayre," wrote Thomas Watson, "Love entred with my will,/And nowe perforce doth keepe possession still." "Oft in a voyce he creeps downe the ear," echoed Phineas Fletcher. "But heare/This syren sing," wrote Carew in "Celia Singing,"

> . . . And on the wing
> Of her sweet voyce, it shall appeare
> That Love can enter at the eare.[58]

This harmonious love in music—or loving harmoniousness —the quality that pleases, that takes the place of beauty, was most often described as "sweetness," and regarded less as a primary cause of love than as a means to increase love.

"Sweetness" might indicate simply "mellifluousness," a smooth and pleasant flowing quality; but it also meant "concord"—another name for love, which was also sweet as honey. Sourness, contrarily, indicated discord or lack of proportion, as in Shakespeare's "How sour sweet music is/ When time is broke and no proportion kept!" Sweetness meant "agreement" in Samuel Rowley's lines, "Another sweetnesse, and harmonious sound,/A milder straine, another kind agreement."[59]

The writings of Castiglione no doubt popularized and literalized for love poets the notion that sweetness had amorous uses. He agreed with Pico that music does not have beauty in the restricted sense; only visual beauty, "a heavenlie shyning beame" that "appeereth in bodies, and especially in the face of mann" is the cause of this "fervent covetinge which wee call Love." Music, however, his speakers concur, possesses another quality that may serve the lover. It has sweetness. This sweetness gives delight; it makes the heart and mind tender, and thus receptive to love; when love already exists, it is the food of love.

Count Ludovico describes a "softe harmonye, that by a delectable waye and full of mourninge sweetnesse maketh tender and perceth the mind, [and] . . . sweetly imprinteth in it a passion full of great delite." Again, he says:

> Many thynges are taken in hand to please women withal, whose tender breastes are soone perced with melodye, and fylled with swetenesse.
>
> Therefore no marvaile that in the olde times and nowe a dayes they have alwayes bene enclined to musitiens, and counted this a moste acceptable foode of the mynde . . . musicke . . . doth not onely make swete the mindes of men, but also many times wilde beastes tame.

Pietro Bembo agrees. The lover, he says, must enjoy not only the brightness of his lady's beauty, but "the sweetnesse of her voice, the tunablenesse of her woordes, the melodie of her singinge and playinge on instruments," and so "with most deintie foode feede the soule through the meanes of these two senses."[60]

Shakespeare's Antony reflects this notion when he calls music the "moody food/Of us that trade in love," as does the lovesick Duke in *Twelfth Night*, who exclaims:

> If music be the food of love, play on!
> Give me excess of it, that, surfeiting,
> The appetite may sicken, and so die.[61]

Poets played with seemingly endless variation on this theme of the power of music's sweetness to prepare the heart for love, to stimulate love, to feed "the greedy hearing." Tunes "Ravish the eare and soul with strange delight,/And with sweet Nectar fill the thirsty sprite." The "sweet voyce . . . sweetly skild withall,/In all sweet stratagems sweete Arte can shew" was the final assault on the heart, for "sweete notes helpe perswasion."[62]

Chiefly, however, love poets drew upon the age-old belief that music, as an image of divine harmony, has power to attract and refine the soul. This attraction of harmony was described in a uniquely literal imagery and often as an amorous experience in which ear or soul could be enamoured of music itself. Harmony, like beauty, could draw soul from body to itself, it was imagined, by natural power, and this ecstasy was described in terms similar to those in which Castiglione, especially, had explained the effects of personal beauty.

As Pico represents orthodox Neoplatonism, so Castiglione represents its popularization. For the benefit of the courtier who preferred to sweeten spiritual philosophy with knowledge and pleasure drawn from the book of nature, he combined into one process the physical and intellectual aspects of Ficino's (and Plato's) account of the operations of love. Enjoyment of physical pleasures need not be condemned, as it was by Neoplatonic purists; they are the first step in love's sublimation, the first step in complete separation of soul from body and its final coupling with the "nature of Aungelles." Herein are the germs of decay that made of Neoplatonic love a travesty of its original intention, that fostered in the court circle of Charles I's queen, Henrietta

Maria, the licentious love cult that so inflamed Puritan ire.[63] But in 1528 Neoplatonism had not yet fallen into disrepute.

The image of beauty enters the eye, Castiglione wrote, and imprints itself on the soul, filling it, as does music, with sweetness and delight. But it also causes heat—"setteth her in heate"—which melts "vertues congeled in the soule." Because of this heat, the spirits of the lover (closely associated with soul) are thrust out through the eyes to see in glorified form the original image, "wherupon the soule . . . with a certein wonder is agast. . . astonied . . . with the pleasure." This heat is nourished by spirits issuing from the eye of the beloved, which "put continually freshe nourishment to the fire," and which also consummate spiritual union.

Spirits and soul can leave the body not only by the eye, but by the mouth in a kiss. The kiss is a symbolic marriage of souls, for by its means the breath, which is soul, passes from one body into the other:

> Although the mouthe be a percell of the bodye, yet is it an issue for the wordes, that be the enterpreters of the soule, and for the inwarde breth, which is also called the soule: and therefore the lover hath a delite to joigne hys mouth with the womans beloved with a kysse . . . bicause he feeleth that, that bonde is the openynge of an entrey to the soules, whiche drawen with a coveting the one of the other, power them selves by tourn, the one into the others bodye. . . . Whereupon a kisse may be said to be rather a cooplinge together of the soule, then of the bodye, bicause it hath suche force in her, that it draweth her unto it, and (as it were) seperateth her from the bodye.

From this first "stayre of love," man may then ascend, by imagination and by intellect, until the soul, purged of all things physical, sees the light of divine beauty.[64]

The widespread influence of these passages on seventeenth-century love imagery in England is obvious and has often been noted. Marlowe's Faustus, kissing Helen, cries, "Her lips suck forth my soul; see where it flies!" "Breake off this last lamenting kisse," exclaimed John Donne, "Which sucks two soules, and vapors Both away." "Eye-beames" were imagined to twist a thread that might unite souls while their bodies lay "like sepulchrall statues," or to pour like wine from eye to eye, joining the spirits of lovers:

> Till my Eyes drank up his,
> And his drank mine,
> I ne'r thought Souls might kiss,
> And Spirits joyn.[65]

It is not surprising to find similar influence in musical imagery, to find that music, even without beauty, also "sucketh sweetly," that it literally draws soul out of the ear as visual beauty draws it from the eye or kissing from the mouth. Here is more sensory pleasure than the churchman defending music's ecstatic power was willing to admit.

Drawing out of the soul through the ear became an ubiquitous metaphor: "sweet Notes" and "Heav'nly sounds" ravished the mind and drew out the soul, as Ficino had written, "like a fish on a hook," to unite not with soul of lover, but with harmony. Sylvester, translating Du Bartas, told how

> . . . six sweet Notes, curiously varied
> In skilful Musick, make a hundred kindes
> Of Heav'nly sounds, that ravish hardest mindes;
> And with Division (of a Choice device)
> The Hearers soules out at their ears intice.[66]

Richard Crashaw emphasized a purer Platonic ideal in his translation of Strada's famous account of a musical duel between nightingale and poet:

> . . . thus doe they vary,
> Each string his Note, as if they meant to carry
> Their Masters blest soule (snatcht out at his Eares
> By a strong Extasy) through all the sphaeares
> Of Musicks heaven; and seat it there on high
> In th'Empyraeum of pure Harmony.[67]

Against this background there is more reason in Sir Toby's boisterous proposal in *Twelfth Night* (in which he refers to the three souls of sense, of reason, and of growth): "Shall we rouse the night-owl in a catch that will draw three souls out of one weaver?" And one feels anew the charm of Lorenzo's lines in *A Merchant of Venice*, for Shakespeare has transformed oddity into the magic of poetry. Through the ear pierced by sweet music, Jessica's soul may be drawn from romantic love to that of the "home" from which it came:

> With sweetest touches pierce your mistress' ear
> And draw her home with music.[68]

Love of the soul, greedy for music and desiring to unite with it, is the subject of a love song in William Cartwright's play, *A Royal Slave*:

> Come my sweet, whiles every strayne
> Calls our Soules into the Eare;
> Where they greedy listning fayne
> Would turne into the sound they heare;
> Lest in desire
> To fill the Quire
> Themselves they tye
> To Harmony,
> Let's kisse and call them backe againe.[69]

This ravishment of the soul by music (the soul being conveniently hermaphroditic) carries, time and again, even more obviously sensual implications, as it does in a masque, *Love in its Extasie*, when Bermudo, hearing music underground, calls on Diana, goddess of chastity, to save him from ravishment:

> Ha! Guard me Diana: A Rape, a Rape;
> Where flies my ravisht Senses?

"Strange violence!" exclaimed William Strode, "thus pleasingly to teare/The soul forth of the body by the eare." And one finds similar suggestion in Benedick's caustic remark in *Much Ado About Nothing*: "Now, divine air! now is his soul ravished! Is it not strange that sheeps' guts should hale souls out of men's bodies? Well, a horn for my money, when all's done."[70]

Music could not only attract the soul from the "enamoured ear"; it could "possess" the soul and inflame it with burning love. As Ficino had said, it "floods us with a wonderful pleasure . . . seizes and claims as its own, man in his entirety." The listener could be in love with harmony as with beauty.

Chapman described this amorous possession of the soul by music in his *Ovids Banquet of Sence*, where each sense in turn is not only banqueted by the food of love, but inspired to passion. Influenced both by Castiglione and by Ficino, he imagined man enamored of music, ravished as by physical love, refined by its flames or by its invading sweetness. Music, sung and played by Corynna, sets the ear on fire. It elevates the spirits, and with their aid marries the soul:

> Never was any sence so sette on fire
> With an immortall ardor, as myne eares;
> Her fingers to the strings doth speeche inspire
> And numbered laughter; that the descant heares
>   To hir sweete voice; whose species through my sence
> My spirits to theyr highest function reares;
>   To which imprest with ceaseless confluence
> It useth them as propper to her powre
> Marries my soule and makes it selfe her dowre.

This image is followed immediately by another: tunes are like bees which carry sweetness (a sweetness characteristic of music, as of honey) that both refines and ravishes. They sting to death but give new life by possession of the soul—an image no Renaissance reader could fail to associate with the pain and sweetness of Eros. Music possesses man in his entirety, as Ficino had claimed:

> Me thinks her tunes flye guilt, like Attick Bees
> To my eares hives, with hony tryed to ayre;
> My braine is but the combe, the wax, the lees,
> My soul the Drone, that lives by their affayre.
>   O so it sweets, refines, and ravisheth,
> And with what sport they sting in theyr repayre;
>   Rise then in swarms, and sting me thus to death
> Or turne me into swounde; possesse me whole,
> Soule to my life, and essence to my soule.

In still another stanza, Chapman turned to the idea that music is air, which fans the flames of love, setting a blaze that purifies the flesh and turns all to spirit. With this image, he combines another: dancing air of music enters the ear and with its "embrace" and "daliance" makes love with the spirits. Sounds touch the ear

> Whose pores doe open wide to theyr regreete
> And my inplanted ayre, that ayre embraceth
> Which they impresse; I feele theyr nimble feete
> Tread my eares Labyrinth; theyr sport amazeth
> They keepe such measure; play themselves, and dance,
> And now my soule in Cupids Furnace blazeth,
> Wrought into furie with theyr daliance:
> And as the fire the parched stuble burns,
> So fades my flesh, and into spyrit turns.[71]

John Norris wrote, a century later, about this love affair with music, in which the lover's death leads to ecstasy:

> Let me soft melting strains of Music hear
> Whose Dying sounds may speak Death to my ear,
> Gently the Bands of life unty,
> Till in sweet raptures I dissolve and dye.[72]

To be a "Lover of Musicke" was to be more than an "admirer." One could fall in love with music itself. Music could draw soul from body as could a kiss, or penetrate the ear, as lover's spirits could the eye, to unite with or refine the soul. The idea that music could cause love for itself and thus effect union with all harmony was not in the orthodox tradition of Neoplatonism as that tradition had passed down from Pico to Donne. It was a debasement of the philosophy of Plotinus, Ficino, and Leo Hebraeus. Poets drew on a rich and varied background to create a unique imagery—serious, whimsical, or humorous—that could have belonged to no other age.

Churchmen who argued the value of music in divine service quite understandably avoided the entire Neoplatonic philosophy of love and turned instead to writings of the ancients, to sources less tainted by trivial eroticism. Only later in the century, when these implications were forgotten, did devout men dare apply Neoplatonic concepts to religious music. Joseph Brookbank turned to them in 1660 when he wrote, wth echoes of Ficino, that "Sweetness of harmonical sounds insinuates it self into the soul of man, prepares the affections for the service of God, delights the mind, kindles Devotion, inflames desire, and ravisheth the spirit with celestial joy."[73] Much later, in 1696, John Newte claimed that "the Grace and Melody of . . . Vocal and Instrumental Musicke together . . . may in time melt us into Love."[74] John Norris, in the same decade, attempted to rescue theories of love and beauty as taught by that "Sublime Platonist divine Marsilius Ficinus" from "those sordid abuses they have hitherto suffer'd," and urged that through contemplation of the beauty and proportion of music we "excite our Passions" and "heighten our Love of God."[75] "What art can teach . . . The sacred Organ's praise?" asked Dryden in "A Song for St. Cecilia's Day":

> Notes inspiring holy love,
> Notes that wing their heav'nly ways
> To mend the choirs above.

By the late seventeenth century, however, this whole concept was anachronistic. Neoplatonism had given way to the new science, metaphysics to physics, feeling to reason. Love and music were no longer identical, nor did one create the other. Before examining some of the trends that led to a changed view of music, however, it is necessary to consider another occult theory that demands attention. Music could be the cause of ecstatic death, but it could also restore life: lovers left lying "like sepulchrall statues," while their souls were gone out in an ecstasy, could be given life again by music.

CHAPTER V

Music: The Breath of Life

When Orpheus descended into Hades and revealed his power to give life to the dead or when by his song he moved trees and rocks or tamed wild beasts, when Amphion caused stones to build the walls of Thebes, they gave many future centuries cause to wonder. If certain philosophers agreed with Clement of Alexandria that Orpheus and the Theban, too, "under cover of music . . . outraged human life, being influenced by daemons, through some artful sorcery,"[1] occult philosophers argued that demons and magic are not necessarily evil. At all events, Orpheus and Arion demonstrated that music not only could cause ecstatic death, but could restore life, and the Renaissance philosopher was not one to let such a miracle go unexplained.

He had at his disposal several explanations of how dead things might be given life by music, but the two most common ones had to do with various kinds of "spirit." One theory originated, to an important degree, in Hermetic philosophy, that body of literature so filled with astrological, cabalistic, alchemical, and Neoplatonic notions that was compiled during the first few centuries after Christ and attributed to Hermes Trismegistus. The other was based on contemporary physiology, as it was interpreted in Platonic love philosophy.

I

Hermetic writings were translated, studied, and brought into prominence by Renaissance Neoplatonists, especially by Ficino and Pico della Mirandola. It was certainly Ficino who formulated from these materials a widely accepted theory of the occult effects of music on "spirits."

As has been seen, spirits, in a medical sense, were believed to be (in Robert Burton's words) "a most subtle vapour . . . expressed from the blood,"[2] which carried out all the functions that today are attributed to the nervous system. Natural spirits aided in carrying out physical functions of growth and reproduction, vital spirits in the functioning of life-giving virtues; animal spirits gave to the soul capabilities of sense and motion. But Ficino, in this connection, broadened the concept of spirits from its medical meaning to a cosmic one in which the whole universe was believed to be filled and animated by spirit, a spirit that linked lowest stone to purest angel.

This expansion of meaning did not originate with Ficino. From Aristotle, from the Stoics, and from Hermetic philosophy, came the idea of spirit, of *pneuma*, which pervaded the universe and gave life and motion to everything, which cemented all parts into a whole. The word *spiritus* or *pneuma*, in ancient science, meant literally breath, and "could be applied to a vapor, a gas, a disembodied spirit or even to the Holy Ghost."[3] This conception was not incompatible with Christian belief; the "Spirit of God," moving "upon the face of the waters" (Gen. 1:2), gave life and form to the world. World spirit was sometimes equated with the soul of the universe, the Platonic *anima mundi*, though it was usually thought to be different. It was the median between soul and body of the world, just as spirits in man were the knot of his soul and body. Aristotle gave authority for the belief (accepted even in the sixteenth century by the famous metallurgist, Georgius Agricola) that spirit not only could generate new forms, but could become form. Metals he described as spirituous exhalations or vapors in the earth: "Metals are the product of the vaporous exhalation, and are all fusible or ductile, for example, iron, gold, copper . . . each is the result of . . . solidification of the exhalation before it turns to water."[4]

Spirit mounted in degree of purity from inanimate objects, through man (where it took the form of natural, vital, and animal spirit in ascending order), to higher forms of spiritual being. Outward material form varied in correspondence with the subtlety of its spirit. Demons and genii were "personalized" world spirit, clothed in air. Angels were pure spirit, with no visible body: in heaven "Bodies are purer, then best Soules are here," wrote John Donne.[5] As Glanvill and others explained, it is not "suitable" to suppose that nature should make "precipitous leaps from one thing to another," from our "grossest matter" to "pure unbodied Spirits."[6] Milton, too, in *Paradise Lost*, described spirit in plants, flowers, fruit, ascending by gradual scale to animal spirits in man. From matter, to spirit in nature, to spirit in man, "by gradual scale sublim'd," man is linked to the angels; from the Almighty "All things proceed, and up to him return."[7]

George Hakewill in 1627 turned to this animating spirit of the universe to combat the misanthropic belief that the world is in a state of decay. It is, he wrote, "the immortall Spirit of the Creator," by which the world "is in some sort quickned and formaliz'd," by which God "is able to make the body of the World immortall, and to preserve it from disolution, as he doth the Angels."[8] From the time of William Gilbert, whose *De magnete* appeared in 1600, to that of Newton, this spirit, or something very like it, explained the operations of magnetism.

The alchemists, following the teaching of Raymond Lully (d. 1315), called this spirit the quintessence, because it was of a higher nature than the four elements (fire, air, water, earth) of which the universe was thought to be composed. It was the quintessence that they hoped by their art to capture for use as a chemical reagent or catalyst or to convert into new forms. For, they reasoned, if the spirit present in an inferior body could be destroyed and replaced by that of one superior to it, the body of the one could be altered to be like that of the other. The "death" of copper, for instance, could be followed by a "resurrection" in the form of gold.

Since the spirits in man resembled, or were a part of, world spirit, it did not seem unreasonable to suppose that his spirits, too, might be altered or replaced by spirit finer than his own. The distillation of alcoholic spirits, called *aqua vitae* (life-giving water), obviously had curative effects. Belief in the beneficent power of these alcoholic spirits combined with spirit drawn from plants (which received their growth from vivifying stellar spirit and thus carried stellar influence) explains, probably, the early monastic production of liqueurs.[9] Many an eminent philosopher devoted his life to an attempt to capture world spirit and infuse it in a philosopher's stone which could then, it was believed, be used to cure all human ills.

Music, as well as plants or stones or talismans, was thought to transmit celestial spirit and influence. On this assumption Ficino projected what a recent scholar calls his "music-spirit theory."[10] His belief in the efficacy of music to carry celestial influence was based on the ancient Pythagorean and Platonic theory of a musically and mathematically ordered universe, an ordering of which the mathematical proportions are similar to those of heard music. This universe, according to Ficino's conception, is animated by spirit, and since the universe is fundamentally musical, its spirit must be musical. "Undoubtedly the world lives and breathes," he wrote in the *De vita*; it is animate, as is man; and its breath is music.[11] Herein lies the significance of the image in Du Bartas (already quoted) of world as organ: as

> . . . one selfly blast breath'd out
> From panting bellows, passeth all-about
> Wind-Instruments. . . .
> . . . .
> Even so th'all quickning Spirit of God above
> The Heav'ns harmonious whirling wheels doth move.[12]

So, in Donne's "A Funerall Elegie," the spirits of the "shee" of whom he wrote tune the organ of the state, creating the music of "wonder and love." So the "blessed Spirit of God" speaks with music through the organ of man in "the Psalmes by Sir Philip Sydney."

By a "personalizing" of world spirit Ficino, in his commentary on Plato's *Symposium*, explained the musical sirens of the spheres and the demons that inhabit every element—

an explanation frequently attributed to Plato, as it was by Milton.[13] These spirits appear in heaven as angels, in the spheres as sirens, in the elements as demons, through the world as genii, man's tutelary spirits. And all are musical. In "Il Penseroso" Milton called on the "spirit of Plato to unfold" the mysteries

> . . . of these *Daemons* that are found
> In fire, air, flood, or under ground,
> Whose power hath a true consent
> With Planet, or with Element.

He wished to hear their music:

> And as I wake, sweet musick breath
> Above, about, or underneath,
> Sent by som spirit to mortals good,
> Or th'unseen Genius of the Wood.

Spirits commanded by Prospero in *The Tempest* appear with "Solemn and strange music."[14] Ariel, more spiritual than the earthy Caliban, is the more musical.

World spirit, because it is the breath of a musically proportioned universe, is musical. Conversely, music, because it images cosmic music, possesses or is spirit. The matter of song, writes Walker in summary of Ficino's *De vita*, "is 'warm air, even breathing, and in a measure living . . . so that it can be said to be, as it were, a kind of aerial and rational animal.' Musically moved air is alive, like a disembodied human spirit." "Sound is a breath," wrote the occult philosopher Agrippa.[15]

It is not in occult philosophy alone that we find this idea. A learned music scholar, Johann Alstedt, writing almost a hundred years later, attributed variation in the quality of musical sound to its spirit. As man is slow to anger or quick of wit from the nature of his spirits, so music is gentle or harsh according as its spirit is "tenuous and asperous": "For every Sound besides the length thereof, is also tenuous or gentle, flat, submiss, small; or sharp, harsh, clear, full, as consisting of a tenuous and asperous Spirit."[16]

The spirit of music, according to Ficino (and innumerable other writers), reflects the mood or emotion of the planet by which it is especially influenced. Each heavenly body has the character of the god whose name it bears, and sounds a music that possesses his characteristics. The music of the sun was thought to be grave and earnest, that of Venus voluptuous. "Saturn, Mars, and the Moon have only 'voices'—no music." These moods were imitated in the musical modes of man-made music.[17] Because the spirit of music shares in world spirit, and because music imitates the proportions and the moods of heavenly bodies, it is uniquely efficacious, Ficino believed, in transmitting celestial spirit and stellar influence to man, whose spirits respond to it by natural sympathy.

The influence of stars and planets on the physical world was rarely questioned, even though a Cassius might exclaim:

> The fault, dear Brutus, is not in our stars,
> But in ourselves, that we are underlings,

or Edmund, in *King Lear*, call it the "excellent foppery of the world, that, when we are sick in fortune,—often the surfeit of our own behaviour,—we make guilty of our disasters the sun, the moon, and the stars." George Hakewill insisted that stars *do* have influence on man, though not on the will.[18] Moon and stars shed that nourishment and heavenly "vertue" that Milton described in *Paradise Lost*, for their

> . . . soft fires
> Not only enlighten, but with kindly heate
> Of various influence foment and warme,
> Temper or nourish, or in part shed down
> Thir stellar vertue on all kinds that grow
> On earth, made hereby apter to receive
> Perfection from the Suns more potent Ray.[19]

By means of this spirit the sun is able to infuse life into dead matter, in a manner analogous to human conception, and to generate worms, flies, frogs, and even mice in dunghill or river mud. Myth had it that human conception could occur in the same way, a legend that accounts for Spenser's story of the miraculous conception of Belphoebe and Amoret from the influence of the sun's rays. This notion is the basis of Hamlet's advice to Polonius. Hamlet enters reading, "For if the sun breed maggots in a dead dog, being a god kissing carrion—" whereupon he breaks off, and asks, "Have you a daughter? . . . Let her not walk i' the sun."[20]

By means of astrologically powerful music, then, Ficino thought it possible to transmit both stellar influence and cosmic spirit to the spirit of man, to alter his temperament and to govern his emotions. By its breathing in of celestial spirit, his own spirit could be revived. By infusion of world spirit, even material objects could be given life: "One can attract into, and retain in, a material object 'something vital from the soul of the world and the souls of the spheres and stars,' that is, celestial spirit, if the object is of a material and form which reflects the celestial source of spirit in question."[21]

For these purposes Ficino composed and sang songs, which he called, for various reasons, "Orphic." They were intended to be like those sung by Orpheus and to possess similar powers. The words were those of the *Orphic Hymns*. The meaning of the text, it must be emphasized, was for Ficino of prime importance, for that alone, he wrote, reaches the mind. The mode fitted that of a particular planet, and attention was given to the daily position and aspect of the stars. The songs were delivered, one may conjecture, in the monodic style made popular in early seventeenth-century musical drama, now called opera.[22]

This notion was not an isolated aberration of a single mind. Its origins were in the past; its influence was a powerful one throughout the sixteenth century and into the seventeenth. It explained for many the use of music for prophetic possession (a practice, still, among primitive people), for as Sylvester translated Du Bartas:

> O! what is it that Musick cannot doo!
> Sith th'all-inspiring Spirit it conquers too:
> And makes the same down from th'Empyreall Pole
> Descend to Earth into a Prophets soule.[23]

It explained the origin of the emotions that seemed to be inherent in music that could sway man even against his will, how music could elevate the soul, why it breathed and revealed heaven. "Musicke breathes heaven, nay more, it doth disclose it," wrote Thomas Palmer in "An Epigram" to Elway Bevin "upon his Canons of three parts in one."[24]

Music might, then, refine the soul to ecstasy, but according to this spirit theory, it was usually not man who was carried to heaven, but heaven that was brought to man. By influx of divine spirit, not withdrawal of soul or spirit, man was made celestial. He need not even have a harmonious soul to be so affected. "The sullenest Creature" could be moved, even stones and trees. "But stone nor tree," wrote Sir Philip Sidney of Stella's singing, "by sences priviledge, can scape from thee." "Orpheus voyce" could "breathe such musicks Love/Through pores of senseless trees, as it could make them move." Amphion gave life to stones which "good measure daunst the Thebane walls to builde."[25] Man himself could be restored to life by music. Why should not the breath of world spirit carried by music give life, since the dust of the earth became man when into it God breathed the "breath of life" (Gen. 2:7)?

Authority for this use of music to infuse prophetic spirit, or to give life where none was before, was to be found in the writings of early Neoplatonists, such as Proclus and Iamblichus. D. P. Walker believes, however, that Ficino's chief sources were Plotinus and the Hermetic *Asclepius*, which Ficino had translated. It was in the latter work, especially, that he found an account of the alchemical infusion of soul into matter. "Our first ancestors," according to the *Asclepius*, "invented the art of making gods." Having made a statue or an image, "they evoked the souls of demons or angels, and put them into images with holy and divine rites." This they did by means of "herbs, stones and aromas, which have in them a natural divine power"; by means of "hymns and praises and sweet sounds concerted like the harmony of the heavens" they retained these spirits. This passage Ficino considered the source of one in the *Enneads* of Plotinus (IV.3.11), which he interpreted to mean that by music "one can attract into, and retain in, a material object 'something vital from the soul of the world and the souls of the spheres and stars.'"[26]

Ficino avoided the idolatry inherent in Hermes' statement. Demons and genii, like angels, were world spirit, but they were personalized world spirit, and because they were personalized, they were thought to have soul. Ficino was firm in his insistence that talismans, odors, music, infuse only impersonal world spirit, which has no soul, and that they affect not the soul of man, but his spirits. He disclaimed any use of "demonic magic"—"black magic"—a practice condemned by the Church, for there was always the danger that bad demons as well as good might be invoked. The air was thought to be full of spirits which could course through the spirits of man. The eminent physician, Levinus Lemnius, referred to these "externall spirites recoursing into his [man's] bodye and mynde," good angels imparting a "pleasant sweete inspiration," bad angels breathing out "a pestiferous poyson." The Devil, wrote Alstedt, uses filthy music "as his Vehicle, by which he slideth himself into the minds of men."[27] Ficino had no intention of encouraging possession by demons and angels. It was "natural magic," not demonic, that he hoped to use. Music was efficacious, according to tradition, to drive *out* evil spirits, but that is another story.

Pico della Mirandola agreed with Ficino in postulating a world spirit that could be controlled and by use of which man could be made celestial. He, too, wrote (in a passage quoted by Henry Reynolds, in *Mythomystes*, in 1633), "In natural magic nothing is more efficacious than the Hymns of Orpheus, if there be applied to them the suitable music, the disposition of the soul, and the other circumstances known to the wise." But he put more faith in the magic of numbers, which had a virtue even apart from music. According to his disciple, Reynolds, the power of Orpheus lay in knowledge of "the mysticall doctrine of Numbers."[28] Seven, four, three, had cosmic significance and magical effect.

Ficino's ideas on world spirit and his use of music were accepted, however, by a procession of sixteenth-century Neoplatonists, many of whom were less cautious about magical infusion of demons and angels than he was, or who combined with his ideas Pico's theories of numerology. Ludovico Lazarelli (according to his *Crater Hermetis*, published 1505) hoped not only to call down demons, in the tradition of the *Asclepius*, but to create them. Sounds themselves became demons. Ficino's warm and living air took on the shape of demons, which possibly were conceived of, writes D. P. Walker, as "separate bits of the Holy Spirit or the spirit of Christ."[29] One recalls Sir John Davies' description in *Orchestra* (stanza xxi) of the mythical musician, Amphion, who by his music "begot" of the air not a demon, but a siren:

> As when Amphion with his charming lire
> Begot so sweet a syren of the ayre.

Ficinos' ideas were repeated—with some variation—in the *Occult Philosophy* of Cornelius Agrippa. The universe is pervaded by spirit, wrote Agrippa, the same in the universe as in man, which carries to man the influences of the stars:

> For this is the band, and continuity of nature, that all superiour vertue doth flow through every inferiour with a long, and continued series, dispersing its rayes even to the very last things . . . as a certain string stretched out, to the lowermost things of all, of which string if one end be touched, the whole doth presently shake, and such a touch doth sound to the other end.

This spirit, which is warm and generative, the source of all life, may be infused by music, for "Musical harmony also is not destitute of the gifts of the Stars." "It is a most powerful imaginer of all things, which whilst it follows opportunely the Celestial bodies, doth wonderfully allure the Celestial influence." In a section "Concerning the agreement of . . . [sound and voices] with the Celestial bodies, and what harmony and sound is correspondent of every star," he attributed to each planet a particular musical tone and mood and quality of sound. Music can thus alter dispositions of bodies and souls, and musical sounds, he wrote, are not used in vain to restore "the minde to wholsome manners, untill they make a man sutable to the Celestial Harmony, and make him wholly Celestial."[30]

In the works of Pomponazzi, Francesco Giorgi, and many other writers, theories regarding the magical power of music recur, as Walker points out. As late as 1588 the theme of Neoplatonic magic was given prominence by Fabio Paolini, a professor of Greek at Venice, in his *Hebdomades,* in which he referred again to the *Asclepius* statues' being animated by "herbs, stones and celestial music." He regretted that the Church frowned on such notions, but he clung to them nevertheless, and he quoted Ficino's rules for composing planetary music in imitation of the *Orphic Hymns*, which contain "divine Mysteries." The power of Orpheus' music to inspire life became a matter of violent debate during a series of lectures given by Paolini in the important *Accademia degli Uranici*, the controversy assuming a seriousness which is difficult for a modern reader to imagine. As influential a philosopher as Campanella believed that music (among other things) could be used for "breathing in the Spirit of the World."[31]

II

These ideas appear in England in two different types of writings—in occult works, especially those associated with Rosicrucianism, which drew heavily on Agrippa and described the alchemical power of music to refine the soul; and also in more popular poetry, which was directly indebted to the *Asclepius* and to Ficino for the notion that music can infuse life.

William Ingpen, in 1624, in a summary of Agrippa's analysis both of world spirit and music, granted to numbers in music (triad or octave) a power above that of all others to attract celestial influence. Having pointed out the "Orphicall" significance of number, without which man cannot learn the secrets of the "Holy Ghost" (which is certainly spirit), he repeated Agrippa's enthusiastic account of the power of music: "Musicall harmony" has such "power and vertues . . . that shee is called The Imitatrix of the starres, of the soule and body of man. And when she followeth celestiall bodies so exquisitely, it is incredible to think, how shee provoketh those heavenly influxes."[32]

A deluge of occult writing followed the translation of Agrippa's *Occult Philosophy* in 1651, inspired presumably by resistance to the new science, which was, in many minds, eliminating God from the universe, which was breaking "the causal chain of descent from God to matter." Many of these writers stressed the magical power of number, but in the work of the astrologer-attorney, John Heydon, one meets again belief in the efficacy of music to call down celestial spirit and genii. World spirit, he related, in the words of Agrippa, is the same in the world as in man, but he departed from his source to explain that this spirit is the medium of genii, which can, by lights and music, be brought down from the spheres. Through lights and sounds, "that consent most sweetly in musick," music sends "down souls so merily to the Moon, and from thence they come down sadly to the belly and Matrix of the Earth in prolific spirited Winds and Waters, and be effectual in the operations of nature."[33] It is not mathematical number that gives music its force, he said, but the "Idea" or the "Genius approaching to the Instruments of sense" and carried inward where it works upon the body.

Current alchemical books also suggest the use of music to aid in control of the alchemist's quintessence or to attract astral influence. From ancient times metals had been associated with planets, from which they derived planetary signs, but they were associated, too, with planetary music, as in Robert Fludd's famous diagram of the universal monochord, where the sign of each metal is paralleled by a note of the scale.[34] Their combination was like that of musical notes ("accords which in Musick be . . . Much like proportions be in Alkimy"):[35] it was numerically the same; and metals were referred to often as the "chymic choir," and personified, each holding a musical instrument.[36] A picture of the alchemist's laboratory in a work by Heinrich Khunrath, published in 1595 and again posthumously in 1609,[37] shows, along with the stills and retorts, a number of musical instruments—lutes, viol, and harp. Michael Maier, in his *Atalanta Fugiens* (1618), appended three-part canons to be used, presumably, in the artist's work.[38] One can only guess that metals responded to musical instruments by sympathy, that law of nature that guaranteed response of like to like, or—judging from Maier's three-part canon (symbolic of the Trinity)—in response to the magic of number.

Metals, however, also had spirit, and it is not far-fetched to guess, too, that music aided in conveyance or control of world spirit, the alchemical quintessence. Elias Ashmole, in his *Theatrum chemicum Britannicum* (1652), intimated as much. The frontispiece (of one copy at least) pictures planetary figures, alchemical vessels, and musical instruments, and carries, beneath, an inscription suggesting the relationship of music to the *anima mundi*: "These Hieroglyphics vaile the Vigorous Beames/Of an unbounded Soule, The Scrowle and Schemes/The full Interpreter: but how's concealed." And in the "Prolegomena" he wrote of how things "Artificially made" may communicate "Celestiall Influences" from the "Soule of the World": "We are to Consider, that the Soule of the World is not confined, nor the Celestiall Influences limited, but doe indifferently emit and communicate their Vertues alike, as well to things Artificially made, as to those that are Naturally generated."[39]

The whole idea of alchemy was an obsession with seventeenth-century writers, who applied its principles or terminology to almost every philosophy. The Neoplatonic lover imagined himself sublimed by the alchemy of love, the religious mystic by the spiritual alchemy of Christ. In "An Elegie," Francis Quarles described music's alchemical breathing in of celestial love, which refined the "ravisht braynes" and made man "ripe for heav'n":

> Musick, the language of th'eternall Quire,
> Breath'd in his soule celestiall straynes,

And fild his Spirits with Seraphick fyre,
Whose gentle flames calcin'd his ravisht braynes;
And made him ripe for heav'n.[40]

Edward Benlowes, in "A Poetic Descant upon a Private Musick-Meeting," described each instrument as a planet, possessing the same powers to move emotions or project influence:

Last Mercury with ravishing strains fell on,
Whose violin seem'd the chymic-stone,
For every melting touch was pure projection.

The sweetness of music could inspire possession by a god:

Form, Beauty, Sweetness, all did here conspire,
Combin'd in one Celestial Quire,
To charm the enthusiastic soul with enthean fire.[41]

This occultism was limited to a comparatively small group of writers, whose ideas had long been under attack. Early in the century Ben Jonson made them the butt of humor in his *News from the New World Discover'd in the Moone*, with remarks aimed both at Cornelius Agrippa and "Cornelius Drible" and at the Rosicrucians. "What is the language in the Moon," asks the Chronicler. "They have no articulate voyces there," is the reply, "but certaine motions to musicke: all the discourse there is harmonie." "A fine Lunatique language i'faith; how doe their Lawyers then?" "They are Pythagorians, all dumbe as fishes." And the account continues: "The brethren of the Rosi-Crosse have their Colledge within a mile o' the Moone."[42] In *Mercurie Vindicated from the Alchemists at Court*, Jonson has his fun with the alchemists who use music to charm new life into old bodies. A grave matron, they think, may be transformed into a young virgin, an old courtier, broiled in the coals, given life again by blowing in of spirit—by use of charms and music:

They will calcine you a grave matron . . . and spring up a yong virgin, out of her ashes, as fresh as a Phoenix; Lay you an old Courtier o' the coales like a sausedge, or a bloat-herring, and after they ha' broil'd him enough, blow a soule into him with a paire of bellowes.

Whereupon Vulcan (entering "with a troupe of threedbare Alchymists" who dance around Mercury) speaks: "Begin your charme, sound musique, circle him in, and take him."[43] In 1656, Abraham Cowley, in a note to his *Davideis*, attacked the "Platoniques" who "fly to their *Anima Mundi*" to explain musical effects, an idea "so false, that I wonder at the negligence of impudence of the Relators."[44]

III

While literal belief in these occult notions was ridiculed, they flourished unchallenged in a large body of poetry. That music could breathe soul into whatever was inanimate, even as Orpheus had proved, was the basis for much poetic imagery less dominated by alchemical notions than that of Quarles and Benlowes.

The most direct debt to the *Asclepius* of Hermes is probably that of Carew in his poem, "Celia singing." Celia's music is as powerful as that of Orpheus to soothe wild beasts, as powerful as that of our "ancient ancestors" to breathe life into idols, which turn idolators of this "choyce music":

> Harke how my Celia, with the choyce
> Musique of her hand and voyce
> Stills the loude wind; and makes the wilde
> Incensed Bore, and Panther milde!
> Marke how those statues like men move,
> Whilst men with wonder statues prove;
> This stiffe rock bends to worship her,
> That Idoll turnes Idolater.[45]

People, too, were brought to life by music. "Here is an instrument," says Amorphus satirically in Jonson's *Cynthia's Revels*, "that (alone) is able to infuse soul into the most melancholique, and dull-disposde creature upon earth."[46] By the magic of music, Hermione, in *The Winter's Tale*, who seems turned to a statue, is given life, as were the statues in the *Asclepius*:

> Music, awake her; strike!
> 'Tis time; descend; be stone no more.

And there follows the oft-made apology for the use of magic:

> If this be magic, let it be an art
> Lawful as eating.

Thaisa, wife of Pericles, is also brought to life with the help of music. "Death may usurp on nature many hours," says Cerimon, "And yet the fire of life kindle again/The o'er-press'd spirits." Then, calling for both fire and music, he commands:

> The rough and woeful music that we have,
> Cause it to sound, beseech you.
> The viol once more, . . .
> . . . .
> The music there! I pray you, give her air.
> Gentlemen,
> This queen will live.[47]

Milton, too, knew his Hermetic philosophy. One of his imagined joys of solitude in "Il Penseroso" is that of watching starry constellations with "thrice great *Hermes*." The Lady in *Comus*, "In stony fetters fixt," is restored to life by the song of the river spirit, Sabrina. The attendant Spirit (*daemon* in the Trinity College Manuscript) hears "At last a soft and solemn breathing sound" (for music is alive and breathing, according to Ficino) that "Rose like a stream of rich distill'd perfumes":

> . . . I was all ear,
> And took in strains that might create a soul
> Under the ribs of Death.[48]

The most imaginative piece of poetry based entirely on this conception of sphere-born influence which can refine the soul, reveal heaven, and give life to the dead, is Milton's "At a solemn Musick." This "solemn" music resembles the "soft and solemn" sounds of *Comus*, that could "create a soul/ Under the ribs of Death." It is the "solemn music" that Prospero calls for in *The Tempest* to evoke spirits and to restore sense to the captive nobles whom he has bewitched. This music, too—music and poetry, born of the spheres—breathes life into the soul of the listener, in Orphic tradition:

> Blest pair of *Sirens*, pledges of Heav'ns joy,
> Sphear-born harmonious Sisters, Voice, and Vers,
> Wed your divine sounds, and mixt power employ
> Dead things with inbreath'd sense able to pierce.

"Voice, and Vers" not only carry the spirit of life; they also present to the phantasy an image of the regions from which they came, a heaven which is musical:

> And to our high-rais'd phantasie present,
> That undisturbed Song of pure concent,
> Ay sung before the saphire-colour'd throne
> To him that sits theron
> With Saintly shout, and solemn Jubily.

The final accomplishment of music is to make the nature of man celestial, to restore man to original purity, to make him one with celestial music:

> That we on Earth with undiscording voice
> May rightly answer that melodious noise;
> As once we did.

Milton was more subtle than the occultists; he enriched Hermetic notions with more intellectual ones. But the idea is the same: music, "The Imitatrix of the starres," breathes in life, provokes "heavenly influxes," and makes man "wholly Celestial."

John Donne lamented that the world had wept out its "vitall spirits," that its binding "Cyment" was "resolv'd," its "Magnetique force" gone, and that the life-giving spirit being lost—"this traffique quite forgot"—the world must now decay:

> What Artist now dares boast that he can bring
> Heaven hither, or constellate any thing,
> So as the influence of those starres may bee
> Imprison'd in an Hearbe, or Charme, or Tree,
> And doe by touch, all that those stars could doe?
> The art is lost, and correspondence too.[49]

Yet the idea persisted, both in occult writing and in metaphor, that music could convey divine spirit, that it could breathe life into stocks and stones. And surely, at the final judgment, the trumpet's sound would wake the dead.

IV

The life, soul, spirit, or living warmth of music was believed by the occult philosophers to derive from world soul and spirit. But it was, by many, attributed not to cosmic spirit but to the spirits of the singer, spirits which, while they might be related to cosmic spirits, carried personal as well as universal qualities. As John of Salisbury had written long before, "Music is . . . a type of conveyance of spirit—now human, now divine, and again prophetic."[50]

There have been many attempts through the ages to explain the response of one person to another. Queries about how man achieves contact with other people and why he responds to their feelings, gestures, words—any kind of utterance—posed problems to which the Renaissance philosophers, as well as later seventeenth-century scientists, devoted endless thought. Why are our teeth set on edge when we see another eat something sour or bitter? it was often asked. Why do we "gape" in sympathy? Why are we moved by an actor to feel whatever emotion he portrays? How must we account for the contact between singer and listener, for the effects of singing that do not seem to derive solely from harmony itself or even from words?

One answer, at least, was that there is a real and almost material contact by means of soul and spirit carried in the breath. Aristotle had implied as much. Sound itself, he wrote, is characterized by motion of the air, "which is . . .

continuous as far as the organ of hearing." Voice, on the other hand, is a kind of sound "produced by a creature possessing a soul." "Voice consists in the impact of the inspired air upon . . . the windpipe," and the agent is the soul resident in that part of the body. "That which . . . causes the impact must have a soul, and use some imagination; for the voice is a sound which means something."[51]

In this context, if song is "warm air, even breathing, and in a measure living," it is so by virtue of the breath and spirit and soul of the singer. In Ficino's words, again, in his commentary on the *Timaeus*, musical sounds convey "as if animated, the emotions and thoughts of the singer's or player's soul to the listeners' souls." In the letter to Canisiano, he described the contact in a similar way: "Since song and sound" arise from the mind, imagination, and heart of the performer, they "move the phantasy, affect the heart and penetrate into the deep recesses of the mind."[52]

Agrippa made a point of prefacing his repetition of this latter assertion by Ficino with the reminder that "We shall not deny, that there is in Sounds a vertue to receive the heavenly gifts," but after this tribute he went on to say that vocal sound is better than that of instrument because, as Ficino had said, it achieves direct contact of mind, imagination, and heart of singer and listener. He described voice in Aristotelian terms. But he added the popular notion that with the voice, which is breath, there is an issue of spirits:

> Sound is a breath, voyce is a sound and animate breath; Speech is a breath pronounced with sound, and a voyce signifying something; the spirit of which proceedeth out of the mouth with sound and voyce; Chaludius saith that a voyce is sent forth out of the inward cavity of the breast and heart, by the assistance of the spirit.[53]

This emphasis on emission of breath and spirit in singing or in speaking was an ancient one and was probably taken for granted, just as it was taken for granted that spirits issue from the eye to carry contagion or to cause love. This assumption had explained for generations the "straunge matters . . .

brought to passe by the woordes and workes of man." Words are generated within, wrote Roger Bacon, "by the thoughts of the Soule." They are emitted by "open wayes, through which is a great passage of Spirits, heate, evaporation, virtue . . . which may bee made by the Soule and heart." These spirits and "virtues" infect whoever is near; they "sometimes hurt us, when they proceede from a crazie body, that is of an evill complexion; and againe they greatly profite and comfort us, when they come from a pure and sound bodie of a good complexion."[54] Francis Bacon considered it not improbable "that there should be some transmission and operations from spirit to spirit without the mediation of the senses."[55] And by emotion-carrying spirit emitted in speech, Lady Macbeth hopes to inspire courage in the heart of her timorous Lord:

> Hie thee hither,
> That I may pour my spirits in thine ear,
> And chastise with the valour of my tongue
> All that impedes thee from the golden round
> Which fate and metaphysical aid doth seem
> To have thee crown'd withal.

Milton's Satan plans to "taint/Th'animal Spirits" of Eve by "inspiring venom."[56]

The contagion of the singer's breath (for tunes could be "contagious" in a literal sense) is the subject of foolery in Ben Jonson's *Poetaster*, when Albius exclaims after Crispinus' song, "O, most odoriferous musicke!" and Tucca joins in, "A, ha! stinkard. Another Orpheus, you slave, another Orpheus! An Arion, riding on the backe of a dolphin, rascall!" The song of the Clown in *Twelfth Night* meets with a similar reception from Sir Andrew and Sir Toby:

> SIR ANDREW: A mellifluous voice, as I am true knight.
> SIR TOBY: A contagious breath.
> SIR ANDREW: Very sweet and contagious, i'faith.
> SIR TOBY: To hear by the nose, it is dulcet in contagion.[57]

But singing did not only carry contagion; it also gave life. Life was given, first, to the music itself. Chapman described

Julia's "sweete tunes" as warm and living children of the brain, conceived in her "mentall wombe" by mind and imagination, in Ficinian tradition, sent out with kisses—and like kisses—on her voice:

> Sweete tunes, brave issue, that from Julia come;
> Shooke from her braine, armed like the Queene of Ire;
> For first conceived in her mentall wombe,
> And nourisht with her soules discursive fire,
>   They grew into the power of her thought;
> She gave them dounye plumes from her attire,
>   And them to strong imagination brought;
> That, to her voice; wherein most movinglye
> Shee blessing them with kysses) letts them flye.[58]

Crashaw likened the nightingale's notes to fledglings born in "the sugred Nest/Of her delicious soule," which finally "forsake their Nest" to flutter on the air. And with the pouring out of this creation, her soul itself is ravished and "pour'd/ Into loose extasies."[59] Lord Herbert of Cherbury imagined the words of a singer given life by her breath, the words then tuned by the soul into harmony that is dismissed into the air as "living, moving, and harmonious noise."[60]

This life given to music by the singer was transmitted, in turn, to the listener. "A young Lord" speaking "to his Mistris, who had taught him a Song," in William Cartwright's verses, exclaims:

> Henceforth I'l think my Breath is due
> No more to Nature, but to you.[61]

These living tunes fly like bees, in Chapman's *Ovid's Banquet of Sence*, to "make love" with the soul of the listener, "possessing" by means of the soul they carry and giving new life:

>   Rise then in swarms, and sting me thus to death
> Or turne me into swounde; possesse me whole,
> Soule to my life, and essence to my soule.

They "flye rejoysing, but . . . in giving others life themselves do dye." By her voice Chapman's Corynna hopes to infuse life into inanimate statues when she woos the gods to add their power to hers to

> . . . try if with her voyces vitall sounde
> She could warme life through those cold statues spread
> And cheere the Dame that wept when she was dead.[62]

V

It was not possible, however, completely to separate human spirit from divine, for the notion that world spirit was shared by man had wide acceptance. This association the love poet, especially, could not ignore. The Neoplatonic lover, like all lovers of earlier centuries who made a cult of worshiping woman, heard not mere woman singing, but the angels themselves. Human spirit was imagined to be a part of cosmic spirit. As in the poetry of Lapo Gianni or of Cavalcanti in the thirteenth century, "the bodily spirits corresponded to the spirits which moved the cosmic organism, the angelic substances in the sky." The lady was of the "species of the heavenly spirits. . . . She was a link with heaven, and her influence was of cosmic significance." In the past, and in orthodox Neoplatonism, this pervasive spirit was seen as the light of beauty that shone pre-eminently through the eye. It "shone in the corporeal world in the appearance of a woman, sending out of the windows of her soul rays of high potency with which to move the hearts of men."[63] But in the seventeenth century it was imagined that these divine spirits could issue also with the voice, that they were distinguished by musicalness rather than by brightness, for world spirit is all musical. "Heare you this soule-invading voyce, & count it but a voyce?" asked Sir Philip Sidney. It is "The verie essence of their tunes, when Angels doo rejoyce."[64] So Milton wrote "To Leonora, Singing in Rome": "Your voice itself sounds forth a god, a very present god . . . or, at least, the Third Intelligence of emptied heaven . . . makes its way through your throat." This spirit that gave life to sound and that was thereby infused into the listener was, in the exaggerated hyperbole of love poetry, not human only but divine.

This notion was combined with another: if spirit is divine, so is its harmony, and whatever harmony images the divine, possesses the power, so often attributed to it in the Renaissance, not only to infuse life but to draw soul from body as in an ecstasy. Singing thus had twofold value: harmony drew out the soul; the spirit that it carried restored life. Its effects thus paralleled those of kissing, as Neoplatonic lovers described it, for a kiss, too, gave both life and death as soul left one body to enter another.

Thomas Stanley, in two poems written to "Celia Singing," described the stealing away of the listener's soul by harmony, the breathing in of another by Celia's inspiring angel. Thus even plants and stones are given life, and thus are achieved the erotic life and death experienced by the lover:

> But if the Angel, which inspires
> This subtile flame with active fires,
> Should mould this breath to words, and those
> Into a harmony dispose,
> The music of this heavenly sphere
> Would steal each soul out at the ear,
> And into plants and stones infuse
> A life that Cherubins would choose;
> And with new powers invert the laws of Fate,
> Kill those that live, and dead things animate.

In the companion verse (in French), he described again the drawing out of soul by the charm of harmony in a kind of death and the reanimation by breath, subtle and warm, which slides through the ear to the heart to infuse new soul:

> Que la vie m'est douce, la mort m'est sans peine,
> Puisqu'on les trouve toutes deux dans ton haleine.[65]

Philip Ayers, in "Cynthia, singing a Recitative Piece of Music," used the image of a body, dead through the power of harmony, and reanimated by the singer's "angelic spirit," which is identified with the spirit that animates the sirens of the spheres. "O thou angelic spirit," he began, "Sweet Syren,"

> Thou canst heat, cool, grieve us, or make us smile
> Nay stab or kill, yet hurt us not the while. . . .
> List'ning to thee, our bodies seem as dead,
> For our rapt souls then up to Heav'n are fled.
> So great a Monarch art thou, that thy breath
> Has power to give us either Life, or Death.[66]

Thus was the power of Orpheus explained, who breathed life into stones and trees and brought his "half regain'd *Eurydice*" from Pluto's doors. Either because he could command demons or because he knew all the secrets of numbers whereby stellar spirits could be invoked or because music itself—or his voice—breathed spirit, he was able to "attract into and retain in, a material object 'something vital from the soul of the world and the souls of the spheres and stars.'" So man's music could bring statues back to life. So the lover lost and won his soul again through his lady's singing. Music was the breath of life.

CHAPTER VI

Musical Humanism: An Anti-Pythagorean Cross-current

For many years there were those who imagined harmony to be the cause of ecstasy or of love or of rebirth, but these ideas obviously could not withstand indefinitely the denigrating rationalism of scientific thought, which was beginning to be felt even in the sixteenth century. Musical thought, too, by re-defining "music," by re-examining its purpose, established a new musical aesthetic that contributed to changing evaluations of harmony. Both these trends openly (not subversively, as did certain aspects of Neoplatonic love philosophy) put the mystery of music in question.

The new aesthetic was most clearly formulated by late sixteenth-century humanists in Italy, who, starting with a Platonic definition of music that ignored its cosmic qualities, set up for it a different set of values. Not all these thinkers rejected completely the idea that the world is governed by harmony or that the right kind of music might "be a pattern and true resemblance of . . . celestial harmonies whence proceed so many good effects and benefits upon earth."[1] but they did believe that "modern" music had no such effects and that what was needed was a renascence of music of the past. In the process of this revival they brought into question the value of musical sound in itself and undermined its metaphysical interpretation. They were not the first to attempt revival of ancient music. Musicians and poets throughout the century had been agitated by this desire, a desire that motivated the famous attempts of the Pléiade and Baïf's Academy to restore the manner and effects of ancient music by careful setting of words. Their theories, however, were still closely allied with the Pythagorean philosophy that explained the entire physical universe in terms of harmony and number imaged in music.[2] The Italian humanists went beyond the French in their questioning of Pythagorean metaphysics; furthermore, they were able to translate theory into musical forms and styles of lasting influence, forms and styles that influenced literature as well as music.

A group of poets, musicians, and scholars (including Count Giovanni Bardi, Vincenzo Galilei, and later the poets Rinuccini and Chiabrera and the composers Peri and Caccini), working together in Florence in a group known as "the Camerata," set out to create music like that of the ancient Greeks, which would produce the same marvelous effects claimed for it by ancient writers. Unfortunately, nothing was known about Greek music. A hymn of Mesomedes, discovered by Galilei, was of no assistance, since its notation could not be deciphered. Greek sculpture and a large body of literature remained, but for the musician interested in ancient musical style—the manner in which the Greek bard had sung his own words or the method of presenting Greek tragedy—there remained as a guide only references to music found in literary and scientific works.

Members of the Camerata turned, then, to writings of the past to discover what that music must have been like. The basic definition they took to be that of Plato in *The Republic*: music is a combination of words and harmony and rhythm.[3] But what is the meaning of "harmony"? Bardi asked, in his *Discourse on Ancient Music* (*c.* 1580). He did not attack the Pythagorean theory of harmony as a universal principle. He simply was not interested in it. "Music," to him, was sound that is heard. "Harmony is a general term, and in speaking of it, Pythagoras says, and after him Plato, that the world is composed of it. But let us come to the particular and treat of the harmony of music as defined by Plato." This harmony intended by Plato was, in Bardi's mind, concerned only with "proportion of the low and the high" in sounds and with "words in rhythm."[4]

From this definition, he and his associates concluded that words come first: "Music is nothing other than the fable and last and not the contrary, the rhythm and the sound." It is this kind of music alone, they said, that can "penetrate the perception of others and . . . produce those marvelous effects admired" by the philosophers.[5]

They saw a model of this music in Greek drama, which they supposed to have been entirely sung, and they judged, therefrom, that the aim of music is not to animate or sublimate but to please, and less to please than to sway the emotions of an audience—to arouse pity and fear. The meaning of the text was, obviously, of paramount importance: the rhythm of melody should be determined by the rhythm of the words. The harmony must suit their mood. Interest focused, then, on projecting the meaning and intensity of the words. The words must be declaimed; music must be the servant of poetry. "In composing," wrote Bardi,

> you will make it your chief aim to arrange the verse well and to declaim the words as intelligibly as you can . . . just as the soul is nobler than the body, so the words are nobler than the counterpoint. Would it not seem ridiculous if, walking in a public square, you saw a servant followed by his master and commanding him, or a boy who wanted to instruct his father or his tutor?[6]

Blame for the decline of "modern" music was placed on the earlier contrapuntists. The polyphonic style used in church music and in motet or madrigal, by a superimposing of words and an unnatural prolongation of syllables or accenting of unimportant ones, obscured the meaning of the words. It lacerated the poetry. The leaders in the new movement felt also that the music of their immediate predecessors, in spite of its development of solo song, fell short in projection of emotion, that it depicted merely graphic details in the text rather than the feeling of an entire passage.[7] Furthermore, its rules of harmony and counterpoint were too restricting.

This last limitation derived in part, they thought (and here they attacked the whole number philosophy), from speculative theories that considered consonance and dissonance to be established by "natural law." Pythagorean measurement based on cosmic law must go, wrote Vincenzo Galilei in 1588. He determined by experiment with strings, tubes, and other sounding bodies—in which he anticipated the later experiments of his more famous son, Galileo Galilei —that the older theory was not valid. The musician must judge by the ear as well as by reason, he wrote. "The only interval with a determinate ratio was the octave; the others were subject to endless variety."[8] While Galilei thus widened the emotional spectrum available to the practicing musician who was concerned with the varied emotion of drama, he at the same time denied the image of the universal in music as the French Academicians had not. In opening the way to a greater use of dissonance, greater flexibility and intensity, he cleared the air of Pythagorean doctrine. Music may have become the slave of poetry, but it was at least freed from the imagined law of nature.

To learn how the dramatic singer might project emotion, he turned to writings of the great orators. (Musician learned from orator, not orator from music.) The objectives of the orator and of the singer were the same—to excite emotions. The "sole aim" of contrapuntal music "is to delight the ear," wrote Galilei, in his *Dialogo della musica antica e della moderna* in 1581, "while that of ancient music is to induce in another the same passion that one feels oneself." These emotions, he believed, with Cicero (with echoes, too, of Ficino), cannot be inspired in the listener unless they are felt and acted by the performer. By words, gestures, affective control of voice, by intense feeling of the executor, rather than by harmony, the audience could be moved, as Alexander had been moved by the singing of Timotheus to leave feasting to take up arms, and then to leave fighting again for banqueting.[9] As the modern romanticists like to say, "It comes from the heart; may it go to the heart." An artificial instrument, Galilei declared, can do no more than tickle the ear, for it is no more than "a simple piece of hollow wood over which are stretched four, six, or more strings of the gut of a dumb beast . . . without sense, movement, intellect, speech, discourse, reason, or soul."[10] The lute was thus no image of the cosmos. Those instruments were best that most nearly resembled human voices. To demonstrate the ideal use of music, Galilei wrote and performed monodies, now lost (foreshadowed by the Orphic monodies of Ficino), which illustrated this oratorical-dramatic style. He chose not the light verse usually found in the madrigal, but the moving poetry of Dante and the "Lamentations of Jeremiah." They were sung by solo voice, accompanied by four viols, and, one assumes, delivered with appropriate histrionics.

Other members of the Camerata, following these suggestions, set out to produce drama entirely declaimed to music, which was, in their judgment, like that of the Greeks. Their works (called *melodramma*, the present-day opera) drew on Italian pastoral drama, especially Tasso's *Aminto* and Guarini's *Il Pastor Fido*, as well as on Greek tragedy, but they were shorter than the pastoral plays, the plots were less complicated, and the stories were based on mythological rather than pastoral themes—legends of Daphne, Orpheus, or Ariadne.

The first "opera" to be performed was Rinuccini's *Dafne* (given in Florence in 1594?), with music by Peri and Jacopo Corsi, the music of which is lost. Two settings of Rinuccini's *Euridice*, by Peri and by Caccini, were produced in Florence in 1600. Their literary value may be questioned, but critical writings of the time to be found in prefaces, dedications, and theoretical works leave no doubt of the sincerity of these attempts to produce drama in the manner of the ancients, which would move by word, music, and gesture. The music (to use the word in the present-day sense) was in the new monodic style of solo singing, with chordal accompaniment, that varied between declamation and melody. The total effect was that of talking in harmony. Caccini wrote that he believed he had "approached . . . ordinary speech." Peri described his settings as "lying between the slow and suspended movements of song and the swift rapid movements of speech." The composer Gagliano called this style a manner "di recitare cantando"—hence the term "recitative."[11]

For the music-theorist the importance of this movement is its contribution to the gradual change from modal to tonal harmony. The literary scholar finds in it significant bearing on poetry. This new style gave to the poet who had musical setting in mind unprecedented freedom in composition and in subject. At few other times in history have words so predominated over music. Musical form was in fact dictated by literary organization and style. The literary part of these productions was not "just a libretto" for a composer to use; it was the heart and soul of the music. Music would be left as body without soul, it was believed, if it were left "without this most important and principal part."[12] The poet *was* musician, not only metaphorically but in reality.

This relationship, ideal perhaps from the standpoint of the poet, could not continue once a composer as great as Monteverdi had appeared on the scene. One wonders what monumental work might have been produced, had he collaborated with a poet of a stature equal to his own. His *Orfeo*, performed at Mantua in 1607, on a text by the poet Alessandro Striggio, was greeted as a "new example of the Florentine style," as indeed it was in its general plan, for it was again a pastoral-tragedy with monodic declamation. It is even closer to the original baroque ideal of "moving" music than are the Florentine productions. It has greater power and variety of expression, more intense pathos, more startling change of mood. His *Arianna*, written and performed at Mantua in 1608 (of which only the famous "Lamento" remains), "was declared by Gagliano to be a living modern example of the power of ancient music, since it 'visibly moved the entire audience to tears.' "[13] Monteverdi himself claimed to have been the first composer to depict anger, also, in music, in his *Il Combattimento di Tancredi e di Clorinda.*[14] Music was obviously asserting itself over poetry. The poetic parts of these works fade in comparison with the emotional quality of the music itself; and Monteverdi, in spite of restrictions, gave to his work an independent musical structure.

Other influences, too, were leading away from the original intention. The attraction of early Florentine drama was apparently limited to serious literary and musical people. Composers and poets who wished to produce a more popular entertainment added elements that would satisfy the prevailing desire for more spectacular amusement. There are obvious signs of departure from the Florentine ideal in Domenico Mazzocchi's *Catena d'Adone*, presented in Rome in 1626—more choruses, changes of scene, greater demarcation between recitative and aria. But for a time the aesthetics of the new music dominated musical thought, and throughout these years, metaphysical notions of cosmic harmony were forgotten or denied.

This philosophy of music was well known in England, but there it was one among many influences—including theories of aesthetics, religious prejudices, national temperament and pride—and it is difficult to trace its direct effects. It merged with other currents of thought that tended also to subject music to words. It was sometimes resisted, or accepted with reluctance, not from any objection to careful setting of words, but because conservative composers felt that established rules of musical art were being ignored. Yet this emphasis on the value of word above harmony, not only formulated into an aesthetic but demonstrated in practice, not only in church music but in secular, did much to attract attention away from the metaphysical associations of musical sound. More than that, it opened up for the poet new possibilities for literary forms.

The humanist philosophy regarding music resembled the Puritan attitude—with its emphasis on meaning of the word, the value of voice over instrument—which had roots deep in patristic writing, but which also indicated Platonic influence. When William Prynne condemned the complicated music of church service because it delighted the ears without care "at all for the vertue, pith, or strength of the words," when he wrote that "we must sing to God with the heart," that the proper singing is "in a manner nothing else but plaine reading,"[15] he did not admit common cause with the Italian Platonists, but he might well have done so. There is close parallel between John Cotton's words, "singing with heart and voyce is significant and edifying by signification . . . which the voyce of Instruments is not," and Caccini's dictum, "unless the words . . . [are] understood, they . . . [can] not move the understanding"; between Cotton's "It was not the sound of David's Harpe that could have this power . . . over the sinfull Passions of Saul himselfe, if the sound of the Harpe had not been quickned and enlived, as it were by a spirituall song," and Vincenzo Galilei's "instruments . . . being without . . . speech, discourse, reason . . . are capable of nothing else" but tickling the ear.[16] There were conspicuous differences, however, in basic philosophy. The Puritan sang to God, not to his fellow men; his only passion was love of God—all others must be subdued; text was limited to scriptural subjects; condemnation of instruments was motivated by fear of distraction rather than by musical aesthetics. And there was no attempt to revive Hebrew music, a task recognized as quite impossible.[17]

Poets, too, from their study of the classics, accepted, independently of contemporary musical theory, the opinion that poetry and music are one, that "music" means "poetry," and they frequently quoted Terence: "for Terence saith, speaking of Poets, *Artem qui tractant musicam*, confounding Musick and Poesy together."[18] Orpheus and Amphion were looked upon as poets, not musicians; it was poetry that accomplished those miracles sometimes attributed to harmony. Poetry—"an apt composition of wordes or clauses"—not music, according to William Webbe, drew "by force the hearers eares even whether soever it lysteth."[19] The poet wrote of himself as a musician who tuned his lyre and sang, as did the bards of old, notes that were words rather than pitch symbols—in which these scholars often showed little interest.

English composers (and poets, too) were as interested as the Italians in careful setting of words, in coupling "words and notes lovingly together," but they were inspired by French and native English influences as well as Italian, and these influences tend to obscure the extent of their debt to Italy. There was considerable interest in the *vers mesuré à lyre* of the Pléiade and in Baïf's *vers mesuré à l'antique*, in which quantitative measures of verse were matched by those of musical notes, in which long syllables were set to long notes, short syllables to short notes. Thomas Campion followed this strict measurement of syllable and note, with only moderate success, in one of the ayres published (with Philip Rosseter) in 1601.[20] This theory, however, unlike the Italian, subjected both poet and musician to insupportable restrictions. Notes were bound to a temporal matching of words, words to classical rhythms. Imitation of ancient lyric forms was not a satisfactory solution for Elizabethan poets motivated by desire for more natural, more varied, rhythms.

The native English ayre, no doubt influenced by the writing of the Pléiade, was more liberating than were experiments in *vers mesuré à l'antique*, but the poet was still limited in style and structure. The ayre did not mark a complete break with older forms. It "explicitly provides for both polyphonic and accompanied-solo" song.[21] And because the ayre, like Ronsard's songs, was often based on strophic form that set numerous stanzas to the same melody, the rhythm, the length, even the subject matter of the poem were to a degree governed by the tune. The result was less a servitude of music than a union of equals. Neither poet nor musician openly attacked musical values.

More obvious Italian influence is evident, however, at an early date. It did not burst dramatically upon the scene. Old ties were not immediately severed. But gradually the idea that the effects of music derive chiefly from the words rather than from musical sound, that poetry is an indispensable part of music, came to the fore, even in the opinion of musicians themselves. Many who were not ready to relinquish older styles of composing or to give up belief in mystical values of harmony still admitted the validity of the Platonic definition as it was stated by members of the Camerata.

There is evidence of direct contact between the Italian theorists and John Dowland. Dowland was in Florence in 1594 or 1595, at approximately the time that Rinuccini's

Dafne was performed with Peri's musical setting, and when he dedicated his first book of songs, in 1597, he described them in the same way that Peri and Caccini described theirs in 1601, as "speaking harmony." He had more faith than did the Italians in the effects of musical sound, which, he wrote, can in itself, "by reason of the variety of number and proportion," stir the mind "to admiration and delight," but he concluded, as they did, that the greatest power is in music "expressing some worthy sentence, or excellent poem," and he gave Plato's definition of music for authority. Thomas Morley, in *A Plaine and Easie Introduction* (1597), decried "the new-fangled opinions of our countrey men, who will highlie esteeme whatsoever commeth from beyond the seas, and speciallie from Italie, be it never so simple, contemning that which is done at home though it be never so excellent." He pointed to the motet as the musical form "chiefest both for art and utilitie." But even he agreed with the Platonists that it is through words alone that man is moved by music: "I see not what passions or motions it can stirre up, being sung as most men doe commonlie sing it: that is, leaving out the dittie and singing onley the bare note." Instruments, he continued, in phraseology reminiscent of the Italians, "never carrie the spirit and (as it were) that livelie soule which the dittie giveth."[22] The musician Thomas Ravenscroft (even while objecting to the new musical trends which brought music, he thought, into disrepute and which violated her laws) still defined music as "Song, or Poetry."[23]

The date of the introduction of recitative proper is uncertain. It was probably not until 1628. But a declamatory element is obvious much earlier in the lutenist ayres of Dowland, Coperario, and Ferrabosco, and in the declamatory ayre, in which "rhythmic forms of words largely governed the rhythmic shape of the music."[24] And after Lanier visited Italy in the mid-1620's he composed a cantata, "Hero and Leander," in the monodic style of Monteverdi's famous "Lamento d'Arianna," a style used later by Henry Lawes for Cartwright's monody on the same theme. By the 1630's the new music had had wide influence not only on settings for masques, but on madrigal and ayre as well. English composers, however, lost sight of the dramatic-oratorical objectives of the original philosophy. The seriousness and intensity of the Italians were lacking. Devotion to an aesthetic was replaced by imitation of superficial characteristics.

Yet their music demonstrates the same subordination to poetry. Madrigal parts could be, and were, played satisfactorily on instruments, without the words. Musical settings for recitative or monody, however, are of little interest apart from words, while words, on the other hand, have slight need of music. One feels no lack because Lawes's setting of Milton's "Arcades" is lost; the songs of *Comus* have as much charm in reading as in singing. It is revealing, comments a present-day musicologist, "that the only tangible result of masques and 'operas' performed during the Commonwealth was literary and not musical."[25] Even English instrumental music, so impressive at the turn of the century, lost its distinction, a loss that may be ascribed, at least in part, to the general trend toward emphasis on the written word.

If, however, music temporarily suffered in this relationship, poetry intended for singing benefited. The possibilities of freedom that it gave to the poet in prosody and diction, in formal structure, in variety of mood, in breadth of subject matter, could not be ignored. The effect of madrigal and ayre on metrical structures has been carefully studied,[26] but no similar work has been done with the effect of monodic style. It is probably not possible to arrive at proved conclusions, for much of the music, for masques at least, is lost—an indication in itself of the value placed on verse over that assigned to music. One may surmise, however, that the new style was responsible for the evident difference between, say, Jonson's "To Celia" ("Drink to me only with thine eyes"), with its two stanzas of identical and regular verse form, suitable to strophic song, and a later lyric in his masque, *Loves Triumph,* which was probably influenced by Italian style and which has two stanzas of different verse form, and words less easily set to music than those of the earlier poem, such words as "emergent," "imprinted," and "signatures":

So love, emergent out of Chaos, brought
The world to light!
And gently moving on the waters, wrought
All forme to sight!

Loves appetite
Did beauty first excite:
And left imprinted in the ayre,
Those signatures of good, and faire.[27]

A song by Carew, written as a dialogue and "sung in a Masque at White-hall, anno 1633," reveals similar influence. The argumentative tone, the speech rhythms, the broken lines, could not have been set by the regular rhythms and strophic form of the ayre:

Quest. By what power was Love confinde
To one object? who can binde,
Or fixe a limit to the free-borne minde?
An. Nature; for as bodyes may
Move at once but in one way,
So nor can mindes to more then one love stray.

There is a distinctly oratorical quality, not found earlier, in the final song of Carew's masque, *Coelum Britannicum* (1633):

Brave Spirits, whose adventrous feet
Have to the Mountaines top aspir'd,
Where faire Desert, and Honour meet,
Here, from the toyling Presse retir'd,
Secure from all disturbing Evill,
For ever in my Temple revell.[28]

The dramatic form of the typical masque is very different from Italian attempts to revive classical drama, yet there is more influence here, too, than is usually recognized. The length, coherence, and seriousness of Carew's masque may well result from Italian influence. It was Milton, however, who seems to have grasped most completely the essence of the new aesthetic, and this subject will be pursued in later chapters.

In time music freed itself from poetry to achieve independent structure and expression. It continued to have admirers who found in harmony an image of universal order. But by the last half of the century it had lost its high place in the philosopher's system of knowledge, a change in which baroque aesthetics surely played a part.

CHAPTER VII

Music and Air: Changing Definitions of Sound

THE power of harmony was brought into question by other influences than those exerted by poets and musicians. More scientific analyses of sound also challenged its innate virtues. The effects of music, it was said, do not derive either from sound itself, no matter how harmonious, or from the projected feeling of the performer, but from the motion of air set up by sound.

This theory had its ground-roots, as did many others, in Ficino, in the two passages on music already quoted,[1] especially that in the commentary on the *Timaeus*:

> Musical sound by the movement of the air moves the body: by purified air it excites the aerial spirit which is the bond of body and soul: by emotion it affects the senses and at the same time the soul: by meaning it works on the mind: finally, by the very movement of the subtle air it penetrates strongly.

This statement, along with a part of the other—"song and sound . . . together with the air they have broken up and tempered . . . strike the aerial spirit of the hearer"—inspired a re-examination of the natures of sound and air, their relation to each other, their effect upon the spirits. It led to hypotheses that mingled with seventeenth-century scientific thought without complete loss of identity. For two centuries this Ficinian formula—musical sound by movement of the air moves the body and spirits—was used by many philosophers and scientists to explain a variety of musical effects. The words themselves acquired new meanings: "air," "motion," "spirits," each changed from something mysterious to something material, "sound," conversely, from something material to something psychological. But even when the source was forgotten, the basic idea lived on, and in its varying interpretations, metaphysical qualities were read out of music.

I

"Air" did not mean to philosophers of Ficino's time what it meant to late seventeenth-century scientists, such as Boyle or Newton. The earlier writers had no conception of the chemical or physical characteristics of air. They did not know, either, what sound is, how it moves the air, or how it is perceived. Occult philosophers imagined that air either was, or was permeated by, the quintessence, the fifth element, the spirit that, in man and in the world, gives life. Air, wrote Agrippa, "is a vitall spirit, passing through all Beings, giving life, and subsistence to all things, binding, moving, and filling all things. . . . It immediately receives into it self the influencies of all Celestiall bodies, and then communicates them to the other Elements."[2] Robert Fludd defined air as "the receptacle of the heavenly spirit," by which it is "informed" and vivified.[3] Poetically speaking, the air was heaven's breath, as in *Macbeth*, when Banquo, seeing the nesting martlet, remarks:

> This guest of summer,
> The temple-haunting martlet, does approve
> By his loved masonry that the heaven's breath
> Smells wooingly here.

Milton's Samson, too, feels "The breath of Heav'n fresh-blowing, pure and sweet."[4]

The air was thought to be filled with disembodied spirits of all kinds—demons, ghosts, angels perhaps, not to mention human spirits spoken or sung into it. It was crowded, too, with all the images of sense perception—"species" of all things—that pass through the air to sense organs, for no one questioned for many centuries that all visible objects somehow project pictures of themselves, which may linger in the air even after the object itself is no longer present, much in the same way that a snail leaves behind its shell. Thus a murderer could depart from the scene of his crime, leaving behind an image that might frighten unsuspecting persons who came there.[5] Sounds also were supposed to leave images of themselves. "Species of audibles," wrote Francis Bacon, "do hang longer in the air than those of visibles."[6]

Although some medium (air being the most favorable) was usually considered necessary for the transmission of sound, sound was thought to have a reality of its own apart from its medium. Today the word "sound" is used to describe both external motion of the air (the primary characteristic) and also the effect of that motion in the mind (the secondary characteristic), a sense perception that is totally unlike the sound waves outside the ear. The two do not coexist: one follows the other. In ancient times and in the Renaissance, however, this distinction was not made. Secondary characteristics of sound were thought to have reality outside of man before they were perceived. Even for Kepler, it has been pointed out, "secondary qualities were out there in the astronomical world, like the primary."[7] Spirit-music or music of the spheres was no less real for not being heard.

There was, nonetheless, serious concern with what is now called "acoustics" and with the physical and psychological aspects of hearing, as Ficino himself showed, both in his analysis of musical effects and in his study of Aristotle's explanations of sound.[8] For centuries, philosophers had attempted to define sound in rational terms. The ancient atomists (Democritus, Epicurus, Lucretius), who inspired later-day scientists, denied the external reality of secondary characteristics of sense impressions—what is seen as color or heard as sound—but even they believed in corporeal sound atoms, existing outside of man although not sounding until they touch the soul. Democritus thought air atoms essential for their transmission; Epicurus apparently did not.[9] Almost all sixteenth- and early seventeenth-century philosophers, however, went to Aristotle (and to later Arabian writers), who had defined sound and hearing in a quite different way.

Sensible objects, wrote Aristotle, are made up of "matter" and "form" or "quality." By sense perception man receives form without matter; what is heard as sound is abstracted from the substance or medium of sound, which is air, air that has been set in motion by sound. He was not explicit about the nature of this motion except to say that air rebounds from the object that is struck, and that it vibrates.[10]

Motion of sound in the air was often described, from ancient times through the Renaissance, as a series of concentric circles similar to those made by a stone dropped into water, "All which infected move with sounding qualitie." According to medieval Arabian writers, sound cuts or breaks up the air,[11] an idea echoed in Ficino's "broken up, and tempered" air, as it was in many other expositions.

This moving air, wrote Aristotle, stirs physically the air that resides in the ear—*pneuma* or connatural air, later identified with spirits.[12] Sound itself, apart from air, has no physical effect (a conviction shared by Francis Bacon), as Aristotle illustrated by what he understood to be the effect of thunder: "For neither light and darkness, nor sound, nor smell, affects bodies at all: it is the objects in which they reside that produce the effect, just as it is the air with the thunderbolt that splits the timber."[13]

He did not discuss the possible effect of the medium (air) of more usual sounds on solid bodies, however, but only its contact with the *pneuma* in the ear, which, he wrote in *Generation of Animals*, connects with outer air and terminates "at the small blood-vessels around the brain which extend thither from the heart." By this route, presumably, sound reaches the heart, seat of the soul and thus center of perception. Aristotle also suggested the possibility of other passages leading directly from sense organ to heart, by which sensory motion could be set up in the heart antecedent to, or independently of, motion around the brain.[14] But by either route perception would depend on the effect of air. "We perceive," he wrote, because the medium of sound "acts on us."[15]

This medium, in spite of its physical contact, was of no consequence beyond carrying the "form" of objects. Sensation is the reception "of the form of the sensible objects without the matter, just as the wax receives the impression of the signet-ring without the iron or the gold."[16] The effects of material motion are insignificant. Aristotle did suggest in the *Movement of Animals* (if the work is really his) the possibility of mechanical animal motion, response to stimuli independent of thought (which was also proposed by Descartes in the seventeenth century). He concluded, however, that animal motion cannot actually be separated from the operation of imagination and thought.[17] It is the soul, using the *pneuma* as its instrument, that causes all sensation, feeling, or motion. As far as sense is concerned (according to the *De anima*), it is indifferent what the substance is; what alone matters is what "quality" it has. It is *sound* then, not *air*, that is significant.[18]

When Ficino said that "song and sound . . . together with the air they have broken up and tempered . . . strike the aerial spirit of the hearer," he incorporated an Aristotelian idea, but he gave added importance to the effect of the air that carries sound apart from the effect of sound itself. "The point which Ficino always emphasizes," writes D. P. Walker, "is that music has stronger effect than anything transmitted through the other senses, because its medium, air, is of the same kind as the spirit," and it was this reason that he gave for combining musical and medical studies.[19] Even Ficino, however, did not completely divorce the effects of air and of sound. Since the soul, he believed, is everywhere present in the body, imagination immediately perceives an image of sound: musical sound "by the movement of the air" excites the spirits and *at the same time* the soul; "song and sound . . . *together with* [italics added] the air they have broken up and tempered . . . strike the aerial spirit of the hearer."

One or the other of these passages of Ficino was quoted for well over a hundred years—by Gregor Reisch, Cornelius

Agrippa, and Robert Fludd,[20] among others—without question and without materialistic emphasis. Air was a mysterious thing, carrying the subtle element called quintessence or world spirit; spirits were akin to soul. Thomas Lodge had no mechanical notion in mind when he applied Ficino's statement to the music of John Dowland:

> Whose Musicall concent (by reason of the aeriall nature therof) being put in motion, moveth the body, and by purified aire, inciteth the aeriall spirit of the soule, and the motion of the body . . . by the very motion of the subtill aire, it pierceth vehemently, and by contemplation sucketh sweetly.[21]

This idea, however, was given more materialistic interpretation long before Lodge wrote about Dowland, by philosophers who followed not Ficinian psychology, but scholastic, a system more complicated than Ficino's. These theories resembled Aristotle's, but since they located only the sensitive soul in the heart, for feeling, the rational soul in the brain, for perceiving, both hearing and emotional or intellectual response were involved processes. It is necessary then to digress briefly to sketch the psychological background within the framework of which many sixteenth- and seventeenth-century writers theorized about musical effects.

Dr. Helkiah Crooke, drawing (in his *Body of Man*, 1615) on an array of authorities from Aristotle and the Arabian writers to the famous sixteenth-century physician Laurentius, summed up the opinion of his day on the subject of sound (as distinct from air) and on hearing (as elimination of air, the "matter" of sound). Sound beats and breaks the air, he wrote, or perhaps air accompanies sound—carries it on its wings. "The fraction of the air is motion," but motion is not sound, for sound is a quality. Outer air does not enter the ear, but by moving the eardrum it moves the inner air. Whether this inner air was spirit, or whether it was merely a subtilized air that resembled spirit, was a question much debated. Crooke thought it similar, at least, to animal spirit. At any rate, it was by means of this airlike substance that motion was transmitted to the auditory nerves leading to the brain, and, in the process, sound was despoiled of all matter. The air in the ear "being altered," he wrote, "doth carie the bare Character and species of the Sound separated from the matter" to the auditory nerve, and thence to higher faculties of the soul.[22]

Further conjecture on the manner of hearing, Dr. Crooke willingly left to the philosophers. According to John Davies of Hereford, who apparently felt no inadequacy to deal with the subject, common sense, which was commonly located in the fore part of the brain, unified the variety of impressions carried to it by the spirits. These impressions, gradually freed of matter (in which he showed no interest), were presented to the phantasy (usually, but not always, the same as imagination) in the middle cell of the brain, which stored some of them in memory, but which referred others to the highest function of the soul, the intellect:

> Th'externall Sences serves the common Sence,
> The common Sence informes the Fantacie,
> The Fantacie, the Minds Intelligence;
> Th'Intelligence doth Knowledge certifie.

Phantasy was the pivotal point in the epistemological process, for whatever reached the intellect from the senses must make a "thorough-fare of the Fantacie." Whatever the intellect or will wished to perform in the body must also be carried out through its mediation. It could, however, operate independently of higher faculties of the soul; it could be what Davies called a "skipp-braine Fancy." Having received a sense impression, it could then, without higher directive, send spirits to all parts of the body, but especially to the heart, which remained, if not, as for Aristotle, the center of thought, at least the center of feeling, and by moving spirits in the heart cause passions.[23]

The way in which imagination aroused passions in the heart was described at length by Thomas Wright in *The Passions of the Minde.* "First then, to our imagination commeth by sense or memorie, some object to be knowne, convenient or disconvenient to Nature," he wrote. Then spirits "flocke from the brayne, by certayne secret channels to the heart, where they pitch at the doore," whereupon the heart "bendeth, either to prosecute it, or to eschewe it." In fear the heart first contracts and forces the spirits out, whereupon nature, to succor it, sends to it heat and spirits from other parts of the body. The face thus becomes pale, the limbs cold, while the heart itself feels heavy. In pleasure and delight the heart creates more spirits and as they are sent through the body, it feels light, while the face may flush and the limbs move more quickly. Love generates heat. Emotion was invariably accompanied by motion of the spirits.[24]

The Elizabethan recognized, as well as modern man, the influence of mental states or of imagination on physical condition. And he realized, too, that the relationship might be reversed, that physical disturbance might be responsible for attitudes and emotions. Sometimes, Thomas Wright concluded, one has feelings that seem to have no origin in will or imagination: "Wee feele our selves, we know not why, mooved to Mirth, Melancholy, or Anger: insomuch that any little occasion were sufficient to incense that Passion."[25] It seemed to him possible that sense impression, passing to the heart by "secret passages," might, without going to imagination at all, create an emotion over which even the imagination had no control. Heating of the spirits in the heart might be the cause and not the result of love or anger.

This assumption could not be accepted lightly, however, for it brought into question the supremacy of the rational soul. It was crucial both for physiologist and theologian. The degree to which spirits could function independently of soul was a matter often discussed, for the beating of the heart, sexual responses, and other bodily motions seemed to be entirely involuntary. Dr. Crooke argued, with Galen, that certain motions are completely "natural," *i.e.*, involuntary. Timothy Bright, on the other hand, believed that even seemingly involuntary motions are controlled by the soul, or at least that the soul has so well disciplined its servants, the spirits, that they carry out behests "although there be no charge or commaundement thereof given." There is no motion of the spirits, he insisted, but by the mind.[26]

Still, man did seem to respond involuntarily to outside stimuli and especially to music. The most famous victim of music's power—as Orpheus was the most famous performer —was Alexander, who had been roused against his will by the playing of Timotheus, first to leave the banquet table and start fighting, then to leave fighting for banqueting. This story was substantiated by a similar tale related by the Danish writer, Saxo Grammaticus, of a musician who, asked by Henry II of Denmark to demonstrate his prowess, put the king first into deep melancholy and then into such a rage that he slew four of his guard. Claude Le Jeune, perhaps the most eminent composer of the second half of the sixteenth century and one of the adherents of Baïf's Academy, was reputed to have similar power.[27] Alexander's "case" was the subject of varied diagnoses. His non-rational response was, by many, attributed to the natural law of sympathy, by which man's passion moves in response to that represented by musical modes. Vincenzo Galilei insisted that it was the inevitable result of similar passion felt and projected by the performer. Ficino had written that Alexander was moved both because the emotion and meaning of musical sound affected his senses and mind and because the motion of the air excited his spirits.

As time went on, however, as scientific trends gained momentum, there was growing belief that involuntary emotions are caused *only* by motion of the air, by the "matter" of sound, rather than by sound itself. From the middle of the sixteenth century, Ficino's analysis began to be interpreted to mean that air, by its very substance, had effect on the spirits, that it could cause emotions independently of imagination, that one might feel even without hearing, a theory that inevitably minimized the value of musical sound.

The great Italian-born physician and scholar, J. C. Scaliger, in his reply to Cardan's *De subtilitate* (1557), literalized Ficino for the physiopsychologists who followed him. Why is one moved by sound? Chiefly, he wrote, because the spirits in the heart are agitated by the trembling and dancing (*tremulum, ac subsaltantem*) air that is received in the breast —whether by way of the brain or directly from the ear he did not say. Everything that is perceptible to the sense, he wrote, arouses the senses, and not only for the sake of the impression—taste, smell, or hearing—as such. Sound, he continued, disturbs man within and directs him to actions that are not properly the result of hearing. It arouses man to pity, love, or madness, as it aroused the followers of Cybele to shed their own blood. In fact, animals, who have no rational soul, react to music as man does, and for the same reasons. As a result of motion in the heart, or of emotions caused by that motion, all other spirits in the body are moved, and they in turn move the muscles or restrain them. They may even mount up under the soul to elevate it. The reason that Scaliger gave for this motion was disappointingly traditional. Spirits move in correspondence to air by the law of sympathy, and the analogy that he used was that of the proverbial two instruments sounding sympathetically, a phenomenon as mysterious to him as the one he was trying to explain.[28] He still had no conception of the possible percussive effects of slight sounds. He would not have admitted, either, any more than Aristotle did, that physical motion in man could be entirely mechanical. But in so far as he asserted that the sensitive soul and the spirits react independently of perception and of reason, he anticipated the later Cartesian view.

John Case, in his *Apologia musices* (1588), quoted Scaliger's passage on trembling and dancing air along with those of Ficino on music, as different phrasings of the same idea. He made the quite logical—to himself at least—assumption that music may move the hearer both by direct action on the heart and also by way of the phantasy (as Cardan said). He became entangled, too, in the occultist discussion of sympathy. But he had in mind, certainly, the force of moving air itself, for he drew a parallel with the force of thunder, which makes man tremble, and he went on to reason, as Aristotle had not, that the soft and gentle pulsation of the air caused by music must give not the vigorous sensation of thunder, but a pleasant and delectable one.[29]

Still, no one seems to have been disturbed by these implications. The motion of dancing air was accepted as a poetic image, as it was by Sir John Davies, who asked in his *Orchestra, or A Pöeme of Dauncing,*

> For what are Breath, Speech, Ecchos, Musicke, Winds,
> But Dauncings of the Ayre in sundry kinds?

or as it was by Chapman in *Hero and Leander*:

> . . . sweet Musick usher'd th'odorous way,
> And wanton Ayre in twentie sweet forms danst
> After her fingers.

Chapman intended no derogation of music when, in the *Banquet of Sence*, he described the "air" of tunes touching the "connatural air" in the ear,

> Whose pores doe open wide to theyr regreet
> And my implanted ayre, that ayre embraceth
> Which they impresse.[30]

Thomas Wright took the next step toward materialism by saying, with no awareness, apparently, of heresy, that sound ("according to the best philosophie") is nothing but a motion of the air (a remark that sounds more materialistic, undoubtedly, than he intended), and by describing the contact of air with spirits as corporeal. In the first edition of his *Passions of the Minde*, in 1601, this passage does not appear. Indeed, there is no study there of musical effects. But in the second edition, in 1604, Wright explained, as had Scaliger, how the "substance" of music affects the spirits. He first summed up older theories, that music works on imagination or by God's providence or by "a naturall correspondence between our diviner parts and harmony." He then set aside these ideas and concluded that the "more sensible & palpable" reason lies in sound itself, which is nothing but "the shaking or artificiall crispling of the aire (which is in effect the substance of musicke)." His explanation of musical effects came from Scaliger, but he was more explicit in his description of the process by which air touches the spirits, for air, he wrote, passes through the ears directly to the heart, the seat of emotion. The spirits move, not for the reason that two instruments sound in sympathy, but for the same reason that one responds to the physical sensation of tickling, from the fact that

> The very sound it selfe, which according to the best philosophie, is nothing else but a certaine artificiall shaking, crispling, or tickling of the ayre . . . passeth thorow the eares, and by them unto the heart, and there beateth and tickleth it in such sort, as it is moved with semblable passions. For as the heart is most delicat and sensitive, so it perceiveth the least motions and impressions that may be: and it seemeth that musicke in those celles playeth with the vitall and animate spirits, the onely instruments and spurres of passions. In like manner we perceive by a little tickling of our sides, or soles of our feet, how we are mooved to laughter, yea and the very heart strings seeme in some sort to be mooved by this almost sencelesse motion.[31]

Here was one explanation at least of the fact that "sometimes wee feele our selves, we know not why, mooved to Mirth, Melancholy, or Anger"; not only extraordinarily loud sounds like thunder can move the hearer in spite of will, but even "this almost sencelesse motion" of music.

It must be remembered that Thomas Wright still postulated a sensitive soul residing in the heart, that his "spirits" were not entirely corporeal, that music, in his opinion, still worked "wonders." In more cautious moments he did not limit the definition of "music" to physical motion. But in this passage, at least, he made significant denial of the "hidden mystery" of sound; this "shaking" and "crispling" air moves in no pattern that images divine proportion. Music tickles "in like manner" as "tickling of our sides, or soles of our feet." Furthermore, the passions that it stirs up are not genuine emotions, but "semblable"; they merely resemble genuine feeling.

Reference to the effect of air on spirits became increasingly frequent, not in poetic metaphor (where it all but disappeared), but in expository prose, and with less interest in its power to rouse emotions than in its ability to cause physical motion or to give pleasure. Descartes, in his *Compendium of Music* (written in 1618, but published only posthumously in 1650), agreed with the Italian humanists that the end of music is to delight and to excite emotions, and this power he attributed (unlike the Italians) mainly to "sympathy." But he pondered, too, the possibility of percussive effects ("the reason whereof is to be referred to the disquisition of Physiology") which result not only in passion but in physical motion: "For certain it is, that a sound doth concusse, or shake all circumjacent bodies, as is exemplified in Thunder, and the ringing of Bells." And he noted that the first beat of a measure in music, being emitted more strongly than the others, "doth more smartly and violently concusse or agitate our Spirits, by which we are excited to motion."[32]

Robert Burton followed this new trend when he recommended music (as was common) for the cure of melancholy. It affects, he said, not only the ears, " 'but the very arteries, the vital and animal spirits.' " "Scaliger gives a reason of these effects," he continued (as Kircher did later): "the spirits about the heart take in that trembling and dancing air into the body, and are moved together and stirred up with it."[33] Owen Felltham, in tune with the temper of his day, concluded that since music "is but wanton'd Ayre, and the Titillation of that spirited Element," "it is more for pleasure, then any profit of Man."[34]

Even writers who were inclined to minimize the value of music because it was nothing but air found, as had Descartes, that it was difficult to shake off occult ideas. Burton added to Scaliger's explanation the equivocation, "or else the mind, as some suppose, harmonically composed, is roused up at the tunes of music." Air remained, in Felltham's opinion, inferior only to the Spirit of God Himself. "Nay, our very thoughts," he wrote, "are not framed without this Ayre. Every breath wee take, it goes unto our heart, to coole it. Our veines, our Arteries, our Nerves, our inmost Marrow, are all vivified by their participation of Aire." Music, then, though it be no more than air, may have great effect, whether that air moved by music enter by ear or by nostril. "Whose dull blood will not caper in his veines, when the very ayre hee breathes in, frisketh in a tickled motion?"[35] Mersenne, who, along with Galileo, later approached a scientific understanding of the vibration of sound, who suggested as early as 1629 that music is, after all, nothing but "le battement de l'air," that the ravishment attributed to harmony is imaginary, added that God had made the air.[36]

II

These gropings for an objective view of music were given direction by three determinative works published on the Continent in the late 1630's: Mersenne's *Harmonie universelle* in 1636, Descartes' *Discourse on Method* in 1637 (to which must be added his *Passions of the Soul*, 1650), and Galileo's *Dialogues Concerning Two New Sciences*, 1638. All gave support to the beliefs that sound, before it is perceived, is nothing but air, and that even slight sounds can have physical effects. Sound is nothing more than corporeal motion, insisted Galileo, until it is translated by the mind. It brings "to the tympanum of the ear a stimulus which the mind translates into sound."[37] He wrote elsewhere:

> If the ears, the tongue, and the nostrils were taken away, the figure, the numbers, and the motions would indeed remain, but not the odours nor the tastes nor the sounds, which, without the living animal, I do not believe are anything else than names, just as tickling is precisely nothing but a name if the armpit and the nasal membrane be removed.[38]

"The thing which we call sound," wrote Sir Kenelm Digby in 1644, "is pure motion," setting up in the eardrum a corresponding motion which is passed on to the brain, "which is all the mystery of hearing." And he warned, "We must narrowly take heed, lest reflecting upon the notions we have in our mind, we afterwards pin those aiery superstructures upon the material things themselves, that begot them."[39]

Languid motions, Galileo demonstrated with his famous pendulum, can set up corresponding motion by impact, not on air alone but on solid bodies; even that vibration made by a musical string is of sufficient force to cause another string tuned in unison to sound, not by occult sympathy, as had long been thought, but by impact. "This undulation," he concluded, "expands through the air and sets into vibration not only strings, but also any other body which happens to have the same period as that of the plucked string." The trembling of small pieces of bristle attached to an instrument and the ringing of thin glass in response to friction seemed to prove his point.[40]

Moreover, both Mersenne and Galileo proved that musical motion of the air is no "wanton" (playful or undisciplined) motion, but mathematically measurable vibration, to be measured not geometrically, in terms of "length, breadth, and thickness," but arithmetically, in time. The pleasure of listening to music, Galileo reasoned, depends on the orderliness with which pulsations of air "tickle" the ear.[41]

The notion that these same external stimuli could rouse passions mechanically was given support by the philosophy of Descartes, which was, in certain ways, a development of those ideas in Scaliger and Wright examined above. Once the rational soul was confined chiefly to a specific area near the brain, and spirits in the heart and elsewhere in the body defined as corporeal, body could be imagined to operate independently of soul, and even to cause emotion for which there was no origin in the mind.

Soul and body, Descartes reasoned, are two separate and distinct substances. There is only one soul, and while it "informs" the whole body, it functions chiefly in the pineal gland, which hangs just beneath the brain (the latter, except for this one small part, not being the center of thought or perception any more than it was for Aristotle).[42] Soul moves body by means of spirits, designated as corporeal (an idea to which William Harvey also contributed), but spirits can be moved by other means as well, without any operation of intellect or will. External motions, wrote Descartes, strike the sense organ and pass to the brain, but at that point two actions may occur: the impetus is transmitted to the soul to effect perception, but independently of this, spirits may be impelled to other parts of the body, to limbs or to heart, to stir up spirits there.[43]

These physical motions could subsequently cause passions of the mind. Descartes clung to the old belief that emotions or passions are accompanied by motion of spirits ("perception, feelings, or emotions of the soul . . . are caused, maintained, and fortified by some movement of the spirits"[44]), as he did to the notion that passions cause or are caused by a change in the heart, even though feeling itself does not occur there. And these old ideas encumbered his physiopsychological scheme. Since he did not admit the existence of a passage from ear directly to heart, and since he denied *awareness* of feeling in the heart itself, he thought that stimuli, if they were to act on the heart independently of mind, and thus to create emotions, must first send impulses to the brain; these would pass thence (avoiding the pineal gland) to the heart to stir the spirits, then back again to the brain, at which time the pineal gland would be moved and the soul "caused to be sensible of this passion."[45] This system, confusing as it was, did give a seemingly rational explanation of involuntary emotional response, of those feelings of sadness or joy, anger or love, for which man cannot otherwise account. Scaliger and Wright could be interpreted in mechanical terms: "tickling" motion of spirits in the heart could cause bodily action or induce passions in the soul by purely physical means.

It is indicative of the changing times that Descartes himself lost interest in music's effects after his early *Compendium.* A few writers did attempt to fit Scaliger's theory into a Cartesian framework. Dr. Thomas Willis (1621–1675) conjectured that involuntary reactions are the result of spirits in the "Cerebel" (not considered part of the brain), which "flow out orderly of their own accord one series after another without any driver, which may govern or moderate their motions." Sounds, he decided, "go to the Cerebel sooner and more immediately than the Brain" and are thus most apt to cause a flow of spirits from this "Fountain" to the heart. As the phantasy may be delighted by the "species" of sound, so the heart, since its spirits derive from the "Cerebel," may be cheered by mechanical motion, which "does as it were inchant with a gentle breath the Spirits there inhabiting, and compose them . . . to numbers and measures of dancing."[46] Anthony Le Grand described the way in which the impulse of sound goes from ear to brain and thence to "Arteries, Veins, and Guts to move the blood and animal spirits." This impulse could also arouse emotions.[47]

These attempts at reconciliation had little effect. The assumption established by Ficino, that music, by motion of the air, moves the spirits, that, as Scaliger added, it rouses emotions independently of the hearing process, the idea that its effects are accomplished, as Wright claimed, not by sympathy, but by contact like that of tickling (a suggestion given support by Galileo and Descartes)—all of these theories led to inevitable results. Music was "anatomized" to the point where its special significance for epistemologist or psychologist concerned with emotion, was minimal. Great philosophers of the second half of the century had little interest in its emotional or ethical effects; some, like Hobbes and Locke, had none at all.

It was primarily the physicists—Boyle, Guericke, Hooke—who, in the second half of the century, studied acoustical vibration, and physicians, more objective than Dr. Willis, who, under Cartesian influence, found new uses for music based on percussive effects that had nothing to do with emotions.

Robert Boyle (who, with Guericke and Hooke, demonstrated scientifically, at last, that there can be no sound without air) took up with enthusiasm the observation of effects of sound vibration both on inanimate objects and on the body of man. When a musician friend reported that a particular note sounded on a bass viol caused a certain window casement to jar, Boyle went quickly to observe the phenomenon. He noted that a certain sung note made an arch tremble. He concluded then, much as had Galileo, that in the agent the necessity was a "determinate tone," and in the receiver, a "peculiar aptitude" of texture or tension, a theory demonstrated by the mutual sounding of strings of musical instruments. Might it not be possible, then, he asked, that animal bodies "of a very different appearance from strings" might "be stretched in a manner requisite, to receive a vibrating motion from some peculiar sounds"? The human body, too, being "an engine," wrote Boyle, "is alterable for the better and worse, by . . . mere mechanical motions." A very languid movement of air (that tickling described by Thomas Wright as taking place only in the heart) may strike any part of the body and thus agitate the spirits. It

> may so determine the motion of the spirits in the body it works upon, as to make multitudes of them act, as if they conspired to perform the same motions: as when a ticklish person . . . has various muscles, and other parts of his body and face put into preter-natural or unusual motions.

This tickling did not induce emotions, however, but only physical change (in which distinction Boyle intended no derogation of music).[48]

Famous physicians seized upon this idea, later, for explanations of how music could be used to cure both poisoning and nervous disorders. Music has a great advantage over other medicines, which touch only fluids of the body, wrote the Italian physician, Giorgio Baglivi, in 1695, "by virtue of the Percussion upon the small Fibres of the Brain." It strikes the skin also and thus (as well as by way of the ear) touches the blood and spirits and dissolves their "Coagulation."[49] Dr. Mead and John Quincy, in England, agreed that music may be of medicinal value "even by a mechanical force" which gives regular motion to the spirits.[50] In spite of their belief that spirits were corporeal and of a fluid heavier than air, that air was made up of atoms, these medical men would have entirely understood the reasons given by that earlier physician, Marsilio Ficino, for combining the study of music with that of medicine—that music, more than other sensations, moves the spirits by motion of the air, that "by the very motion of the air it penetrates strongly." They would not, however, have accepted his occult music-spirit theory, for music, they thought, worked by a mechanical force. The fact that nerves, in time, took the place of spirits did not impede the development of this idea, for nerves were thought to be strung up to such tension as could make them apt to vibrate to musical sounds.

This stream of thought did not progress as directly or as smoothly as such a brief review may indicate. Occult notions had not been completely filtered out; islands of resistance (or scientific ignorance) remained, defended with the aid of past ideas; rivulets were channeled into backwaters where they were lost in a confusion of new theories entangled with old. Many writers—occultists, Neoplatonists, churchmen—tried to stem the current that threatened to sweep away ancient belief in the significance of music. Defenders of church music argued that music "carries such extasies, and Rapture, with it, as elevate the Soul of man into a higher Region." If music could accomplish these wonders in the past, as authority revealed, why should it not do so now, for "the Nature of the thing is always the same"? Enthusiasts like Thomas Mace lamented music's decline in reputation, and claimed that without doubt it had magical and mysterious powers, "there being no Passion in Man, but it will Excite, and Stir up. . . . It is a bemoanable pity to consider how few there are who know, but fewer who consider, what wonderful-powerful-efficacious Virtues and Operations Musick has."[51]

In this age of skepticism, however, the fact that the ancients had claimed marvelous effects from music no longer carried weight. The powers of music to enchant man and beast and to change their very nature had been "really and irrecoverably lost, if ever they were had," wrote William Wotton in 1697. "Music is a Physico-Mathematical Science." Its "great End . . . is to please the Audience."[52] Dr. Wallis reported to the Royal Society in 1698 that he considered ancient reports of the power of music "highly hyperbolical," and Alexander Malcolm agreed. It was the historians, wrote Malcolm, who were to blame for accounts of "those amazing Transports of Mind, and hurrying of men from one Passion to another, all on a sudden, like the moving of a Machine."[53] The Puritan who insisted that "All that Musick of its self can do, is only to put a pleasing Motion upon the Blood and Spirits,"[54] was closer to the thought of his time than was the lover of church organ. Music was believed by many to be nothing, literally, but a motion of the air.

MILTON AND MUSIC

CHAPTER VIII

Speculative Musical Imagery in Milton's Poems

PERHAPS no single body of writing sums up so many of the conflicts, confusions, and enthusiasms of musical speculation as does the poetry of Milton. Born in the still golden sunset of an animated and musical-spirited universe, he lived into the new scientific age in which the world was believed to operate like a machine. Yet his thought does not follow the chronological pattern of the century. Past, present, and future meet in one poet, who belongs to his time, yet is apart from it. His musical backgrounds are in Plato and Cassiodorus, St. Augustine and Boethius, Hermes, Agrippa, Ficino, and Spenser. Yet there is nothing "archaic" in his imagery: it is for all time. He was, early and late, both a lover of music and a Puritan—and, most of all, a poet. Out of these conflicts and this diversity, he created a uniquely beautiful imagery. The sweetness that he gathered from the philosophers was transformed by poetic alchemy into his own kind of music.

Milton could use the speculative ideas of his time without making of them a philosophy. Like his contemporaries, with their world of instruments, he described the spheres in terms of an organ: "Ring out ye Crystall sphears. . . . And let the Base of Heav'ns deep Organ blow." Instruments might be heard in nature: "rocking Winds are Piping loud"; "the Gray-fly winds her sultry horn." False churchmen spoke through "their scrannel Pipes of wretched straw." But this imagery did not serve for him, as it had for Donne and Shakespeare, to explain the relation of God to man or of men to each other. While he may have been influenced, as Saurat suggests, by the cosmology of Robert Fludd, he did not, like

Fludd, imagine the universe a musical monochord tuned by God, the Master Musician. He did not confuse Pythagoreanism with Christian theology.[1]

Like his fellows, Milton turned now and then to music as a book of knowledge. In the sonnet written on his twenty-third birthday he stated his determination to govern his life as music is governed,

> . . . in strictest measure eev'n,
> To that same lot, however mean or high,
> Toward which Time leads me, and the will of Heav'n.
> (Sonnet VII, lines 10–12)

In *Paradise Lost*, the archangel Raphael finds in the tension of musical strings a lesson for society, which can exist only by equality of its parts:

> Among unequals what societie
> Can sort, what harmonie or true delight?
> Which must be mutual, in proportion due
> . . . .
> The one intense, the other still remiss
> Cannot well suite with either. (VIII.383–388)

The sound of choir and organ brought all heaven before his eyes; "Voice, and Verse" presented to his phantasy the "undisturbed Song of pure concent." But this poetic "vision" Milton did not confound with "learning."

Although Milton referred often to the ecstatic effects of music, he always avoided the literalism of lesser poets—a fault that he only narrowly escaped when he so fortunately eliminated from an early draft of "At a solemn Musick" the line, "Snatch us from earth awhile."[2] His metaphor is less specific than that of many other poets, as may be seen in the *Nativity Ode*, when the shepherds hear heavenly sounds "As all their souls in blissfull rapture took," or in *Comus*, when the attendant Spirit's singing moves "even to extasie" (623), or in *Paradise Lost*, when angels' song awakens "raptures high" (III.369).

Milton does give hints of a more positive musical philosophy. One aspect of it is revealed in the sounding through his poems of a musical world spirit—that spirit described by Ficino, which finds voice in all kinds of individual spirits, whether sirens of the spheres, angels in heaven, or genii and demons in the elements, and which may be transmitted to man either to refine or to give life. With this idea of "spiritual" music goes Milton's interest in the "Platonic" approach to music, which defined music as primarily words, secondarily melody, an idea which is seemingly incompatible with the first, and which was never completely reconciled with it. With these two patterns of thought is interwoven a third—his changing ideas of the relation of music and love.

From the *Nativity Ode* to *Paradise Lost*, Milton imagined a universe filled with "aerial music." In the early poems he restricted use of the word "music" almost entirely to designate this kind of harmony neither heard nor made by man. For man-made music he used the words "ayre," "song," "madrigal," "anthem," but seldom the word "music." "At a solemn Musick" may be an exception, but this "musick," although it was audible, possessed qualities that made it extraordinary. "Soft Musicke" is indicated in the stage direction for the banquet scene in *Comus*, with a use of the word not given it in the text.[3] Later, in the sonnet to Henry Lawes, Milton used the word by necessity (what other could he have chosen?) to name a national art and practice of composing, "our English Musick." In *Paradise Lost* and *Paradise Regain'd*, the word had still other implications. But in the early poems it usually indicated either musical sounds (no less real for not being heard) of a Hermetic world spirit, or a principle of concord or love (of which world spirit is a symbol), audible, if man had not fallen by original sin, as harmonious sound.

This cosmic music is described in the *Nativity Ode*:

> Such Music (as 'tis said)
> Before was never made,
>   But when of old the sons of morning sung,
> While the Creator great
> His Constellations set. ("Hymn," stanza xii)

The shepherds were enraptured by "such musick sweet... As never was by mortal finger strook":

> Divinely-warbl'd voice
> Answering the stringed noise,
> As all their souls in blissfull rapture took.
> ("Hymn," stanza ix)

"Such harmony alone" (seen as light in stanza xi) could bind the universe with love, could "hold Heav'n and Earth in happier union" (stanza x). Milton referred again in "The Passion" (lines 1–2) to this "Musick, and Ethereal mirth,/Wherewith the stage of Ayr and Earth did ring," and in "Upon the Circumcision" (lines 2–3) to the "Musick, and triumphant song/First heard by . . . watchful Shepherds ear," this music that was pure harmoniousness, still not defiled by man's misuse. The word "music" has this meaning in the "Arcades," when the "Genius of the Wood," personified spirit, dreams of those other spirits, the celestial sirens, whose harmony turns

> . . . the Adamantine spindle round,
> On which the fate of gods and men is wound.

This music alone governs the world, music that none of "human mould" can hear:

> Such sweet compulsion doth in musick ly,
> To lull the daughters of *Necessity*,
> And keep unsteddy Nature to her law,
> And the low world in measur'd motion draw
> After the heavenly tune, which none can hear
> Of human mould with grosse unpurged ear. (61–73)

The music that Milton did hear in "At a solemn Musick" was no ordinary harmony, for it was born of the spheres and carried with it life-giving world spirit that could pierce "Dead things with inbreath'd sense," that could transmit celestial influences in Ficinian tradition.

One of the many remarkable virtues of this poem, however, is that with the line, "And to our high-rais'd phantasie present," it may be interpreted, also, within the framework of Ficino's philosophy of love. Having perceived beauty "in the harmony of several virtues," in the harmony of colors and lines, and in "the best harmony of several tones," wrote Ficino, man experiences one of three kinds of love. Those born with an inclination to the contemplative life "are lifted immediately from the sight of bodily form to the contemplation of the spiritual and divine"; those inclined to the voluptuous life descend to "desire to touch"; those inclined to the practical life are content with the pleasure of seeing or hearing. The soul, he wrote, "sees the images of bodies shining in it [spirit] as though in a mirror," and "while it sees these images it conceives in itself," through the phantasy, "images like them, but much purer." Through these images "the eyes of the soul are wakened to behold the Universal Ideas of things." By beauty man is led to understand divine love and is fired with desire to unite with it.[4]

Milton, born, indeed, with an inclination to the contemplative life, heard and saw in the wedded sound of voice and verse, by means of "high-rais'd phantasie," the image of divine concord (like earthly concord, but much purer), which is both love and music. He imagined the "Saintly shout" of seraphim, angels of love. But the intellect went beyond the image to the idea of the love of God and the inaudible "musick" of man that is also the concord of love,

> . . . the fair musick that all creatures made
> To their great Lord, whose love their motion sway'd
> In perfet Diapason.

In this music of perfect love Milton desired to become a part; he longed to be united with this "celestial consort," the "unexpressive nuptiall Song" of "Lycidas."

Yet there is no naming of "beauty" and only at the end of the poem a mention of the "love" of God. The debt to Neoplatonic doctrine, fallen into disrepute in Milton's day, is well disguised. Kinship with it is clear, however, when one compares this poem with the final stanza of Spenser's Platonic *Hymne of Heavenly Love* (where visible or spiritual beauty only, not audible, lifts thoughts to God):

Then shall thy ravisht soule inspired bee
With heavenly thoughts, farre above humane skil,
And thy bright radiant eyes shall plainely see
Th'idee of his pure glorie present still
Before thy face, that all thy spirits shall fill
With sweete enragement of celestiall love,
Kindled through sight of those faire things above.

Milton imagined a different kind of musical experience in "L'Allegro," when he asked for "Aires,/Married to immortal verse" (not called "music") that "pierce" the "meeting soul" —a phrasing reminiscent both of Ficino's passage on the penetration of "song and sound" and of his suggestion that soul leaves body to hear. Milton wished to indulge here in the more sensuous pleasures of listening to the sweetness of audible sounds themselves, to

. . . notes, with many a winding bout
Of lincked sweetness long drawn out,
With wanton heed, and giddy cunning,
The melting voice through mazes running.

Phantasy alone was stimulated to imagine Orpheus, free now of love's grief, who is wakened from "a bed/Of heapt *Elysian* flowres" to hear

Such streins as would have won the ear
Of *Pluto*, to have quite set free
His half regain'd *Eurydice*.

Music of world spirit sounds again in "Il Penseroso," to be heard, if at all, by the contemplative man:

And as I wake, sweet musick breath
Above, about, or underneath,
Sent by som spirit to mortals good,
Or th'unseen Genius of the Wood.

The climax, however, comes with the earthly sound of "pealing Organ" and "full voic'd Quire," sound that both dissolves with sweetness and reveals heaven. Again Milton completely avoided any suggestion of Neoplatonic love and of the eroticism implicit in the idea of penetrating and ravishing sweetness so congenial to Castiglione and Chapman, an eroticism welcomed by the Catholic poet, Richard Crashaw, whose soul "melts down in sweet desire" in the ecstasy of religious love. Milton avoided, too, any notion of complete ecstasy, for heaven is carried to the soul, not the soul to heaven:

> There let the pealing Organ blow,
> To the full voic'd Quire below,
> In Service high, and Anthems cleer,
> As may with sweetness, through mine ear,
> Dissolve me into extasies,
> And bring all Heav'n before mine eyes.

Gradually, however, man-made music, as described in the early poems, loses contact with divine. Although *Ad Patrem* again describes a "never-dying melody" sung by "the fiery spirit that flies round and round 'mid the swiftly whirling orbs," this harmony is not echoed in that of man, for Milton clearly places poet above musician. "Song," not harmonious sound, is evidence of our "heavenly source." By song, "not by his lyre," not by "warbled" notes as in "Il Penseroso," Orpheus compelled the ghosts of the dead to tears. (*Ad Patrem*, lines 35–37, 17–18, 52–55.) The poet, not the musician, is seer. Milton had often implied in earlier poems the necessity of verse with sound of voice or instrument. The "Sisters, Voice, and Vers" in a uniting of "divine Sounds" imaged, by their "mixt power," the "undisturbed Song of pure concent"; "*Lydian* Aires,/Married to immortal verse" pierced the meeting soul; organ and choir together dissolved the hearer into ecstasies. He had thought of himself, from youth, as a bard, like Orpheus, who sang to musical accompaniment, or whose poetry was song, whose words were "notes." The verse of "The Passion" demands "softer airs . . . and softer strings/Of lute, or Viol.":

> For now to sorrow must I tune my song,
> And set my Harp to notes of saddest wo. (8–9)

The "singer" of "Lycidas" "touch'd the tender stops of various

Quills,/With eager thought warbling his *Dorick* lay" (188–189). But one senses in *Ad Patrem* a sharpening of opinion, a critical view that takes on new dimension in *Comus*.

Earthly music, in *Comus*, is still imagined to perform miracles, for when the Lady sings, she breathes sounds "that might create a soul/Under the ribs of Death"; and the River Spirit, "invok't in warbled Song" (song aided by "the power of som adjuring verse"), animates the Lady "in stony fetters fixt," as the Asclipean statues were animated in antique lore. Although occult concept colors imagery, however, this idea is balanced, virtually obscured, by a more Puritan and a more purely Platonic view. The entire theme of the poem concerns the dangers of sensory pleasure (in criticism, it has been suggested, of current Neoplatonism, the pastime of the Queen's coterie at court[5]), and music shares in this scrutiny.

Song, Milton declared, may be harmful as well as beneficial, and he judged it not by aesthetic or Pythagorean, but by ethical standards. The singing of Circe and the sirens inspired false ecstasy, which robbed the soul of perceptive power. They

> . . . as they sung, would take the prison'd soul,
> And lap it in *Elysium*,
> . . . .
> Yet they in pleasing slumber lull'd the sense,
> And in sweet madnes rob'd it of it self. (255–260)

This kind of music, designated for use in the banqueting scene, is the seductive music of Acrasia's Bower, where men are transformed to beasts. Yet the singing of the Lady is "ravishing," too, in an entirely acceptable sense, without any perceptible distinction in musical sound itself, in tempo, dynamics, pitch, harmonic texture, or style of singing. What then determines the value of music? The words are undoubtedly important, although the reader is not given those of Circe's song, but only those of the Lady's, words impersonal, free of sensuous suggestion, imploring but not enticing. The singing of the Lady is praiseworthy not because music in itself is good, but because the Lady is, because "something holy lodges in that brest. . . . /To testifie his hidd'n residence," because she is motivated by faith and virtue, just as the singing of Circe was evil because she was evil and because she used music for the wrong purposes. The difference in effects does not derive from the relation of earthly music to divine, or even from differences in musical modes—Phrygian, Dorian, or Lydian—but from the character and emotion of the singer, for singer, like orator, arouses in the listener the same feelings that he himself experiences, as Cicero and Galilei had said. Comus, himself, for the moment, reveals his better self, even lifts his thoughts to the "home-felt" delights of heaven as he listens to the Lady sing.

Music does not figure in the serious Platonic philosophy of *Comus*. Neither from visual beauty nor from auditory, but from the beauty of virtue alone can man hope to reach "Celestial *Cupid*." In silent contemplation, in "retir'd Solitude," not through pleasures of sense, Wisdom "lets grow her wings, for "musing meditation most affects/The pensive secrecy of desert cell" (375–386). The food of the soul is not the sweetness of song, but the music of divine philosophy, in which there is no surfeit by which man may "sicken and so die":

> How charming is divine Philosophy!
> Not harsh, and crabbed as dull fools suppose,
> But musical as is *Apollo's* lute,
> And a perpetual feast of nectar'd sweets,
> Where no crude surfet raigns. (475–479)

Whether poet-philosopher or Puritan or austere Platonist speaks here, Milton's attitude toward music is changing. The change is gradual, however. Although, in the basic conflict in *Comus* between Reason and Sense, Reason emerges the victor, Milton had not, apparently, won a similar victory in his own mind, for he still admitted the "inchanting ravishment" of vocal sound.

None of Milton's poems is more "musical" than "Lycidas." It is dominated by the Orpheus image; it is "sung" in liquid verse. Yet in few other poems of Milton is there less obvious musical imagery. The subtle references to dolphins won to love of Arion by his singing, in "O ye *Dolphins*, waft the haples youth," to heavenly music, in "the unexpressive nuptiall Song," convert specific image to conceptual symbol. The fact that *Comus*, as a masque, was partly set to music, that "Lycidas," as an elegy, needed none, is not an entirely satisfactory explanation of the difference in use of musical metaphor. One suspects conscious avoidance of it.

The sonnet to Henry Lawes, written some years later, gives the reader a sense of stepping into an entirely different musical environment from that of the earlier poems. "Music" here means merely notes written for words. Milton did not praise Lawes, as did other poets, because his notes "the ravished ears do fill" or because in his music the soul, "Meeting a glance of her owne harmonie,/Moves to those sounds she heares,"[6] but because (although one may rightly question the historical accuracy of the statement) it was he who

> First taught our English Musick how to span
> Words with just note and accent, not to scan
> With *Midas* Ears, committing short and long.

Not harmony, but setting of words, matters. Lawes is honored not for imaging divine harmony, but for serving the poet:

> Thou honour'st Verse, and Verse must send her wing
> To honour thee, the Priest of *Phoebus* Quire
> That tun'st their happiest lines in Hymn, or Story.[7]

Milton, however, had not relinquished the "music" of his youth. Spiritual music resounds in *Paradise Lost*, written at a time when, for most men, the musical universe had been replaced by a mechanical one. In his own way, Milton resisted the breaking of the cosmic chain: he imagined a universe filled still with the musical breath of divine spirit. In heaven, angelic spirits sing and dance in motions resembling those of the spheres:

> And in thir motions harmonie Divine
> So smooths her charming tones, that Gods own ear
> Listens delighted. (V.625–627)

Over the earth walk "Millions of spiritual Creatures . . . Unseen," who

> . . . oft in bands
> While they keep watch, or nightly rounding walk
> With Heav'nly touch of instrumental sounds
> In full harmonic number joind, thir songs
> Divide the night, and lift our thoughts to Heaven.
> (IV.677–688)

The fallen angels sing "With notes Angelical to many a Harp," with harmony that is ravishing because they, the singers, still are immortal:

> Thir Song was partial, but the harmony
> (What could it less when Spirits immortal sing?)
> Suspended Hell, and took with ravishment
> The thronging audience. (II.552–555)

From musical spirit Pandemonium is built, spirit resembling the spirituous exhalations in the earth that Aristotle described, in his *Meteorologica*, as congealing to copper or gold. These exhalations, like all world spirit, are musical, as the organ's breath is musical. The "massie Ore," having been melted by "liquid fire," takes shape again as a temple overlaid with "Golden Architrave," with roof of "fretted Gold." (I.700–717.)[8]

Music produced by man, however, does not reflect divine origins. Beauty, as in orthodox Neoplatonic tradition, comes from light, not proportion. It shines not in music, but in the face of God's earthly image, man himself, and this "grace" alone inspires love in man that leads back to God. It is love of man for woman (governed always by Reason), not love for music, "By which to heav'nly Love thou maist ascend." Love is music of a higher order than audible sound, "Harmonie to behold in wedded pair/More grateful then harmonious sound to the eare." (VIII. 589–592; 605–606.)

As in *Comus*, Milton contrasts song worthy of admiration with sound that seduces, the singing of Adam and Eve before the Fall with the music heard in the tents of their descendants, fallen from goodness as a result of original sin. And again, as in *Comus*, the value of music depends not on the music *per se*, but on the virtue of the performer and on its use. The music that Adam first hears when he is permitted a vision of future times on earth seems to a modern reader above reproach:

> . . . whence the sound
> Of Instruments that made melodious chime
> Was heard, of Harp and Organ; and who moovd
> Thir stops and chords was seen: his volant touch
> Instinct through all proportions low and high
> Fled and pursu'd transverse the resonant fugue.
> (XI.558–563)

Yet these sounds are not approved above those heard echoing from other tents of the wicked, the harp and "amorous ditties" that weave nets of love and raise the heat of physical desire (sounds which Milton calls "Musick," an indication perhaps of his waning interest in the special meaning of the word). Both are equally condemned, because, while the performers may seem "studious . . . Of Arts that polish Life," all are "Unmindful of thir Maker." All fail to acknowledge His gifts. To enjoy music for its own sake, for the pleasure that it gives, is wrong, warns Michael:

> . . . Judg not what is best
> By pleasure, though to Nature seeming meet
> Created, as thou art, to nobler end. (XI.580–611)

Adam and Eve, in their state of perfection, sing only in praise of God, nor have they need of "Lute or Harp" to add "sweetness" to their orisons of love expressed "in fit strains pronounc't or sung" that "Flowd from thir lips, in Prose or numerous Verse" (V.145–152) as by a kind of spoken music. The right music resembles speech. This is no longer the Milton who was dissolved into ecstasies by the sweetness of pealing organ, who had, through music, a vision of "That undisturbed Song of pure concent,/Ay sung before the saphire-colour'd throne," who imagined melodious song that "might create a soul/Under the ribs of Death." The victory of

Reason over Sense is not yet completely won, however, i not even in his youth did Milton describe instrumenta sounds with more love than in *Paradise Lost*. The victory is still to come.

When Satan tempts Christ, in *Paradise Regain'd*, to

> . . . learn the secret power
> Of harmony in tones and number hit
> By voice or hand,

Christ replies that these are

> . . . little else but dreams
> Conjectures, fancies, built on nothing firm.

For Him, "music" *is* poetry. The music or poem with which He would delight His private hours is to be found "in our native Language":

> Or if I would delight my private hours
> With Music or with Poem, where so soon
> As in our native Language can I find
> That solace? (IV.254–334)

The poet is, himself, the musician; music is verbal language.

The universe of *Samson Agonistes* is not a musical one. No "aerial music" sounds to comfort Samson. Milton, like his age, found himself in a world changed by scientific thought from one "rich with colour and sound . . . speaking everywhere of purposive harmony and creative ideals" to "a world hard, cold, colourless, silent and dead."[9] Milton here reflects at last the changing ideas of the century that discovered music to be nothing but air, nothing but physical motion.

Yet he reveals in his late poems even less interest in the acoustics of sound than he does in the new astronomy. Music at its worst is still a seduction. He would seem to have been more influenced by puritanical judgment of music than by scientific thought. But Puritan bias does not seem to account entirely for his thought about music, for even in *Paradise Lost* he still described with enthusiasm not only the singing of the angels, but the resonant fugues of a fallen people.

Above all, Milton was pre-eminently a poet, a poet who

almost always regarded music as an adjunct to verse. The relationship of music to poetry was often in his mind, and in that relationship music had a progressively less important role, reduced as it was from a position of "misterious spousall" with verse (as he described it in an early draft of "At a solemn Musick"), to one of servitude in the Lawes sonnet, to one of extraneous ornament in the singing (more pronounced than sung) of Adam and Eve. Finally, in the preface to *Samson Agonistes*, music, even for choral odes, was dismissed completely, as "not essential to Poem, and therefore not material." In taking this view, Milton was undoubtedly influenced by Puritan rationalism, as he was by a first-hand knowledge of the classical background, but in many respects he agreed also with the Italian poets and musicians who, late in the sixteenth century and early in the seventeenth, believed with Plato that "music is nothing other than the fable and last and not the contrary, the rhythm and the sound," and who attempted to revive this "music" in odes and in dramatic forms "in fit strains pronounc't or sung."

The problem of Milton's awareness of the Italian "school" remains a tantalizing one. Did he recognize his kinship with Italian theorists, poets, and composers, who had, like himself, judged music by its effects, who were also, to a degree, Platonists, who denied, as he did in maturity, that man-made music is based on a natural law that makes of it an inevitable image of the universe? What was the extent of his acquaintance with the early experiments in producing a new music that would project the meaning of words, without which music merely pleased the ear? There are no positive answers to these questions, but one can find illumination, perhaps, by turning from the musical imagery of Milton's poems to their themes and their structural organization.

CHAPTER IX

Comus: dramma per musica

MILTON left surprisingly few comments about specific musical works he had heard or about the new Italian experiments in musical drama. It is known, of course, that he saw an operatic production in Rome in the early spring of 1638 and that he was much impressed, more by the occasion and the spectacle, apparently, than by the drama itself, for he made no reference in his letter to Holstenius either to poet or to composer. He later praised Henry Lawes (the only composer whom he ever named) for his setting, in monodic style, of Cartwright's imitation of Monteverdi's famous "Lamento" from the *Arianna—Ariadne Deserted.* The early sketches for *Paradise Lost* were "operatic," a plan that Dryden may well have sensed in the finished work when he adapted it to opera, and that Milton himself seems to have admitted when he gave Dryden permission to do so. But surely he knew about the Italian experiments well before he went to Italy. The theories that led to the new musical style were familiar to English composers by the time Milton was born, in 1608. In 1607 Monteverdi's *Orfeo* was produced, and in 1608 his *Arianna*, bringing to the composer, already known as a madrigalist, immediate fame. His libretti, and others, were published and widely distributed and imitated. From Elizabethan days, large numbers of Englishmen had traveled or studied in Italy, among them the composers, Coperario (born Cooper) and Lanier; the architect and stage designer, Inigo Jones; the poets, Thomas Carew and Aurelian Townshend.

The prominent new musical-dramatic productions of Milton's university and Horton years were the court masques, in which Lanier, Jones, Carew, Townshend (all back from

Italy) had a part. And although the masques were more influenced by French *ballet de cour* and Italian *intermezzo* than by Italian opera, while they were not dramas but combinations of lyrics and dance, there had long been, in their performance, imitation of recitative style, which in itself reveals acknowledged debt to Italian opera. With almost all these masques, Milton's friend, Henry Lawes, was connected as composer or performer. He sang in Jonson's *Chloridia* in 1630; he had a part during the following year in Townshend's *Albions Triumph* and in his *Tempe Restored.* In 1633 he was active in the production of James Shirley's *Triumph of Peace* and in Carew's *Coelum Britannicum*, the influence of which on *Comus* has frequently been noted.[1] Milton, himself, essayed this type of entertainment, probably at Lawes's suggestion, in the "Arcades." Since Lawes's music is lost, one can only guess that it was in the same quasi-recitative style that he used later for the songs of *Comus*, in 1634.

These two works are strikingly different in literary structure. The "Arcades" is fragmentary, limited in form by the very nature of the masque, and, in spite of lovely lyric passages, not, one would suppose, the sort of work with which Milton, as an ambitious poet, would have been content. *Comus* is a drama, "complete and of a certain magnitude," unrestricted by demands of musical setting, a vehicle for the declamation of serious philosophical ideas.

That the form of *Comus* is different from that of the typical masque has been generally granted. *Comus* does not depend upon dance and setting as essential features of the entertainment, but rather upon the "spirit of drama." There is, in *Comus*, a much more consistent dramatic effect than in the Jonsonian masque, a greater dramatic unity, a deeper seriousness, a more sustained lyricism. *Comus* is more genuinely pastoral. The masque is episodic. It depends for its success upon startling and extravagant effects. It is not subjected to dramatic laws. "If, in short," says a modern critic, "we allow *Comus* to be rightly called, as Milton called it, a Masque, we must add that it is one in which the spirit of drama has broken free from the Masque, in everything that concerns scheme and composition, while retaining a few unimportant traces of nominal allegiance."[2]

If *Comus* is not a typical masque, neither is it a typical pastoral drama, which is more complicated as to plot and more suited to the public stage. It is, as Greg suggests,[3] a poetical drama, essentially in the classical tradition in regard to simplicity and unity, but with the addition of songs and dances usual to the masque. Even this classification does not find for *Comus* a place with other works of its own kind, and yet Milton did not usually create new forms for his expression.

The derivation of subject matter in *Comus* has disturbed critics much less than that of form—so much less that the variety of the suggested source material is incredible, including, as it does, Homer, Spenser, Ben Jonson, the Greek tragic poets, and George Peele, not to mention parallels from the book of Job and Thomas Randolph's *Muses Looking-Glass.* Such diversity of source implies a complexity of background that does not suit a work that is fundamentally simple and direct.

Is it not possible, however, that Milton was not working from the masque form at all, but had another already crystallized scheme in mind? It seems not too fanciful to suggest that he found that form in the Italian productions, the motivating philosophy of which suited in so many ways Milton's own ideas about music. Is it not possible that Milton, with his background of Italian language and literature, his knowledge of music, his love of the classics, and especially his constant approval of the use of music to present words, might have turned from the popular court entertainment (the dramatic part so formless, the notes so inferior in expressiveness to Italian monody) to the famous musical-dramatic productions of Italy, which attempted to create a "music" like that defined by Plato? If, as seems probable, the theme of *Comus* was intended to be an attack on the debased Neoplatonism that dominated the queen's court,[4] since it preached return to a purer Platonic love of virtue, is it not possible that its literary structure, too, was patterned on a more classical or Platonically oriented sort of production? To find the answer, one must turn to the work itself.

I

Comus has many characteristics in common with the early Florentine attempts to imitate the Greeks, as critics have implied in comparing it to the *Bacchae* or to *Iphigenia in Tauris* or to *Prometheus. Comus*, also, is a pastoral drama on a mythological subject which aims to arouse pity, which adheres to the unities of time and action, and which contains moral and philosophical comments. In *Comus*, too, may be found indirect narration of action and other "ancient dramatic practices"—in the handling of dialogue, in the use of irony, in the prologue. Milton, however, Christianized his theme, treated it allegorically, added more lyrics and more dances, and avoided a tragic conclusion.

In these latter respects *Comus* resembles more nearly the productions of the 1620's in Rome, where composers and poets attempted to relieve what seemed to them the monotony of the comparatively pure classical style of the early Florentine sung drama, with its preponderance of recitative and its serious plot, by the introduction of the songs, dances, and spectacle which had hitherto been characteristic of the *intermedio*. The result was, again, sung drama with the same mythological plot, the pastoral setting, and adherence to the unities, at least to those of time and action; but in the later works there are more changes of scene than formerly, more changes of costume, and more dancing, and the recitative is varied by arias and duets. These *drammi per musica* were neither classical musical drama as it was conceived by the Florentines nor conventional *intermedio*, but a combination of the two. The proportion became overbalanced, in time, in favor of the more spectacular entertainment, but in the second decade of the century the Tuscan drama was still recognizable in the Roman, and it is with this early musical drama in Rome that the present study is most concerned. For *Comus*, being a combination of serious drama which is under the influence of the ancients, and of masque song and dance, is obviously of the same genre. Sir Henry Wotton, long Ambassador at Venice, who wrote to Milton in praise of the poem, appears to have recognized its source, since he referred to its combination of "Tragical part" with "Lyrical . . . in . . . Songs and Odes, whereunto I must plainly confess to have seen yet nothing parallel in our Language."

Comus has other characteristics in common with the musical drama of this particular decade. The poets and musicians in Rome, unlike the earlier group of experimenters, were not satisfied merely to set forth a pagan story. At times the intrusion of the Christian idea seems to have been merely an unconscious use of Christian terminology, as of "god" for "gods." Again the author made definite apology for the use of such terms as "fate," "fortune," "destiny" as the language of ignorant pagans, somewhat as the Elder Brother does in *Comus* (586–587) when he speaks of "that power/Which erring men call Chance." But often the dramas were written on definitely Christian themes, or else the mythological subject was interpreted as a Christian allegory. *Comus*, more successfully than the Italian works, blends the two. Its plot absorbs mythological material; yet its moral is entirely consistent with Christian belief.

The Italian dramas, unlike *Comus,* were completely sung —the narrative or explanatory passages in recitative, the lyrics, both solos and choruses, in a more melodic style. But metrically they resemble *Comus*, in as far as they are written with variety of verse form. These changes in verse form, which in the Italian musical drama were made to suit different kinds of musical setting, raise the question whether Milton may not have hoped to have his play completely set to music. The blank verse suggests recitative; the shorter lines are better adapted to aria. The first song of *Comus*, for example, "The Star that bids the Shepherd fold" (93) must, it seems, have been intended for singing. Although there is no indication in the text that Milton intended to use the chorus for singing as well as for dance, the first section of this song suits choral style and could, reasonably, have been sung by the chorus, especially the lines beginning "We that are of purer fire," where use of the plural pronoun also suggests group singing. The introduction of a longer line, such as is found beginning with line 115 ("The Sounds, and Seas with all their finny drove"), would indicate, to judge by the style of the Italian works, the entrance again of a solo part. The inserted songs in *Comus* are, of course, definitely lyrical and for solo voice; and Lawes's settings for them are clearly in the Italian style of the time, for they represent a departure from strict recitative—which, as a matter of fact, was never entirely compatible with the tastes of the English composer—toward a semi-recitative which is more tuneful and more lyrical.

Of these musical dramas—or *drammi per musica*—which were given in Rome in the early part of the seventeenth century, there is one to which *Comus* has peculiar similarity, *La catena d'Adone,* by Ottavio Tronsarelli and Domenico Mazzocchi, performed and printed in Rome in 1626. Not only is this particular work typical, in general, of the dramatic form to which *Comus* would seem to belong, but the striking similarities between it and *Comus* in plot, setting, allegory, and details of structural plan, point it out as a source upon which Milton almost certainly drew in the writing of *Comus.*

There can be no question of either the prominence or the availability of Tronsarelli's work. It was one of the first musical dramas of this sort to be presented in Rome.[5] Not only was it given an auspicious first performance, to judge by the editor's preface to the published score,[6] but Erythraeus says, in connection with his praise of Tronsarelli in his *Pinacotheca*, that it was repeated seven times.[7] It was published in musical score and twice as an independent dramatic work in the same year (1626); the libretto was republished in 1627, and copies of the work are not, even now, excessively rare.[8] Mazzocchi, who composed the music, was a famous musician in Rome. The drama is based upon an incident in one of the most widely read poems of the time, *L'Adone* of Giambattista Marino, and was probably written with advice from Marino.[9] There can be no doubt regarding Milton's knowledge of this latter work, not only because of its popularity, not only because of Milton's known admiration of Marino, evident in his poem *Ad Mansus*, but also because of the internal evidence of *Comus* itself.

La catena d'Adone begins with a prologue sung by Apollo, who descends from the sky, as did the Spirit in *Comus* from "Regions milde of calm and serene Air," to address the more distinguished guests and to state his part in the development of the plot:

> De' puri campi Regnator lucente
> Abbandono del Ciel la via serena,
> E scendo a l'altrui danno, a l'altrui pena
> Nume più d'odij, che di raggi ardente.[10]

His intentions are very different from those of the attendant Spirit of *Comus*, for he asks the Cyclops to procure from Vulcan invisible chains, to be used to keep Adonis from Venus who represents true love. But the plot, as in *Comus*, is a conflict between sensual love and divine. A chorus by the Cyclops follows. The first scene of Act I opens in a dark wood, with Falsirena, a sorceress, and her companion, Idonia, who represents concupiscence. Idonia tells Falsirena about a beautiful youth who is lost in the forest, and Falsirena, as Adonis approaches, feels, as Comus does at the approach of the Lady, "the different pace" of an alien personality, and she asks, as Comus asks,

> Can any mortal mixture of Earths mould
> Breath such Divine inchanting ravishment?
> (*Comus*, 243–244)
>
> Dimmi dunque, qual Nume
> Raccolto in mortal velo
> Qui spande eterno lume,
> E lieto cangia queste Piagge in Cielo.
> (*La catena d'Adone*, I.1, p. 15)

Even before she sees the youth, she desires him, and Idonia suggests that she use her magical powers to transform the wood into a beautiful garden, the better to ensnare him. In the second scene Adonis appears, frightened by the anger and jealousy of Mars. He is lost in the wood, like the Lady in *Comus*, and cries out, as she does,

> A thousand fantasies
> Begin to throng into my memory
> Of calling shapes, and beckning shadows dire,
> And airy tongues, that syllable mens names.
> (*Comus*, 204–207)

> Ch'odo di flebil voce
> Risonar la Foresta.
> Folle: l'aura mi scherne.
> Anzi pietoso il vento
> In si misti susurri
> Forse parla con me del mio tormento.
> (*La catena d'Adone*, I.1, p. 21)

There follows, as in *Comus*, an echo song, in which Adone calls upon and is answered by Echo, who comforts him. He soon falls asleep. Falsirena, seeing him, recognizes him at once as the youth whom Idonia has described. She wakens him and begs him to follow her to the beautiful spot which she has prepared, tempting him, as Comus tries to tempt the Lady, with "Refreshment after toil" (686): "ristoro/Da i travagli la vita" (I. iii, p. 26). Adonis follows her, hoping to find his way back to Venus. A chorus of nymphs, the followers of Falsirena, dance and sing the pleasures of love.

In Act II Oraspe brings the chains which Vulcan has forged. Arsete (Reason) tries, vainly, to dissuade Oraspe from using them, and, left alone finally, pleads for reason in a style worthy of the Lady in *Comus*: "La Ragion perde, dov'il Senso abonda" (III. i, pp. 43 ff.). The scene changes, then, to a palace of gold, "magick structures rear'd so high" (*Comus*, 797), in which Adonis, again like the Lady, is made captive with invisible chains. He bewails his fate, tries to flee and cannot, but continues throughout Act III to repulse the advances of Falsirena, who finally faints, and who, when revived, expresses a frenzy of despair, portrayed by a dance of nymphs. Falsirena's own magical powers having failed her, she determines (Act IV) to appeal to Pluto. Idonia describes the frenzied rites of Falsirena before an altar "in thick shelter of black shades embowr'd," "immur'd in cypress shades,"

> Di Pini cinto, e di Cipressi chiuso.
> Ivi di negre spoglie il seno cinse,
> (*Comus*, 62, 520; *La catena d'Adone*, VI, i, p. 58)

where Falsirena invokes the powers of the lower world as Comus does those of Cotytto. Pluto explains to Falsirena Adonis' attachment to Venus, whereupon Falsirena decides to disguise herself as her rival. However, Venus and Love arrive (Act V) in time to save Adonis from the false enchanter, as providentially as do the Spirit and the two brothers in *Comus*. Love frees Adonis; Falsirena takes on her true shape as a witch; and Adonis is reunited with Venus. An appended allegory explains that Falsirena is the spirit which is torn between reason and sensuality. Adonis is man, who is loved by God, but who loses his way and becomes bound by chains of flesh and evil, ultimately to be freed by love and reunited with God.

Both in *Comus* and in *La catena d'Adone*, there is the story of a sorcerer who tries, by enchantments, to win to sensual pleasures a beautiful young person who is lost and separated from loved ones. The failure of the enchanter and the rescue and release of the captive provide the subject of both. Even details of plot are alike: the occult sense by which the enchanter feels the new presence before it is seen; the desire for that person; the use of magic to deceive and captivate; the fear—or at least uneasiness—on the part of the lost person, and the appeal to Echo for direction; the frenzied sensual dance by the followers of the magician; the description of magical rites; the binding with invisible chains of the victim, who resists all persuasion to sin; the rescue of the captive and dissolution of the magic chains by the arrival of the loved ones from whom the lost person has been separated. The settings also are the same; both dramas open in a dark and formidable wood, shifting to a magically created and luxurious palace, and later to a pastoral scene.

The chief difference is that Milton has localized the setting of *Comus*, making it, as far as possible, British. The allegory of *Comus* is more one with the plot than is that of *La catena d'Adone*; the characters are nearer the abstractions for which they stand. Moreover, Milton makes the allegory his own by placing more emphasis on the virtue of the Lady's chastity than on the virtues of faith and patience represented by the brothers. But the idea of the lost soul's resisting evil and being finally restored through steadfastness to its heavenly state is common to both.

Formally—in proportion, in plan, in length—the two works are surprisingly similar. Each opens with a prologue (somewhat longer in *La catena* than in *Comus*) delivered by a supernatural being, who has descended from heaven to explain the action of the play. The prologue is followed in both works by the introduction of the enchanter (again slightly longer in *La catena*); and in both the enchanter with his or her companions retires to permit the entrance of the lost person, who expresses his fears, then sings an echo song. In *Comus* this soliloquy is 74 lines, in *La catena d'Adone*, 63. The enchanter then reveals himself and urges the lost person to follow him. In length, these two sections are identical. The ballet in Comus precedes the entrance of the lost person; in *La catena d'Adone* it follows the meeting. Milton uses this occasion for an anti-masque effect, and the dancing is unaccompanied by singing, unless one imagines the first song of Comus as the dance song. The dancing in *La catena d'Adone* is more conventional ballet, accompanied by chorus, which adds here 48 lines. Both dramas go on to a moral controversy—debated in *Comus* by the two brothers, in *La catena d'Adone* by Arsete and Idonia, the forces of good and evil—ending in the one case with the brothers setting out to free the victim, in the other with Falsirena's setting out to ensnare Adonis (a section appreciably longer in *Comus* than in *La catena*). The temptation of the captive by the enchanter and the vanquishing of the latter is prefaced in *La catena d'Adone* by another song on the subject of virtue and concluded by choruses and by Falsirena's expression of rage; but the core of the entire section is, as in *Comus*, the argument (similar in length) between victim and enchanter. There follows, in *La catena d'Adone*, a section describing the orgies of Falsirena and her descent to the realms of Pluto—material included by Milton in the first entrance of Comus and in the descriptions of him by the attendant Spirit—and a further attempt by Falsirena to seduce Adonis. Both dramas end with the entrance of rescuers and the joyful restoration of the lost person to loved ones (again scenes of nearly equal length). There are no dances indicated at the end of *La catena*, as there are in *Comus*, and the epilogue takes the form of a double chorus. Milton has, on the whole, pruned unnecessary repetition of idea. He has made of *Comus* a purer dramatic form.

The verse form is also, needless to say, Milton's own. There is no blank verse in *La catena d'Adone*, which is irregular in line and rhymed. The lyrics of *Comus* may be "related primarily to Jonson and Fletcher," as F. T. Prince has decided[11]; the similarities to Tronsarelli may well be due to common source. There are, nonetheless, interesting similarities between the rhymed sections of *Comus* and certain parts of *La catena d'Adone* in the use of couplets and more especially in the irregular form of the songs. "Sweet Echo," for instance, resembles the echo song in *La catena d'Adone* in the combination of couplets with an irregular rhyme. In length the two differ by only one line. (*Comus*, 229–242; *La catena d'Adone*, I. ii, p. 21.) The group of songs connected with the invocation of Sabrina is, again, almost identical in length with the group of pastoral songs in *La catena d'Adone* which is sung for the first ballet; and Sabrina's song is identical in length and amazingly similar in rhyme scheme to one of the choruses in that group, where one finds the *abc bcb dd ee fb* rhyme of *La catena d'Adone* compared to the *aab ccb dd ee fg* of *Comus*. One notes, also, the pastoral quality of both:

Qui d'or la Rosa
Colora il suo crin,
E cinge spoglie
Di vivo rubin.
Diamanti accoglie

Il bel Gelsomin.
Porporeggianti
Son gli Amaranti,
Avorio è'l viso
Del bel Narciso,
Son de l'argento
I Gigli più fin.
(*La catena d'Adone*, I, iii, pp. 28–29)

By the rushy-fringed bank,
Where grows the Willow and the Osier dank,
My sliding Chariot stayes,
Thick set with Agat, and the azurn sheen
Of Turkis blew, and Emrauld green
That in the channell strayes,
Whilst from off the waters fleet
Thus I set my printless feet,
O're the Cowslips Velvet head,
That bends not as I tread,
Gentle swain at thy request
I am here.
(*Comus*, 889–900)

Milton uses couplets more consistently than does Tronsarelli, who never uses them for an entire speech or song; but in the second scene of Act II the chorus in *La catena d'Adone* sings of the pleasures of love, as does Comus in his first song, in short-line couplets which are contrasted with a longer line. (*Comus*, 93–144; *La catena d'Adone*, II.ii, p. 40.)

One cannot deny other literary influences in *Comus*, and yet many of the elements that are usually traced to other sources are to be found in this Italian work. The central plot in *Comus*, drawn from the Circe episode in Homer, resembles also the attemped seduction of Adonis by Falsirena. Neither the abduction and rescue idea nor the echo dialogue need be traced to Peele's *Old Wives Tale*. Adonis, as well as Spenser's chaste Florimel, is robbed by his captor of power to move. In fact, most of the differences between *Comus* and *La catena d'Adone* in plot and in characters are changes demanded by the occasion for which *Comus* was composed: the scene was easily transferred to England by bringing the magician to "Celtick . . . fields" (60) and by introducing a goddess, Sabrina, who is descended from British kings; and the characters of the Italian plot had to be adapted to the young actors, the Egerton children. First of all, it was necessary to give to Lady Alice Egerton the part of a young and beautiful heroine. She was, therefore, given a part corresponding to that of Adonis. Comus was played, probably, by a professional actor, since the role of Falsirena did not fit the young Egertons, and he absorbed the qualities and words of Idonia, the voice of evil. The ideas of Arsete, or Reason, were expressed by the Lady, who was ably supported in the task by her two brothers. Venus, whose popular reputation, especially in this period of debased Neoplatonism, did not suit a treatise on chastity, came to be mentioned only twice, once by Comus, with an implication of sensual love, once by the attendant Spirit, as "th' *Assyrian* Queen," with Adonis in Elysium, far below "Celestial *Cupid* her fam'd son" (1000–1004). Her role, as defined by Marino, was divided among the brothers, Sabrina, and the parents, who receive the lost soul at the end.

There remained, of the characters in the Tronsarelli play, the speaker of the prologue, in itself a minor role, and of the possible actors upon whom Milton could draw, the best, Henry Lawes. Lawes did, of course, speak, or sing, the prologue (from which the doubtful ethics of Apollo were eliminated), but a larger part, that of the attendant Spirit, was also given to him. That part was not created by Milton, however. It appeared elsewhere in Adonis fiction. The existence of this role in *Comus* proves, rather than disproves, Milton's use of the Italian work, for this character is to be found in the source of *La catena d'Adone*, the famous *L'Adone* of Giambattista Marino.

II

L'Adone is the most important work of a poet who was the idol of his age, a poet of whom Milton himself wrote later to Manso—referring to this very work—"wherever . . . the fame of immortal Marini shall grow with fresh brightness, . . . you will press swiftly along an imperishable way" (*Ad Mansus*, 50–53). It was reprinted in each of the five consecutive years following its first printing in 1623, always with the appended allegory of Don Lorenzo Scoto. It was endlessly admired and imitated.

There is, of course, no similarity in form between *Comus* and Marino's epic, and Milton followed so closely Tronsarelli's choice and arrangement of plot material that there can be little question of the determining influence of the Tronsarelli work. But there are, in *Comus*, details of allegorical interpretation and of characterization, especially in the descriptions of Comus, which are not found in *La catena d'Adone*, but which do exist in *L'Adone*. There is, further, the character of the attendant Spirit in *Comus*, which is not in the Tronsarelli libretto, but which is paralleled in Marino's work in the role of Mercury. Moreover, the ending of *Comus*, especially in the freeing of the Lady by the river goddess, follows *L'Adone* just where Tronsarelli departs from it. And lastly, the textual parallels between *Comus* and *L'Adone* are even closer than those between *Comus* and Tronsarelli's drama, as is evidenced by the adequacy of Milton's lines as at least a free translation of the corresponding passages in Marino.

In *L'Adone* Adonis is driven from Heaven by the anger of Mars, as he is in *La catena d'Adone*, but in Marino's work he is given by Venus, before he goes, a magic ring, "a hidden strength," which affords him the protection which the Lady in *Comus* has in her virginity. Although Milton, in this particular instance, omitted the symbol, he retained the abstract interpretation of it. While Adonis has the ring, he, like the Lady, can be harmed by

> . . . no evil thing that walks by night
> . . . or stubborn unlaid ghost,
> That breaks his magick chains:

> . . . incontr'a lui non hanno
> Malie possanza, ò magiche fatture.

Mentre teco l'havrai, nulla potranno
Nocerti i neri Dei del'ombre oscure.
(*Comus*, 431–434; *L'Adone*, XII.77)

Adonis arrives, finally, at the garden of the goddess of delights. Guarding the gateway is a serpent, who has been changed into that form by the goddess, and who represents, as did the creatures of *Comus*, those who follow sin, whose

. . . human count'nance,
Th'express resemblance of the gods, is chang'd
Into som brutish form:

"chi cera l'occasioni del peccare, per la qual cosa perdendo l'humana effigie, ch'è ritratto, della divina somiglianza, vien condannato a vivere bestialmente nelle tenebre come cieco" (*Comus*, 68–70; *L'Adone*, "Allegoria," XII).[12]

This goddess, Falsirena, who rules over the island—for it *is* an island, as is the abode of Comus—is not "Of *Bacchus*, and of *Circe* born" (*Comus*, 521), but "Di Proserpina figlia, e di Plutone" (*L'Adone*, XII.123). Some of her victims, as is revealed later by Mercury, she destroys; others she changes into the "inglorious likenes of a beast," as does Comus, or, as Comus threatens to do, into stone, "chain'd up in Alablaster," or into plants, "Root-bound":

Molti uccider ne suol, talun n'incanta
Volto in fera, in augello, in sasso, ò in pianta.
(*Comus*, 527, 659, 661; *L'Adone*, XIII.133)

Falsirena tries to seduce Adonis, and, failing to beguile him by arguments, finally resorts to charms and incantations. She and her followers gather, therefore, at night around an altar, "immur'd in cypress shades," to perform "In their obscured haunts of inmost bowres," "abhorred rites to *Hecate*":

Sorge nel sen più folto, e più confuso
D'un bosco antico un solitario altare,
D'alti cipressi incoronato. . . .
. . . .
Opaco horror l'ingombra, e lo nasconde
Sotto perpetue tenebre di fronde.
(*Comus*, 520, 535, 534; *L'Adone*, XIII.8)

Tronsarelli imitated closely, here, the details of Marino's description, but Milton followed them even more closely. Falsirena and her followers burn their sacrifices, and then the sorceress takes her "Charming Rod" and calls to Pluto, with dissonant words, imitating the howl of "stabl'd wolves," which again recalls Comus:

> Poi prende nela man verga nefanda,
> . . . .
> Viè più ch'altra efficace indi discioglie
> La fiera voce, ch'a Pluton comanda,
> E move ai detti suoi sommessa e piana
> Lingua, ch'assai discorde è dal' humana.
>
> De' Cani imita i queruli latrati,
> Et esprime de' Lupi i rauchi suoni.
> (*Comus*, 549, 533; *L'Adone*, XIII.54, 55)

Then, in order to steal the ring, the safeguard which Venus has given to Adonis, the enchantress offers Adonis an "orient liquor" in a goblet, again a Miltonic detail not found in Tronsarelli:

> D'oppio forte e gravoso è quel licore
> Composto, e di mandragora, e di loto.
> (*Comus*, 65; *L'Adone*, XIII.112)

The potion works quickly; Adonis is overcome by oblivion. His ring is taken away, and he is bound in chains, in "fetters fixt, and motionless." (*Comus*, 818; *L'Adone*, XIII.113–114.)

Yet he may be still saved. Venus has asked of Jove the services of Mercury, who, like the attendant Spirit, "by quick command from Soveran *Jove*/ . . . dispatcht for . . . [his] defence and guard":

> Pregandol quanto può, mentre che'l manda
> Spia fidata e secreta a questa impresa,
> Che'n ogni rischio il suo intelletto astuto
> Gli sia saldo riparo, e fido aiuto.
> (*Comus*, 41–42; *L'Adone*, XII.82)

There is more than one hint that Milton thought of the attendant Spirit as Mercury. Together with Athena, Mercury escorted and protected heroes in perilous enterprises. He was a patron of music and oratory and could charm by his speech. But he was also the conductor of the souls of the dead, and thus intermediary between upper and lower worlds. The attendant Spirit, too, comes down "Swift as the Sparkle of a glancing Star" (80) to aid one in distress. He, too, can sing so that his auditors "hearken even to exstasie" (624). He points the way to the other world. He resembles significantly the Mercury who opens Carew's masque, *Coelum Britannicum*, who also descends from "the high Senate of the gods" to spread the doctrine of the exemplary life and the beauty of virtue.[13] Milton surely had Mercury in mind elsewhere in *Comus*: the attendant Spirit's *haemony* is like the moly "that *Hermes* once to wise *Ulysses* gave"; the dances at the close are such "*As* Mercury *did first devise*" (636, 962).

At any rate, the activities of Marino's messenger, Mercury, parallel those of the attendant Spirit. He, watching invisible all who are loved by Venus, sees Adonis and flies down to his aid, assisted, as is the attendant Spirit, by a magic herb "of divine effect," useful " 'Gainst all inchantments":

> Hor colta hà l'herba rara, e vigorosa,
> . . . .
> Contro la cui virtù maravigliosa
> Con mille chiavi indarno uscio si serra.
> (*Comus*, 629, 639; *L'Adone*, XIII.127)

This herb, later given by Mercury to Adonis, affords to Adonis the power which the *haemony* gives the attendant Spirit to know "the foul inchanter though disguis'd":

> E benche sappia esser beltà fallace
> L'inganno è però tal, ch'agli occhi piace.
> (*Comus*, 644; *L'Adone*, XIII.144)

Mercury comforts Adonis and frees him from his prison, but he is not able completely to liberate him, any more than the attendant Spirit is able, unaided, to free the Lady. Adonis is, after that, changed into a bird, although he can still say, as did the Lady,

Thou canst not touch the freedom of my minde
With all thy charms, although this corporal rinde
Thou haste immanacl'd:

Questa catena è tal, che solamente
Ritiene il corpo, e non n'è il core offeso.
(*Comus*, 663–665; *L'Adone*, XIII.154)

Of the two protectors of Adonis in *L'Adone*, Tronsarelli chose Venus and omitted Mercury: Venus and Love finally free Adonis. Milton chose Mercury and omitted Venus, and he followed Marino's solution for freeing the captive. Adonis, in order to recover his true shape, must return to the magician's garden and bathe in a fountain there, dipping his wings seven times in the water. Free, then, he hastens to find his ring and escapes. The Lady, too, is freed by water, which touches her seven times. Sabrina sings,

Thus I sprinkle on thy brest
Drops that from my fountain pure,
I have kept of pretious cure,
Thrice upon thy fingers tip,
Thrice upon thy rubied lip,
(*Comus*, 910–914; *L'Adone*, XIII.217, 218)

and after the seventh magic touch, Sabrina places her hands on the marble chair, and the Lady, too, is free. Milton has not made the allegory of this event explicit. Scoto interpreted it in Marino's story as representing salvation by grace, since Adonis was powerless to save himself.

Marino's story continues to the killing of Adonis by the wild boar and Venus' commemoration of his death with games and dances, designed to show that true virtue deserves suitable acknowledgment, "*a crown of deathless Praise*":

. . . L'honesto, e'l bene
Del meritato honor non si defraude.
Non dee vera virtù, nè si conviene
Senza premio restarsi, e senza laude.
. . . .
E [Vener] fattasi recar la statua d'oro
Del' istessa Virtù, la donò loro.
(*Comus*, 972; *L'Adone*, XX.92)

These concluding festivities remind one further of the ending of *Comus*, for the jousts and contests are followed, as are the country dances in *Comus*, by more courtly ballet, by music more soft than that of the warriors. After the rougher sports there are, as in *Comus*,

> *Other trippings to be trod*
> *Of lighter toes, and such Court guise*
> *As* Mercury *did first devise.*
> (*Comus*, 960–963; *L'Adone*, XX.62)

The festivities in *L'Adone* end in lengthy praises of France and of its early rulers and their "*fair branches*," "*so goodly grown*," which are reminiscent of the compliments with which the young actors in *Comus* are returned to their parents:

> Narrate io t'hò gran maraviglie, e talii
> Che volto forse havran di favolose;
> (*Comus*, 968, 967; *L'Adone*, XX.484 ff., 463)

Marino concludes, as the attendant Spirit begins his narrative to the brothers: I have told marvels "Storied of old in high immortal vers." And the tale being finished, the spirits return to their proper abodes—the evil to Tartarus, the good, like the attendant Spirit in *Comus* (and Milton was surely thinking of Adonis in the epilogue), to

> . . . those happy climes that ly
> . . . .
> Up in the broad fields of the sky:
> . . . .
> Where young *Adonis* oft reposes,
> Waxing well of his deep wound.
> (*Comus*, 976–978, 998–999)

It is not conceivable that this succession of parallels could be accidental. On the other hand, it is scarcely possible that Milton, using the material of *L'Adone* and casting it into the form of a musical drama, would not have been conscious of another musical drama based on exactly that same material

—*La catena d'Adone.* What is important, however, is not the relative influence of these two works, hardly even that Milton was drawing upon them for his plot material, but the joint proof they offer of the fact that Milton was writing a musical drama in the Italian style, that he did have in mind in writing *Comus* a crystallized dramatic form, with which he must have been acquainted before his Italian journey.

CHAPTER X

A Musical Backround for "Lycidas"

Of all the poems of Milton, "Lycidas" has best withstood the test of centuries, the ebb and flow of criticism. It remains for many the touchstone of poetic taste. Yet even those critics who love it most reveal some discomfort when they attempt to make its structure clear, to simplify its "elaborate art," for the poem has a design that eludes definition. "Lycidas" is, without question, "a splendid experiment in a traditional form, the pastoral elegy as that had been composed by Theocritus, Bion, Moschus, Virgil, Clement Marot, Spenser, Drummond."[1] Many of the old devices and conventions are there—the lament of nature, the questioning of the nymphs, the procession of mourners. In its rhythmic pattern and to a limited degree in its organization, "Lycidas" owes a debt to the Italian *canzone*, for both are made up of a series of "six to eight stanzas of medium length, of relatively complex structure," framed by a prelude and a brief conclusion. But the *canzone* does not have, as does "Lycidas," a "controlling principle . . . of logical progression," a "central theme." The *canzone* is a love song—charming but inconsequential.[2] It lacks the action, the drama, the tragic element of "Lycidas." In spite of its derivative elements, "Lycidas" is unique, not merely in those poetic qualities definable only as "Miltonic," but also in details of organization which are apparently without precedent in literary history.

Few structural analyses of the poem reflect complete peace of mind in the critics. Many scholars have rested content with a free stanza or paragraph analysis with a possible reference to the two "digressions"—the attack of St. Peter and the

Fame passage—admitting thus a degree of formlessness or a momentary deviation from convention. One critic, in a discussion of the metrics of the poem, concludes that "Lycidas" shows a definite contempt for formalities, that Milton "is uneasy, sceptical, about the whole foundation of poetry as an art." But has Milton succeeded, he asks, in this new venture, whatever it is? "Where then is Milton the individualist, whose metrical departures would seem to have advertised a performance which in some to-be-manifested manner will be revolutionary?" The "garden" which is "Lycidas" may be formal, but it is nonetheless a "somewhat tangled garden," which many find "confusing."[3]

It is, however, scarcely conceivable that Milton, with his sense and mastery of form, would have composed for publication a poem lacking the careful plan and skilful construction of which he was so entirely capable. The meticulous balance and parallelism of "L'Allegro" and "Il Penseroso" prove an already self-conscious artist. Nor would Milton, with his classical training and Renaissance heritage, have felt the need or advisability of "originality"—that modern criterion of excellence, with which few great authors of the seventeenth and eighteenth centuries would have agreed. If, in all his other mature works, Milton drew from sources, it is not likely that in "Lycidas" alone he would have attempted to be in any way "revolutionary."

Along with critics' questioning of form goes a doubt of the emotional sincerity of the poem. Can it be, many ask, an expression of deep personal grief? From the time of Samuel Johnson's verdict that "It is not to be considered as the effusion of real passion; for passion runs not after remote allusions and obscure opinions," this aloofness has been felt. One defense has been that Milton was not writing about the death of a friend, but about himself, his own ambitions, his own problems, his own fear of death. Tillyard, in this interpretation, has many followers who feel that it explains a unique emotional quality in "Lycidas."[4] For John Crowe Ransom, this detachment is no fault, but shows, rather, a "dramatic sense" which goes with greatness. The first-rate poet must be a "dramatis persona," the poem "nearly anonymous."

The stature of "Lycidas" is not obscured by these enigmas. Still, the questions recur. By what precedent did Milton contrive so seemingly intricate a composition? Was he merely elaborating ingeniously on classical models, or was he, to the contrary, defying formalities? "*Lycidas* cannot be dissected without a knowledge of the Italian poetry of the sixteenth century," writes a recent critic, "but it must be said that there is no exact parallel in Italian literature to the pattern of Milton's poem."[5]

Many critics, attempting to grasp this elusive structural and emotional quality of "Lycidas," and not finding any entirely satisfying literary source, have found analogy in music. They have compared the plan of "Lycidas" to that of a sonata or symphony. "No symphony was ever composed," writes Hanford, "of more varied emotional elements or blended them more consummately into artistic unity." Again, he compares its changing moods to "changing keys" of music. Saintsbury, too, describes its effect as "symphonic."[6] Laurence Binyon thinks that "in his use of language Milton seems to be powerfully influenced by the art of music and to aim at producing an analogous pleasure."[7]

These specific parallels are anachronistic, because they depend upon modern denotations of musical terms whose meanings have changed since Milton's day. If Milton used musical forms, they were those of his own day, not of the present. One feels with Allen Tate the necessity "to find out what the poets have done . . . and to guess what it was possible for them to do in their times."[8] Furthermore, the musical productions known to Milton provide fruitful comparison with "Lycidas" and can explain many of its puzzling qualities.

There are three ways of approaching this problem. One is to analyze the poem itself for internal evidence as to how it differs from the classical elegy, and to see whether "Lycidas" in its individual structure and its special sequence of moods suggests to a modern reader any definite musical form or setting. It is possible, in the second place, to search for musical forms that Milton would have known, and upon which he might have drawn, forms which so definitely resemble the style and organization of "Lycidas" that similarity seems beyond the range of coincidence. And, finally, there is one other method which may be employed to supplement the more obvious ones: it is to ask, does Milton subconsciously give himself away? Does he show dominant interests and presuppositions which would add weight to the theory that in his composition of "Lycidas" he drew upon music as well as upon literature? Granted that the analysis of "Lycidas" affords internal evidence that Milton had in mind a musical production as his source, granted that one may find in contemporary music, available to Milton, form and structure resembling "Lycidas," is it also possible to find unconscious evidence of Milton's interests at this period? If each of these three considerations leads to the same conclusion, the contention will then be justified that the ultimate source of "Lycidas," which explains its unique contribution to English literature, was as much a musical as a literary one.

I

Only a close and careful analysis of the "verse paragraphs" of "Lycidas" from the point of view of possible musical setting can serve to establish the first point—that the poem shows definite structural parallels with sung poetry of Milton's day, and that it suggests a definite manner of musical setting which was peculiar to a specific musical form.

The first paragraph is obviously a prologue, which falls naturally into two parts, the first of nine lines, the second of five. The passage has two striking characteristics: first, it is spoken—or sung—by one person, although the reader is not told specifically who that person is; second, if sung, certainly it would be sung in recitative. It has the lofty style, the declamatory character, the typical phrasing of recitative. In fact, Milton has accomplished with words alone something that is usually the result of a combination of declamation with interposed chords. One recalls Binyon's sensing of

Milton's aim to produce "pleasure analogous to that of music." These lines cannot be read without definite pauses; it is not necessary that the chords themselves should be there:

> Yet once more, O ye Laurels,/and once more
> Ye Myrtles brown,/with Ivy never sear,/
> I com to pluck your Berries harsh and crude,/
> And with forc'd fingers rude,/
> Shatter your leaves before the mellowing year./

Compare these lines with the next five lines of the paragraph, especially with the last three of them:

> Who would not sing for *Lycidas*? he knew
> Himself to sing, and build the lofty rhyme.
> He must not flote upon his watry bear
> Unwept, and welter to the parching wind,
> Without the meed of som melodious tear.

These latter flow along much more melodically. The declamatory quality is gone. The large, open vowel sounds and harsh consonants of the first group are superseded by the short vowels and liquid alliteration of the second. One is oratorical, the other lyrical. The reader is not told specifically that this second part is sung or spoken by one person. The more general subject, the comment on preceding statement, suggests chorus. These lines could be adjusted to a straightforward 4-4 time commonly used for choral singing. On the other hand, they could be sung as an aria, by a single voice above a simple bass.[9]

The next ten lines, the invocation of the muse, "Begin then, Sisters of the sacred well," are suggestive of recitative, the speaker definitely a shepherd. Again there is the formal address; there are the broken phrases. But with "So may som gentle Muse" the passage becomes more meditative. The whole is less grand, less oratorical than the introductory paragraph.

After an introduction and an invocation to the muse, comes the first subject of the poem:

> Together both, ere the high Lawns appear'd
> Under the opening eye-lids of the morn.

One person is singing, still the shepherd. Rhythmically, this paragraph begins in the same style as the preceding one, in a kind of recitative, but there is an interesting change in rhythm starting with the lines:

> Mean while the Rural ditties were not mute,
> Temper'd to th'Oaten Flute,
> Rough *Satyrs* danc'd, and *Fauns* with clov'n heel,
> From the glad sound would not be absent long,
> And old *Damaetus* lov'd to hear our song.

These lines are lighter, more gay. If they were to be set to music they might be set to a pastoral 6-8 or 12-8 meter in which the two or four large beats of the measure are subdivided into threes, comparable to the dactyl in poetry.

One notices a slowing down of tempo in the last line, "And old *Damaetus* lov'd to hear our song," a ritard that introduces the slow tempo of the next paragraph, which is a direct contrast to the preceding both in mood and rhythm:

> But O the heavy change, now thou art gon,
> Now thou art gon, and never must return!

This passage might be choral. There is no specific indication that it is solo and, as might be said also of the second part of the first paragraph, the subject is more general than that of the section that precedes it. Rhythmically it is broader and more regular. The iambic, five-foot line suggests a slow 3-2 or 3-4 meter in which the three large beats subdivide into twos. Such a pairing of dance rhythms, slow and fast, combining duple and triple meter, was basic to early baroque instrumental forms.[10]

It is only possible, of course, to make general comparisons between rhythms of poetry and of music. There are irregularities in verse, especially in verse as subtle and intricate as Milton's, that are not easily reproduced in the more regular musical rhythms. The musician, therefore, in setting words, must be more concerned with quantity than with the formal syllabic scansion. But one may safely say that the first of these sections is fast and suggests compound-duple time, and that the second section is slow, obviously in contrast to the first, and suggests a simple three-beat measure.

The next paragraph returns, with the questioning of the nymphs, to a more declamatory style:

> Where were ye Nymphs when the remorseless deep
> Clos'd o're the head of your lov'd *Lycidas*?

This passage again is clearly a monologue. Rhythmically it is most like the invocation to the muse, a quasi-recitative—a recitative less oratorical than the opening lines, but less lyrical and less consistent in rhythmical effect than the definitely melodic passages.

The sixth paragraph is a dialogue between the shepherd, who is tempted by the pleasures of the flesh, and Phoebus, who expounds the rewards of intellectual achievement. The first six lines are meditative and suggest a recitative in the nature of a chant:

> Alas! What boots it with uncessant care
> To tend the homely slighted Shepherds trade.

The next seven lines, however, beginning "Fame is the spur that the clear spirit doth raise," and the reply of Phoebus, are again declamatory, a quality accentuated by the couplet at the end.

In this "higher mood," then, the first large division of the poem ends, a division made up of prologue; invocation; two contrasting rhythmical sections in pastoral mood; a section of questioning which expands the material of the eclogue to include the British scene and which links Druid, Greek, and modern bard; and, finally, the flesh-spirit dialogue which forms the climax.

The second division of the poem, extending through the St. Peter passage, is indeed different in mood and tone from the first, though similar to it in plan and in development of idea. It, too, begins in a pastoral mood; like the first, it proceeds to a questioning section which serves by its juxtaposition of symbols of the past with those of Milton's own day to link ancient and modern, Greek and British elements;

each concludes with a moral discussion of the life of self-denial that belongs to "the faithfull Herdmans art" as against a life of pleasure and self-aggrandizement. These two large divisions are linked by three lines which are both a comment on the controversial section just finished and a reassertion of the pastoral scene. There follow a fourth and fifth line which definitely focus attention on a new subject:

> O Fountain *Arethuse*, and thou honour'd flood,
> Smooth-sliding *Mincius*, crown'd with vocal reeds,
> That strain I heard was of a higher mood:
> But now my Oat proceeds,
> And listens to the Herald of the Sea.

In their function of pivotal link these lines recall a tragic chorus, such as that in *Samson Agonistes*, which, having commented on Samson's guilt, turns to announce a new episode:

> Down Reason, then, at least vain reasonings down,
> Though Reason here aver
> That moral verdit quits her of unclean:
> Unchaste was subsequent, her stain not his.
> But see here comes thy reverend Sire. (323–326)

While the second division is structurally very much like the first, the two differ in mood and in general treatment of the theme. The first is secular, pastoral; the second, while it begins in a pastoral vein, is ecclesiastical, moral. Moreover, this second division is less stylized than the first. Instead of being a series of set songs, of small forms, it is a free treatment of a large subject which is not bound by a formal design. This entire second division is in recitative, with the variety in style that recitative permits. There are no arias and no parts that would naturally be sung by a chorus. As a result, it is less melodic than the first. The speaker is still the shepherd, but his lines now are neither monologue nor part of a dialogue. He is a narrator who stands aside and introduces a procession of personages who speak in turn.

In general, there are here two recitative styles, one for the shepherd-narrator, another for the characters whom he introduces. The shepherd's introductory lines are quiet, not at all dramatic, almost prosaic:

> But now my Oat proceeds,
> And listens to the Herald of the Sea
> That came in *Neptune's* plea.

The next twelve lines, Triton's questioning, are at once more oratorical:

> He ask'd the Waves, and ask'd the Fellon Winds,
> What hard mishap hath doom'd this gentle swain?
> And question'd every gust of rugged wings
> That blows from off each beaked Promontory.

At the conclusion of the Triton passage, the narrator, quietly again, announces the entrance of Camus, who recites one dynamic line,

> Ah; Who hath reft (quoth he) my dearest pledge?

before the narrator continues, in the same manner in which he began,

> Last came, and last did go,
> The Pilot of the *Galilean* lake.

One can imagine an intensification of vocal quality, with a crescendo from the light vowels of "He ask'd the Waves, and ask'd the Fellon Winds," to the passionate intonation of St. Peter:

> How well could I have spar'd for thee, young swain,
> Anow of such as for their bellies sake,
> Creep and intrude, and climb into the fold?

This speech, with its attack on all who are faithless to the "Herdmans art," concludes the second large division of the poem with a return to the "homely slighted Shepherds trade" which concluded the first. In the first division, however, the reader is conscious of the shepherd as a poet, in the second, of the shepherd as priest—a dual interpretation natural to the Renaissance poet with his background in both classics and Scripture.

As at the end of the first division, there is a choral effect in the two lines that connect this part of the poem to the last division, which is, like the first, more conventionally pastoral. These two lines are marked by an interesting change of rhythm. The first line and a half are recitative, as was the preceding passage. The last half line is lighter in style and carries on into the lyrical passage that follows:

Return *Alpheus*, the dread voice is past,
That shrunk thy streams;/Return *Sicilian* Muse.

The general form of the third division of the poem is similar to that of the other two. It opens, as did the others, with a pastoral section, the flower passage, introduced by "Return *Alpheus* . . . Return *Sicilian* Muse," which takes the reader back both to the "Rural ditties" of the first division and to "O Fountain *Arethuse*" of the second. It proceeds then to a section of questioning and "surmise" which is comparable to "Where were ye Nymphs" and to "What hard mishap hath doom'd this gentle swain?" It then expands geographically the classical setting, and the conclusion is again an elevation of the eclogue idea to a higher philosophical and religious plane, where the rewards of a life of self-denial are defended first by Phoebus, then by St. Peter.

There can be no question that the flower passage with which this division begins is a return to the lyrical, pastoral style of the first part of the poem. But this whole passage is in a slower tempo than was the gay dance movement of the first division. In tempo and in its elegiac mood it is more like the slow movement, the lament of nature, which followed. And here Milton does not couple a light pastoral dance with a stately one, but combines certain qualities of each in a single paragraph, and gains contrast by proceeding from a graceful, melodic movement to a particularly forceful recitative. One notes the slowing down of tempo in the line "To strew the laureate Herse where *Lycid* lies."

A couplet links this melodic pastoral passage to the next paragraph, the questioning surmise:

For so to interpose a little ease,
Let our frail thoughts dally with false surmise.

These lines again sound as if they were being spoken by a narrator or chorus; they are an explanation of what follows, rather than a part of it. The "Ay me!" however, definitely announces the opening of a recitative section:

> Ay me! whilst thee the shores, and sounding Seas
> Wash far away. . . .

The recitative is of the modified character used earlier, in the questioning of the nymphs. It suggests an oratorical delivery, which at its height becomes melodic. One is impressed by its grandiloquence, the loud, open vowels, the prolonged quantity of the words.

The climax, however, is reached in the victorious ascent to "the blest Kingdoms meek of joy and love," with its "solemn troops" of "all the Saints above" who "singing in their glory move." Such a crescendo in music would depend on dynamics, on increase in the volume of tone. The flower passage is light, with short vowels and delicate consonants. The recitative is strong and forceful; it demands full voice. The next paragraph then, the final, triumphant song, would have to be still louder and still more majestic. One way to gain that climax would be to make it choral:

> Weep no more, woful Shepherds, weep no more,
> For *Lycidas* your sorrow is not dead,
> Sunk though he be beneath the watry floar,
> So sinks the day-star in the Ocean bed,
> And yet anon repairs his drooping head,
> And tricks his beams, and with new spangled Ore,
> Flames in the forehead of the morning sky.

This passage suggests chorus. It is too melodic to be read in the declamatory manner demanded by recitative, and the thought is so sustained through successive lines that the phrases should not be broken by punctuation. The rhythm is fairly regular, easily adapted to choral singing. In attitude and ideas it is like the concluding semichorus of *Samson Agonistes*:

But he though blind of sight,
Despis'd and thought extinguish't quite,
With inward eyes illuminated
His fierie vertue rouz'd
From under ashes into sudden flame. (1687–1691)

The epilogue brings the reader back suddenly to the conventions of the classical eclogue, which was sung by one person, and which had a strictly pastoral setting, with no audience beyond an imaginary group of shepherds. It may be noted, however, that in mood—in "peace" and "calm of mind"—it is still close to *Samson.*

Obviously, "Lycidas" differs in many ways from its classical models. Some of the differences have been sufficiently suggested in the analysis of the poem—the clearly defined three-part structure, each part progressing consciously, almost geometrically, as the pastoral leads into query, query into dynamic answer, each reply rising in crescendo over the one before. The first section and the last, with even more conspicuously obvious parallels in rhythm and mood, are frame for the second. This contrived architecture is not typical of classical models. Structurally, "Lycidas" is more like *Comus.* The prologue and epilogue, the large sections or acts divided by changes of rhythm and idea into smaller parts, the philosophical argument separating more distinctly pastoral sections are common to both.

There are other suggestions, also, of a dramatic quality in "Lycidas." In the middle section especially, there is an impression of stage which is found neither in Virgil nor in the *Lament for Bion* by Moschus. In these older works, one does not see the events that are described as happening immediately before one's eyes. Even in the first *Idyl* of Theocritus when a procession of personages questions Daphnis, the narrator is clearly separated in time from the events he describes. The repeated refrain emphasizes this time difference, as does the fact that Thyrsis, in introducing the questioners, uses the past tense. In "Lycidas," the shepherd says, "But now my Oate *proceeds* and *listens* to the Herald of the Sea." "There pass then across the visionary stage three figures in succession."[11] The reader sees them standing before him and hears them speak.

Furthermore, this impression of pageantry projects the events of the poem and makes the reader part of an audience. The suggestion of recitative also contributes to such a feeling. The prologue, especially, has an oratorical style which would be entirely out of keeping except in a formal dramatic presentation. Such a narrative song as that of the shepherd, "Together both, ere the high Lawns appear'd," is less for a companion than for a spectator. There is certainly no such theatrical implication in the Eclogues of Virgil or in the *Lament for Bion*. Even in Theocritus, one shepherd sings to another quietly under a shady tree. The musical suggestion is different, also, from that of the Greek pastoral: recitative is dramatic, not lyric; the lyrical refrain is gone; there is more sudden variety and contrast.

These distinguishing qualities define within close limits the kind of musical composition that the present study is seeking: a large vocal form, dramatic in character, which has at least three divisions, each made up of a series of solos, both aria and recitative, and probably choruses. For a complete parallel, such a form should have prologue and epilogue. It should deal seriously with a pastoral subject in which classic and Christian ideas are combined. The parallel would prove still more complete if that musical form emphasized dialogue, and a certain type of narrative method that combines narration and action.

II

The signs point unerringly toward the most prominent form of production of the seventeenth century, the "sensation" of Europe—Italian musical drama, which, like "Lycidas," is rooted in pastoral eclogue, but which, like "Lycidas" again, is theatrical. With it and its allied forms—oratorio in Italy, the masque in England—recitative style was chiefly associated. The libretti of these musical dramas usually begin with a prologue declaimed, to music, by an allegorical figure, such as "Music" or "Tragedy," which sets the mood of the piece. Frequently there follows a section that serves to introduce the plot and the main characters of the story, made up of solos in contrasting moods and rhythms, sung in recitative or semi-recitative by one of a group of shepherds or nymphs, and of choruses by the rest of the group. The plot then proceeds in this pastoral setting and is unfolded by a series of arias and passages in recitative, with choral elaboration. At the end there may be an epilogue or a *balletto* to be danced and sung by the chorus. Act division is implied, although not always designated. One sees that the form of "Lycidas," especially that of the first and last parts, is not incompatible with this literary-musical type. It too is pastoral, opens with a formal declamatory prologue, and proceeds in a style suggestive of recitative varied with more melodic aria and with contrasts of mood and rhythm, to a climax well suited to chorus.

The middle section of "Lycidas," however, immediately suggests oratorio, which is, loosely speaking, a religious variant of musical drama. The oratorio had its roots in older church drama and was, originally, mainly choral, but by the late 1630's it had felt the influence of the secular musical drama and taken on many of its characteristics, notably greater use of solo voice, and the new style of singing, *stilo recitativo*. It is, however, static drama. The story is told, usually in recitative, by a narrator who introduces the characters, who in turn sing, but do not act, their parts. The theme is usually Biblical rather than pastoral. The method, at least, is the same in "Lycidas" as in oratorio, for the narrator presents other speakers—the Herald of the Sea, Camus, the Pilot of the Galilean Lake—who step foward in turn.[12] This section, however, in the anger of St. Peter (who, in Ciceronian tradition, moves his audience because he is himself moved), adds an emotional dimension to the poem in keeping with the new baroque dramatic style—anger being a mood that Monteverdi claimed to have been the first to portray in music. "Lycidas" is obviously not drama for the operatic stage, any more than is *Samson Agonistes*, nor is it the sung drama of the oratory. But its structural organization indicates the possible influences of these two related musical forms.

Before searching for more specific parallels, however, it is necessary to consider other possibilities of musical source. No complete musical forms have come down from the Greek. Medieval church music is so unlike anything in "Lycidas" that it is needless to look there. The medieval music is essentially choral; it is non-personal. The anthem, Service, and Mass of Milton's own day provide no sustained likeness in structure or intent. Even if one were willing to brave the risks of comparing "Lycidas" to an instrumental musical form of the time, there is none that invites parallel. There are various pieces, such as the canzona and ricercar, that derive their structure in one way or another from early polyphonic vocal forms.[13] There are dance movements extended by variations or divisions or linked into suites. "Lycidas," with its closely knit structure and its climactic composition, cannot be compared to these light pieces. Neither do secular lyric forms provide suggestive material for a background to Milton's poem. Madrigal verse is usually of one stanza only. It tends to be light in mood, and impersonal. The repetition of phrase and superimposing of line common in the madrigal would not suit the compressed thought and balanced construction of "Lycidas." "On May morning" might well have been intended for such a setting, but not "Lycidas." The English ayre follows more in ballad tradition, the verse usually in regular stanza form, set to a repeated melody. Both these forms imply a subordination of word to music, a dependence of verse on musical form to which Milton would not have been likely to confine himself.

As one turns to Italy, however (and it is inevitable that one should turn to Italy, in view of the amazing musical activity there at that time, and of Milton's enthusiasm for Italian culture), one finds a style ideally suited to the subtlety and freedom of rhythmic pattern so characteristic of "Lycidas." This is the new musical style of Caccini and Peri, which was attracting the attention of all Europe, and which reached its culmination in the music dramas of Monteverdi and his distinguished contemporaries.

The affinity of Milton's musical ideals with those of the early Florentine poet-musician is obvious, his knowledge of their activities beyond the realm of mere probability. Granted, then, that the structure and musical suggestion of "Lycidas" point to the musical drama, and to musical drama alone, as a possible musical influence in its composition, granted that that particular literary-musical form of production would surely have been known to Milton and have been of special interest to him, are there to be found, in the subject matter of the poem, ideas and presuppositions which lead to the same conclusion—that the characteristics of "Lycidas" which make the poem unique derive from Milton's interest in this Italian art form?

III

The subject of "Lycidas" is, obviously, the life and death of Edward King—only a little less obviously the life and fame of John Milton. It is inspired by the death of a young man—poet, lyric singer, priest—who, deserted by his tutelary deity, dies, his body lost in the sea. But it is not his fate to lie forgotten: he takes his place in the heavens as a new star. This is the story of Orpheus, too, poet and prophet, who, forsaken, was destroyed and cast into the sea, a singer, mourned by all nature. Even like Christ Himself, he charmed the lion and the lamb; like David, that "Israelitish Orpheus,"[13] he foretold secrets of the future. His life was cut short by the "blind fury." His head was claimed by the "remorseless deep." He, to, according to certain of the ancient stories, took his place in the heavens as a new constellation. Milton himself calls attention to the similarity:

> What could the Muse her self that *Orpheus* bore,
> The Muse her self, for her inchanting son
> Whom Universal nature did lament,
> When by the rout that made the hideous roar,

His goary visage down the stream was sent,
Down the swift *Hebrus* to the *Lesbian* shore.

Significantly enough, Milton proceeds from this parallel to another reference to the muse and another element inherent in the Orpheus stories—the conflict in Orpheus' life and death between the power of Phoebus Apollo and that of Bacchus. The association was evidently close in Milton's mind, for he goes on with no need of expressed transition to the conflict between the desire for pleasure and the desire for fame defended by Phoebus:

Alas! What boots it with uncessant care
To tend the homely slighted Shepherds trade,
And strictly meditate the thankless Muse,
Were it not better don as others use,
To sport with *Amaryllis* in the shade,
Or with the tangles of *Neaera's* hair?

The Orpheus reference in "Lycidas" is not an isolated one. Milton's work is filled with references to the Orpheus legend. In "L'Allegro" and "Il Penseroso," it provides merely a charming poetic image: Orpheus in "golden slumber on a bed/Of heapt *Elysian* flowres" or singing "Such notes as warbled to the string,/Drew Iron tears down *Pluto's* cheek" (146–147; 106–107). In the sixth Elegy, he is a symbol of the serious poet, as contrasted with Bacchus, who invites light verses and a life of pleasure. *Ad Patrem* crystallizes Milton's identification of himself with Orpheus. In placing the poet's calling above that of the musician, he asks, "In brief, what pleasure will there be in music well attuned if it is empty of voice, empty of words and of their meanings, and of numbers that talk? Such strains befit the woodland choirs, not Orpheus, who by his songs held fast the streams, and added ears to the oaks by his songs, not by his lyre" (52–55). This parallel is deepened in *Paradise Lost*, where Orpheus becomes a symbol of Milton's own tragic suffering:

But drive farr off the barbarous dissonance
Of *Bacchus* and his Revellers, the Race

> Of that wilde Rout that tore the *Thracian* Bard
> In *Rhodope*, where Woods and Rocks had Eares
> To rapture, till the savage clamor dround
> Both Harp and Voice; nor could the Muse defend
> Her Son. (VII.32–38)

In "Lycidas" are reflections of all these conceptions. The reference is more than an idyllic image. As a symbol of the young poet—indeed as a uniquely apt symbol of the poet-priest— who is not only Edward King, but Milton himself—Orpheus is again Milton's own prototype, in calling, in gift, in conflict of opposing aspects of life.

There are countless references to the Orpheus story in the works of Renaissance poets and Neoplatonic philosophers. For the musician it provided the subject not only for lyric songs, but for at least five different operatic productions. The mythical powers of Orpheus in music invited musical presentation, and the expression of emotion suited the medium of song. The story has variety of mood, joy, and sorrow. Both the elegiac quality and the implication of pastoral background fitted in with the general interest in the pastoral eclogue. Four libretti, written between 1597 and 1619, used this subject: Rinuccini's *Euridice*, which was set by both Peri and Caccini and presented first at the marriage of Maria de' Medici in Florence in 1600; *La favola d'Orfeo*, by Alessandro Striggio, music by Monteverdi, first performed in Mantua in 1607; *Il pianto d'Orfeo*, by Chiabrera, written and probably produced in 1608, reworked and set to music by Domenico Belli in 1616 as *Orfeo dolente*; and, finally, *La morte d'Orfeo*, words and music by Stefano Landi (1619). All these works were printed (either as separate libretti or in musical score, or both) at about this same time.[15] There is every reason to examine them more closely.

While the Rinuccini and Chiabrera libretti are, in general plan, obviously of the literary genre discussed above, they offer few specific parallels with "Lycidas" in treatment of theme. Rinuccini's poem, in spite of the fact that "Tragedy" speaks the prologue, is not really a tragedy, nor is it especially somber in mood. Chiabrera's is purely lyrical; it includes no narrative, no moralizing. But the other two, those of Striggio and Landi, are of special interest.

The more famous, then, as now, was Striggio's libretto, *La favola d'Orfeo*, set by Monteverdi, a work with greater emotional intensity, sharper contrast of mood, higher degree of seriousness, than its predecessors. Even a casual perusal of the work reveals striking similarities to "Lycidas" both in organization and in treatment of subject. Certain obvious similarities suggest themselves, many of which are coincidental with common interest in the pastoral eclogue—the device of shepherds and nymphs, invocation to the muse, well-known pastoral elements such as the lament of nature for the dead singer. But there is a progression of similarities, for the most part between the first and last parts of each work, that are unexpected.[16]

The opera begins with a prologue in recitative declaimed by "Music," which is a statement of the purpose of the drama —I come to tell you of Orpheus, of Orpheus, who drew wild beasts by his singing and by his prayers enslaved the ghosts of the dead:

> Dal mio Permesso amato a voi ne vegno,
>
> . . . .
>
> Quinci a dirvi d'Orfeo desio mi sprona,
> D'Orfeo che trasse al suo cantar le fere,
> E servo fe' l'Inferno a sue preghiere,
> Gloria immortal di Pindo e d'Elicona.

The recitative prologue in "Lycidas" is spoken by a shepherd, but in a style general and noble enough to suit a personification of tragedy:

> Yet once more, O ye Laurels, and once more
> Ye Myrtles brown, with Ivy never sear,
> I com to pluck your Berries harsh and crude,
>
> . . . .
>
> For *Lycidas* is dead, dead ere his prime
> Young *Lycidas*, and hath not left his peer.

Act I of *Orfeo* opens with another introductory section, sung in recitative by a shepherd, outlining the plot—the shepherds will sing of Orpheus and Eurydice in accents worthy of Orpheus, who was also a singer:

> Del nostro Semideo, cantiam, pastori,
> Con sí soavi accenti
> Che sien degni d'Orfeo nostri concenti. (I.23–25)

In "Lycidas," the shepherd similarly continues:

> Who would not sing for *Lycidas*? he knew
> Himself to sing, and build the lofty rhyme.

In both, there follows an invocation to the muse, in *Orfeo* sung by a nymph—may your song, on well-tempered strings, be in accord with ours:

> Muse, onor di Parnaso, amor del Cielo,
> . . . .
> Su ben temprate corde
> Co' 'l vostro suon nostr'armonia s'accorde. (I.43–50)

In "Lycidas" also is the plea:

> Begin, then, Sisters of the sacred well
> That from beneath the seat of *Jove* doth spring,
> Begin, and somewhat loudly sweep the string.

There is less similarity throughout the middle parts of the two works, where *Orfeo* is more definitely narrative than is "Lycidas." Common to both is a startling intrusion of the Christian conception of the deity, though less radical in *Orfeo* than in the attack on the church in "Lycidas." A choral passage in the second act of *Orfeo*, a comment on the fruitless labor of man, who is faced with inevitable oblivion, suggests the first part of Milton's Fame passage:

> Non si fidi uom mortale
> Di ben caduco e frale
> Che tosto fugge, e spesso
> A gran salita il precipizio è presso. (II.258–261)

The conclusion of *Orfeo*, however, is strikingly like the conclusion of "Lycidas," both in the imposition of a Christian conception of death on an essentially classical poem and in a remarkable similarity of phraseology. In the first edition of the libretto, published in 1607, the work closes with the destruction of Orpheus by the Bacchantes. In the musical score published in 1609, Apollo comes down from heaven in a chariot to carry him above to enjoy celestial honor, rather after the Christian manner. The lamented dead in Theocritus and Virgil did not share everlasting bliss with the saints above, yet both Orpheus and Lycidas—conceptions of their Christian authors—are granted that fate. As Orpheus mounts with Apollo, the chorus sings of how he will receive celestial honor amidst incense and prayers where sorrow is no more:

> Vanne, Orfeo, felice a pieno
> A goder celeste onore,
> Là 've ben non vien mai meno,
> Là 've mai non fu dolore,
> Mentr'altari, incensi e voti
> Noi t'offriam lieti e devoti.[17]

The chorus (if such it be) in "Lycidas" sings of "*Lycidas* sunk low, but mounted high . . . in the blest Kingdoms meek of joy and love" where the saints "wipe the tears for ever from his eyes."

There is also in this "ascent" chorus a stanza which again recalls the Fame passage of "Lycidas": it is in heaven that man receives his rewards for earthly sorrow. The chorus sings, as Orpheus ascends to heaven,

> Cosi va chi non s'arretra
> Al chiamar di nume eterno,
> Così grazia in ciel impetra
> Chi qua giù provò l'inferno,
> E chi semina fra doglie
> D'ogni grazia il frutto coglie.[18]

It is interesting that the plaintive instrumental epilogue which closes *Orfeo* is written in the ecclesiastical Dorian mode, and that the final pastoral epilogue of "Lycidas" ends, too, with the shepherd "warbling his *Dorick* lay."

A study of *La morte d'Orfeo* of Stefano Landi further strengthens the supposition that Milton was interested in the story of Orpheus and in the form of the musical drama as a means of expression. While it is more diffuse than Striggio's poem and more elaborate, as was usual in the musical dramas of the second and third decades of the century, and while there are more songs included simply for the sake of the singing, it provides a few close textual parallels.[19]

Some of the similarity is probably, as with *La favola d'Orfeo*, the result of common pastoral derivation, as, for example, the calling of flowers to cover Orpheus:

> Tu, ricca primavera,
> De' fiori tesoriera,
> Di croco e d'amaranto,
> Di bianchi gigli e rose
> Tessi ad Orfeo il prezioso manto. (V.844–848)

In both works appears the not unusual conception of the creation of a new God who will protect mortals. Lycidas, become the "Genius of the shore," Orpheus, seated in the luminous light of the heavens, both guard men from evil:

> Quivi, del centro alla più luminosa
> Seggia del ciel, tra fortunati eroi,
> Orfeo, qui ti riposa,
> Novello nume ai Traci e ai lidi Eòi;
> E già inchina l'orecchio, e de' mortali
> Pietosa accogli i voti e caccia i mali. (V.826–831)

There are throughout the drama other scattered similarities to "Lycidas"—satyrs dancing to the music of Orpheus, the advice of Apollo to flee women and their delights:

> Fuggi pur, fuggi pure
> Le donne e i lor diletti; forse a morte
> Non giungerai, seguendo infide scorte. (II.253–255)

Many characters of the drama are at least named in "Lycidas": Orpheus, his mother Calliope, Apollo, Jove, Tethys, queen of the sea (as compared to Triton), the Furies, Fate, and, of course, the inevitable shepherds. *La morte d'Orfeo*, having been written for the ecclesiastical group in Rome, was intended, also, to carry Christian significance.

Of more interest, however, are the following passages from the concluding scene of *La morte d'Orfeo* which invite comparison with very similar lines from the conclusion of "Lycidas." Two shepherds begin, as the heavens open to disclose a new and shining light among the troops above:

> Ecco, fra le più belle
> Schiere del ciel divine,
> Qual òr lampeggia. . . . (V.814–816)

The entire chorus continues in the style of almost unison singing, known as chorody: lament no more, for his rays are not spent. Orpheus still lives, not on earth but on eternal shores:

> Non più, non più lamenti,
> Non più, non più querele:
> Non son i raggi spenti,
> Son giunte al ciel le fortunate vele:
> Orfeo ancora vive,
> In terra no, ma nell'eteree rive. (V.820–825)

Fosoro, the morning star, adds the image of the Graces bringing serenity again to the face of Orpheus, who now outshines all others:

> E voi, Grazie. . .
> . . . .
> Rasserenate il viso
> Al nostro Orfeo, che sovra ogni altro avvampi.
> (V.852–856)

There is similarity both in idea and in phrasing in "Lycidas," in the final chorus of shepherds:

> Weep no more, woful Shepherds weep no more,
> For *Lycidas* your sorrow is not dead,
> Sunk though he be beneath the watry floar,
> So sinks the day-star in the Ocean bed,
> And yet anon repairs his drooping head,
> And tricks his beams, and with new spangled Ore,
> Flames in the forehead of the morning sky:
> . . . .

There entertain him all the Saints above,

. . . .

And wipe the tears for ever from his eyes.

The story of Lycidas is the story of Orpheus, and Milton's treatment of it is similar at many points to that in two of the most prominent sung dramas of the time. Milton, through the Orpheus image, has again led the reader to the Italian musical drama. In structure, mood, and subject as well, "Lycidas" suggests these musical productions, which Milton surely knew and with which he would have been in sympathy.

Finally, Milton has left one more significant clue. "Lycidas" is a "monody." The term is often dismissed today as a purely literary one. But it was used in the seventeenth century quite as often (as indeed it is today) to denote a musical style. A music scholar, Johann Alstedt, explained in a work first published in 1611 that "melodie is simple or compounded. That is called Monodie, this Symphony."[20] His entire emphasis is on musical composition. In Italy, the word *monodia* was used specifically for music sung by a solo voice in the new recitative style, by Pietro della Valle in his *Discorso della musica dell'età nostra* (1640)[21] and by Giovanni Battista Doni in a "Discorso sopra la perfettione della melodia" (1635).[22] It was this same Doni, one of the most prominent of the music theorists of the time, whom Milton may have met later in Italy.[23] Monody was discussed usually in connection with musical drama, which was after all its chief reason for being. A complete libretto was published as a "favola in musica," "tragicomedia pastorale," or "tragedia per musica," but in musical discussions, the songs which made up these works were called *monodie* because they were for solo voice, in a style which was thought to resemble that used for the monodies of Greek tragedy. Even when they were not definitely a part of a sung drama, however, they were performed with appropriate gestures and facial expression.[24] Since they expressed an emotion, it was necessary that the singer put himself in the place of the person whose emotions were being expressed, that he represent that person. The monody, even out of a larger setting, was thus a dramatic form.

Milton chose the inevitable word to describe his "splendid experiment," for "Lycidas" is a monody in both the literary and musical senses. It is rooted in the classical traditions of the past, but shaped to the broad formal pattern of the musical productions of its own time. "*In this Monody the Author bewails a learned Friend, unfortunately drown'd in his passage from* Chester *on the Irish Seas,* 1637."

CHAPTER XI

Chorus in Samson Agonistes

MILTON wrote in his preface to *Samson Agonistes* (1671) that "*Chorus* is here introduc'd after the Greek manner, not antient only but modern, and still in use among the *Italians*," that "In the modelling therefore of this Poem . . . the Antients and *Italians* are rather follow'd, as of much more authority and fame." It is not unreasonable, therefore, to expect to find in Italian drama of the seventeenth century these evidences of classical usage to which he referred. When he went on to explain the stanzaic form of his choruses as being monostrophic—"without regard had to *Strophe, Antistrophe* or *Epod*" he wrote of stylistic characteristics that had been anticipated in Torquato Tasso's *Aminta* and Battista Guarini's *Il Pastor Fido*, in the sixteenth century. In his previous statement, however, he referred not to style, but, first of all, to the fact that he used chorus at all, and second, to the manner in which it was used—a manner like that of the Greeks and "still in use among the *Italians*." He implied that there was common in Italy in his day an imitation of Greek drama that differed from similar efforts elsewhere in the handling of the chorus.

The phrase "still in use" cannot be accepted as a reference to drama of the sixteenth century, however convenient it would be to fall back upon proved relationships. Giovanni Trissino's *Sophonisba*, for example, so close a copy of Sophocles and Euripides, presents many parallels to *Samson Agonistes,* but it was written more than a century and a half earlier, in 1515, and was presented in 1562. Certain sixteenth-century Italian pastoral plays, such as the *Aminta,* use chorus in a manner suggestive of Greek drama, but the *Aminta* was written in 1573, and can scarcely answer for chorus "still in use."[1] Even the seventeenth-century revivals of it were too infrequent to account for a statement as broad as Milton's. Much the same may be said of the *Pastor Fido*. Moreover, had Milton been thinking of the sixteenth century, he could not have singled out Italian drama as unique, for between 1550 and 1590, Etienne Jodelle and Robert Garnier in France were writing tragedies at least as much after the Greek manner as those of Tasso and Guarini.[2] One must return to the fact that Milton was concerned with a trend in his own century.

Italian models have been overlooked from the time of Dr. Johnson, who evidently thought them not even worth mentioning. "It would only be by long prejudice, and the bigotry of learning," he wrote, "that Milton could prefer the antient tragedies, with their encumbrance of a chorus, to the exhibitions of the French and English stages."[3] Later critics, likewise, persisted in ignoring them. Because of this neglect, Edmundson wrote in his *Milton and Vondel*: "He alone [Vondel], of all the modern writers of so-called classical tragedy, has grasped the fact that the Hellenic drama had its origin in rhythmic song." His attempts to revive it, declared Edmundson, were entirely original and self-evolved."[4] Saurat gives the impression that the use of chorus in *Samson Agonistes* was a novel rediscovery, for in speaking of Milton's interjection of personal comments in *Paradise Lost*, he wrote: "Later on he found the trick of the chorus in *Samson Agonistes* to fulfil the same function."[5] Even a later excellent treatment of the debt of *Samson Agonistes* to Greek drama leaves out of consideration the Italian use of chorus, a usage that possibly offers partial explanation of certain peculiarities in Milton's choral speeches for which the author can find no precedent.[6]

I

Because the revival of classical drama in Europe in the sixteenth century was, on the whole, dominated by Senecan models rather than by Greek, and thus used chorus sparingly within the act, and because in the seventeenth century, especially in England and France, chorus in tragedy tended more and more to be omitted altogether, *Samson Agonistes* with its actor-chorus has always seemed isolated from contemporary practice. There is justification for this view. In France, later in England, Corneille came to dominate the scene, and he, in his passion for "vraisemblance," omitted chorus entirely until late in the century, and saw no necessity for it except to furnish a song to cover up the noise of adjusting stage machinery.[7] Madame de Scudéry, Rotrou, Racine, and a host of lesser writers followed his example. Not until late in the century did French writers turn again to use of chorus, notably through the influence of the operatic productions at the Académie Royale de Musique.

In England the popular stage play of the age of Elizabeth, with its nationalistic influences, its individual character, and, not least, its appeal to a popular audience, had little in common with classical drama, and scarcely ever introduced a chorus.[8] John Webster, in his preface to *The White Devil* (1612), commented as follows on popular objection to "sententious" chorus and "waighty Nuntius":

> If it be objected this is no true Drammaticke Poem, I shall easily confesse it. . . . willingly, and not ignorantly, in this kind have I faulted: for should a man present to such an Auditory, the most sententious Tragedy that ever was written, observing all the critticall lawes, as heighth of stile, and gravety of person, inrich it with the sententious Chorus, and as it were lifen Death, in the passionate and waighty Nuntius: yet after all this divine rapture . . . the breath that comes from the uncapable multitude, is able to poison it.[9]

In following decades, the tragedies of Corneille and later the heroic play—both consciously omitting chorus—became the standards of literary judgment. Even in Davenant's strange attempts at "Declamations and Music: after the manner of the Ancients" (1656), there is little use of chorus, and Dryden, in the preface to his tragedy *Oedipus* (1679), in which the nearest approach to chorus is a passage comparable to the witch scene in *Macbeth*, implied a pride in the English stage as differing from the Athenian, where one sees "in every Act a single Scene, (or two at most), which manage the business of the Play; and after that succeeds the chorus, which commonly takes up more time in Singing than there has been employ'd in speaking."[10] The two points of view represent a basic conflict in seventeenth-century drama, a conflict in which Milton stood with the Greeks and—he said—with the Italians.

Many historians of the Italian theater report a similar disappearance of chorus. A modern critic, for example, declares: "This suppression of the chorus [in Italy] is the most important innovation in the seventeenth-century pseudo-classic tragedy."[11] The strictly literary plays do, indeed, indicate a tendency to minimize its function.[12] Esteban Arteaga, however, in his well-known work, *Le rivoluzioni del teatro musicale italiano* (1783), heaped disdain on the opinion of an earlier critic, Giovanni Mario Crescimbeni, for discounting the use of chorus in Italian tragedy of his own century. He asked irefully if Crescimbeni had not read the five choruses that end the five acts of *L'Euridice*, if he had not examined "la Dafne, l'Arianna, il Rapimento di Cefalo, la Medusa, la Flora, la Sant' Ursola," and a thousand others. Did he not know, Arteaga asked, that no celebrated Italian *melodramma* was without a chorus until the middle of the 1600's, and that many continued its use during the rest of the century? "Cotanta ignoranza si rende pressochè incredibile in uno de' primi storici della italiana poesia."[13] This eighteenth-century critic illuminates Milton's comment.

Music was an important and controversial element in much of the pseudo-classical drama of the sixteenth and seventeenth centuries. No criticism of one can ignore the other. This mutual attachment is traceable, in large degree, to a curiosity about the music of the Greeks and performances of Greek drama—how it was sung and how much of it was sung. The English classical drama, it is true, was never concerned with music as an integral part of the play, but on the Continent, use of chorus was always closely bound up with that of music. Even in the most academic works of the sixteenth century, the choruses, at least, were expected to be sung, and, for this purpose, were written in strophic form.[14]

Decline of chorus in France in the seventeenth century was recognized as a curtailment of music. "Le retranchement que nous avons fait des choeurs a retranché la musique de nos poëmes," wrote Corneille,[15] assuming that chorus involved music.

The artistic group in Florence that was most responsible in the late sixteenth and early seventeenth centuries for the revitalized interest in classical dramatic practice came to the considered conclusion that Greek drama was entirely sung. It is only to be expected, then, that in Italy there should have been renewed interest in chorus. In drama completely sung, chorus became practical and natural because it was a definite part of a unified whole. It was acceptable because there had developed a new musical style that made possible a clear declamation of the words. It was desirable because of the musical effects to be gained, not only by choral singing, but by divided choruses, and combination of chorus with solo leader. The unusual character of *Samson Agonistes* lies in the fact that Milton used chorus even though he did not intend to use music. Even he, however, associated the chorus with music by saying that absence of music determined the measure of his verse—"without regard had to *Strophe*, *Antistrophe* or *Epod*, which were a kind of Stanza's fram'd only for the Music."

A matter of more concern is whether or not the chorus in *melodramma* resembles at all the classical chorus. Does the literary form of these works represent an interest in the classics that Milton might have felt at all similar to his own? There is no doubt that the musical drama is closely akin to, and was enormously influenced by, the pastoral drama of Tasso and Guarini, but there is no doubt, either, that it often was intended to be tragedy in the accepted sense of the term. The prologue of Rinuccini's *Euridice* is delivered by "La Tragedia," as is that of Striggio's *Favola d'Orfeo*. Campeggi's *Andromeda* is a "tragedia de recitarsi in musica." Chiabrera's *Angelica in Ebuda* is a "tragedia per musica." Milton's friend, Carlo Dati, referred to "*L'Arianna*, nobil Tragedia d'Ottavio Rinuccini."[16] The fact that these works were pastoral did not prevent their being tragedies. Milton, himself, did not distinguish sharply between pastoral drama and tragedy, for he discussed them in close juxtaposition (following a reference to the productions of Sophocles and Euripides) in the *Reason of Church-government*:

> . . . the Scripture also affords us a divine pastoral Drama in the Song of *Salomon* consisting of two persons and a double *Chorus*. . . . And the Apocalyps of Saint *John* is the majestick image of a high and stately Tragedy, shutting up and intermingling her solemn Scenes and Acts with a sevenfold *Chorus* of halleluja's and harping symphonies: and this my opinion the grave authority of *Pareus*, commenting that booke is sufficient to confirm.[17]

The difference that he implied was one of mood or subject rather than of form. There is no reason to suppose that he would have ignored the use of chorus in Italian plays that confused pastoral and tragic elements. And the fact remains that the present discussion is concerned, not with a strict dramatic form, but with use of chorus.

The strict classicist could find innumerable faults in these apparently trivial attempts to revive Greek tragedy. The composers were more interested in the wedding of music and poetry than in the unities. Above all, they were showmen first, classicists second. Nonetheless, their works often reflect the broader characteristics of ancient Greek tragedy—general adherence to unities, absence of strict act division, limited number of characters, and especially use of chorus, which, as in ancient times, took an active part in the drama. The chorus often remained on the stage during the entire action. It attempted to copy the patterned step and dignified gestures that are associated with Greek chorus.[18]

The first musical dramas—*Dafne* and *Euridice*—use chorus even more than do plays of any of the Greek tragic writers except Aeschylus, and the chorus is lyric rather than dramatic.[19] The similarity to *Samson Agonistes* and to Greek drama is only general. In proportions, in feeling, and in use of chorus, Rinuccini's *Arianna* provides closer parallel. The play is 1114 lines long, the choral parts taking up just under 30 per cent of the whole, which approaches the proportion in *Samson* and in certain dramas of Sophocles.

Gabriel Chiabrera, however, famous for his interest in the classics, used chorus in the most authentic manner and was most like Milton. Even in the slight dramatic pieces that he called "Favolette"—*Polifemo geloso*, for example—the chorus is used in a manner suggestive of classical drama.[20] Arteaga referred to *Il rapimento di Cefalo*, but that particular work is of less interest in connection with the present study than are some others. The chorus is used as a group only at the end of acts. In *Angelica in Ebuda, tragedia per musica*, however, one finds a plan and use of chorus obviously modeled on the Greek. The chorus does not speak until the second scene, where it begins with a long choral ode, as does the chorus in *Samson*, and throughout the pursuant alternating of solo dialogue with choral, there is striking similarity between the two works. *Samson Agonistes* is more weighted with meaning, but the common source is evident.

In other ways, too, these Italian choruses resemble those of *Samson*. One of the characteristics of Milton's chorus that has puzzled scholars seeking for source is the fact that its speeches are, on the whole, longer than those in Greek tragedy. William Riley Parker discusses this peculiarity of Milton's choral passages:

> When we come to examine the actual length of the speeches and odes, we face another interesting problem. Milton's drama has ten speeches of the Chorus between five and ten lines in length. This circumstance, which the reader is likely to take for granted, is extremely rare in Greek tragedy . . . there are no Greek plays which have, like the *Samson*, more choral speeches between six and ten lines long, than choral speeches one line long. Indeed, there are relatively few Greek plays which have not more . . . one, two, and three-line speeches than *Samson Agonistes*. . . . The problem of a specific debt seems insoluble.[21]

Yet one rarely finds in the choral speeches of these Italian works, any more than one does in Milton, half lines or single lines. Most of the speeches are between two and eight lines.

They differ from those in *Samson Agonistes* in tending to be three or four-line speeches rather than the longer five or ten lines, but Chiabrera, for example, although he does favor the three-line speech, has more speeches over three lines than under, none of one line. *La favola d'Orfeo* (Mantua, 1607), by Allessandro Striggio (set by Monteverdi), shows the closest parallel with *Samson Agonistes* (as it shows parallels of a different sort with "Lycidas"), not only in the contemplative function of the chorus, but in the length of the choral speeches, for all but three of them are between six and eight lines long, and again there are no one-line speeches. The reason is probably a practical one—that it is difficult to shift convincingly from a series of solo passages to a choral passage of only a few words. But if one is interested in finding a precedent for the long choral speeches in Milton, the musical drama provides at least a similarity.

II

As time went on, operatic chorus gradually expanded beyond classical limits. There were many forces at work, even aside from public demand, that encouraged expansion. From the beginning, this pseudo-classical movement in Italy was interested not only in ancient tragedy and the ancient satirical play, but in every kind of ancient show and spectacle, both Roman and Greek—games, combats, festivals, and triumphs—and there was, from the first of the century, an attempt to copy them.[22] These performances were bound to have an effect on the more serious drama in adding dancing, changes of scenery, and all sorts of spectacular effects. This development was first obvious in Rome in the 1620's, in such works as Tronsarelli's *Catena d'Adone*—the similarity of which to *Comus* in plan and idea has been noted —and in Venice. But in Florence, too, in 1625, in the theater of the Grand Duke of Tuscany, where the first musical drama had been performed, appeared *La Regina Sant'Orsola* of Andrea Salvadori, which used nine choruses, and which was given in a manner, according to the author, "degna dell'-antica grandezza Romana."[23]—words similar to Milton's in his description of the spectacle that he saw in Rome in the next decade.

Throughout the 1630's the Barberini family, under the aegis of the Cardinals Francesco and Antonio, nephews of Pope Urban VIII, continued this trend of magnificent entertainment by means of musical dramas on religious themes—most of them written by Giulio Rospigliosi (later Cardinal and then Pope Clement IX) and set by the most popular musicians of the time, including Stefano Landi, composer of *La morte d'Orfeo.* Rospigliosi's *Sant' Alessio* (1634), *Vita de Santa Teodora* (1635), and *Erminia sul Giordano* (1637) were performed in the new Palazzo Barberini, probably before the famous theater wing was completed. All were produced with ingenius use of stage machinery, some perhaps the work of Bernini, who had also helped to design the palace.[24]

By the time Milton was in Rome, in 1638–1639, the audience wanted even greater variety, and the work that he presumably saw—written also by Rospigliosi—was quite different in subject if not in general effect. It was a comedy, on a secular pastoral subject, *Chi soffre, speri* ("Who Suffers May Hope"), with music by Marco Marazzoli and Virgilio Mazzocchi, brother of the composer of *La catena d'Adone.* Milton, in his letter to Holstenius (custodian of the Vatican library, through whom he had received an invitation to the event), called it a "musical entertainment with truly Roman magnificence," thus associating it with the current interest in the revival of ancient spectacle. The work was a direct development of the earlier dramas, but it bears little true resemblance to them.

The plot of the drama portrays the loves of shepherds and nymphs, amusingly complicated by disguises of sex, and elevated only by a prefatory moral allegory. Chorus is used here in the pastoral tradition. But the fame of the production rested less on the drama itself than on its *intermedii.* At the end of the first (a *ballo,* with dances and songs by shepherds and nymphs), the group is dispersed by a storm, with thunder, lightning, rain, and wind. The second pictures a village fair, the stage being filled with vendors, storytellers, charlatans crying their wares. Grand seigneurs arrive in their carriages; a litter appears, pulled by mules and followed by a horse. A group of young men dance; one strikes a dog; the owner in anger draws his rapier and a duel ensues in which blood flows.[25]

Is this surely the work that Milton saw? Alessandro Ademollo, the authority on seventeenth-century theater in Rome, states definitely that in the last part of 1638 and the first months of 1639 only this entertainment, presented at the end of Carnival season, could fit Milton's description.[26] There are two contemporary accounts of the performance, Ademollo points out, that are similar to Milton's, one in the "Avissi di Roma," one in archives at Modena. The latter, a dispatch from Massimiliano Montecuccoli to the Duke of Modena, dated the second of March, 1639, states that the writer saw on the preceding day the "comedia Barberini." (The Carnival in that year lasted until the eighth of March, and the Barberini entertainments usually came near the end of Carnival.) He says in this dispatch that it was Cardinal Antonio Barberini (not Francesco, as Milton reports—correctly, to judge by the personalities of the two men) who stood at the door in "so great a Crowd," greeting everyone who came. Montecuccoli comments, as does Milton, on being greeted personally, as was everyone else in his party, and says that both Cardinals worked with the greatest diligence to seat as many as possible of the thirty-five hundred guests—a throng that indicates the use, by then, of the new theater. Cardinal Francesco went from bench to bench, "Con modi humanissimi, e di somma cortesia," urging people to sit closer and to make room for more. Cardinal Antonio undertook the more active task of forcibly removing from the audience a young man of twenty-five who was noisy and impolite.

One can only surmise who, of the many famous artists and musicians in Rome at the time, joined the throngs of Cardinals and Princes of the Church who invariably attended these entertainments—Frescobaldi, perhaps, who was subsidized by Antonio Barberini, or his pupil, Froberger; the composers of earlier Barberini productions, Stefano Landi and Domenico Mazzocchi; Giambattista Doni or Pietro della Valle, both of whom wrote about the musical trends of their time[27]; perhaps Pietro da Cortona, who was still working on the magnificent ceiling frescoes in the palace, frescoes that make of the Palazzo Barberini today a monument of seventeenth-century art. Mazarin, it has been suggested, may have been present, for he headed the list of Cardinal Antonio's domestic officers from 1637 to 1639.[28] The composers of *Chi soffre, speri* were surely present, and one may conclude, also, that the famous castrato, Loreto Vittori, saw the performance, for he acknowledged debt to the market scene in the preface to his own poem, *La Fiera.* Leonora Baroni, the famous singer to whom Milton wrote the Latin poems, was probably not present on this occasion, for Ademollo states definitely that no women were allowed to sing in the performance or even to attend unless they were accompanied by their husbands, and at this time Leonora was not married.

The well-known poet, Fulvio Testi, was probably not in Rome during the winter of 1638–1639. Two years before he had published an exceedingly influential "tragedy" intended for musical setting, *L'Isola d'Alcina,*[29] which was in a more restrained classical style than was popular at the time. His name appears, also, with two poems (in the same general vein as Milton's on the same subject) in the volume of verses written to Leonora and published in the fall of 1639. It is disappointing not to find Milton's, also, in the volume, for a Latin poem by Holstenius is included, as well as others by poets with whom Milton might have enjoyed association—Bracciolini, Bonarelli, Achillini, Rospigliosi, and others. One can only guess that his poems to Leonora were written with the hope that they would be printed in this famous volume, which may already have been in preparation.

In any case, his own statement proves beyond conjecture that Milton saw in Rome a musical drama which was at least a variation of the earlier Florentine productions, and it is equally sure that he heard about many others.

III

Even in musical drama the use of chorus waned after 1640. The public tired of long choruses; there was an ever-increasing demand for solo singing. And after the first public opera house was opened in Venice in 1637—two years before Milton's visit—the public came to be more and more of an influence. The matter of expense in a public theater was also a factor, as was the matter of space which would permit large groups on the stage. Further, the development of instrumental music substituted symphonic music for choral. When chorus was used, as in the operas of Cavalli, the words were often set in madrigalesque style, for purely musical effect. The interest in opera shifted from classical dramatic form and ancient usage to novelty and mass effect. Where, then, may one find a continuation of the use of chorus which would justify Milton's reference both to ancient and modern usage?

The classic chorus, at approximately the time it began to recede in musical drama, began, and continued, to be used in another musical form, the oratorio, one of the most popular musical attractions in Rome when Milton was there. The oratorio is a tempting field for a student of *Samson Agonistes*, because the Samson story was a favorite one for writers of oratorio from its beginnings up to the time of Handel's *Samson* (1741), which is based on Milton's work.[30] It is tempting, too, because there are static qualities in *Samson Agonistes* which suggest oratorio, a form designed to be sung, but not acted. Oratorio appealed to the ear, not to the eye. Action was merely suggested. It was not meant for the stage —"to which," wrote Milton of *Samson Agonistes*, "this work was never intended."

The development of the oratorio form is too complicated a story to be treated here with any adequacy. Generally speaking, it was, to quote Bukofzer, "a sacred, but non-liturgical dramatic composition in which a Biblical subject was presented in the form of recitative, arioso, aria, ensemble, and chorus, usually with the aid of a narrator or *testo*." It was presented in the prayer hall, also called an *oratorio* (oratory), which was "the meeting place of a devout congregation of laymen, the *Congregazione dell'Oratorio,* where the members met for prayer and the singing of devotional songs," and where in time more elaborate entertainment was provided.[31]

The oratorio derives from the purely meditative *lauda spirituale*, which was sung by a chorus, with the same music for each stanza. The *lauda* came in time, however, to portray the story of the sermon, to be a narrative with dramatic qualities, but still entirely choral. The chorus then became narrator, with the dialogue sometimes sung by solo voices. The final formative contribution came from *melodramma*, which developed dramatic qualities through the emphasis on solo singing and use of recitative. The dialogue was expanded and personalized; the narrator was personified. The resulting productions were considered dramas.[32] The chorus had always been an important part of religious music. When, therefore, the oratorio began to feel the influence of drama, it was natural that the chorus should assume characteristics of the classical chorus and that it should survive in the oratorio.

The purpose of the oratorio was to attract people to the service by means of music, and, by combining morals and entertainment, to lure the audience, in spite of itself, to a contemplation of the divine: "allettate le genti dal canto e dall'affettuose parole."[33] In attracting crowds, the oratorio was eminently successful, and it became so popular that the best musicians of Rome devoted their energies to writing works for the brothers of the congregation whose aim it was to sweeten religious instruction. The Oratorio della Vallicella, the most famous of them all, was approaching the peak of its popularity when Milton was in Rome, and several contemporary accounts give an idea of what Milton may have heard. A manuscript in the archives of the Oratorio della Vallicella tells how travelers thronged there and how they marveled at the heavenly music: "non solamente quei della città, ma i forestieri e gli ultramontani istessi venivano in nostra Chiesa alla Messa Cantata et a' Vesperi p. urdirlo . . . e dopo tutti le faceano applauso, dicendo taluno: *questi che canta è anzi angelo che huomo.*"[34] Erythraeus wrote in his *Pinacotheca* (1642) about Loreto Vittori, the composer and castrato, then singing in Vallicella, who stirred his audience to indescribable exaltation, so that they could scarcely breathe and many had to loosen their garments.[35] One wonders if Milton, having accepted an invitation to the Barberini Palace, may not have further overcome his religious scruples and gone to hear the famous singers at Vallicella, with the crowds who, when they could not get into the oratory, stood outside to catch a trill of the famous Loreto. It is in the works of Balducci (1579–1642), one of the composers at Vallicella at this time, that there may be found the first significant use of the chorus in oratorio as one of the protagonists.[36]

A description of the other famous oratory, the Oratorio del Crocifisso connected with San Marcello, was given by Maugars in his *Responce faite à un curieux sur le sentiment de la musique d'Italie*, written in Rome in October, 1639.[37] He had been in Rome for over a year, at the same time that Milton was there. He, like Milton, had heard the great Leonora. He had been on numerous occasions to her home, had himself played the viol for this "merveille du monde," and had gained no little notoriety thereby. He had been in England, too, in the 1620's, and thought Ferrabosco the greatest performer upon the lyre whom he had ever heard. There is no evidence that Milton met him either in London or in Rome, but he does describe performances of oratorios in Rome that Milton might well have heard, especially those at the oratory of San Marcello,

> où il y a une congrégation des Frères du Saint-Crucifix, composée des plus grands seigneurs de Rome, qui par conséquent ont le pouvoir d'assembler tout ce que l'Italie produit de plus rare; et en effet les plus excellens Musiciens se piquent de s'y trouver, et les plus suffisans Compositeurs briguent l'honneur d'y faire entendre leurs compositions. . . . Les voix après chantoient une Histore du Viel Testament, en forme d'une comédie spirituelle, comme delle de Suzanne, de Judith et d'Holoferne, de David et de Goliat. Chaque

chantre représentoit un personnage de l'histoire et esprimoit perfaitement bien l'énergie des paroles.

The greatest composer for the Oratorio del Crocifisso was Carissimi, a member of the German-Hungarian College of Jesuits and *maestro* at the church of Sant' Apollinare, who was almost certainly there in 1639. His *Jefte* (1650), the best known of the published oratorios, is of interest here because of its classical use of chorus.[38]

One of the most interesting examples of seventeenth-century oratorio, which shows many of the classical influences of sung drama, is actually based on the Samson story: *Il Sansone*, by Benedetto Ferrari.[39] At the time of Milton's visit, Ferrari was one of the most prominent composers in Venice, where he had gone from Rome in 1637 with Francesco Manelli to open the first public opera house, San Cassiano.[40] It is difficult to imagine Milton's not knowing about Ferrari, who shared with Monteverdi, head of music at San Marco, the fame and popularity of the day, and he was the more likely to know of him since Ferrari's patron was the English Ambassador to Venice, Basil Feilding.[41] The date of *Il Sansone* is not known. There are many indications (one being the limited use of the chorus) that it should be dated about 1660. But since there is no necessity of finding a further source for *Samson Agonistes, Il Sansone*'s interest for this study lies in the fact that it is a seventeenth-century oratorio on the Samson theme, with which Milton's drama has elements in common. *Il Sansone*, like the typical oratorio, is divided into two parts—one to come before the sermon, one after—a narrator being used for the introductory and transitional narrative. But Ferrari keeps to the classical number of characters and to the unity of time, although not to that of place. He uses the device of the messenger, and some chorus. Ferrari, like Milton—and like Quarles, in his *Historie of Samson*—portrays a Dalilah whose motives include not only money and fame, but patriotic duty as well, and the idea expressed in the Philistine Captain's prophecy, "Palestine already bows to your great merit, and will pay tribute of flowers and soft odors," very much resembles that of Dalila in *Samson Agonistes*:

> I shall be nam'd among the famousest
> Of Women, sung at solemn festivals,
> . . . .
> . . . . my tomb
> With odours visited and annual flowers. (982–987)

It is entirely possible that Milton had oratorio in mind when he asked in *The Reason of Church-government*, in 1642, that the Commonwealth plan entertainment for the public which would elevate the mind even while it furnished amusement, "not only in Pulpits, but after another persuasive method, at set and solemn Paneguries, in Theatres, porches, or what other place, or way may win most upon the people to receiv at once both recreation, & instruction." At about this same time the oratorio was exerting a strong influence on German religious music, notably through the compositions of Heinrich Schütz. The music of the Puritan church had no place for such semi-dramatic works as either the Catholic oratorio or the Lutheran passion, but Milton, feeling the need for some attractive means of elevating the public—"at set and solemn Paneguries, in Theatres, porches, or what other place, or way may win most upon the people"—may very well have recalled these Italian works with their similar aim.

IV

Although the works discussed above bear out Milton's statement that the chorus was used in Italian drama up to the time of his writing *Samson Agonistes*, there is doubt of his being familiar with oratorios written after he left Italy. Of the Latin oratorios, not even a libretto was published, apparently, before 1678. They were used for a religious service and left in manuscript. Only a very small percentage of them have been printed. They are not dated, and it is difficult to tell which ones he may have heard while in Italy.

The conclusion must be, therefore, that Milton employed the expression "still in use" on the basis of his acquaintance with Italian *melodramma* and oratorio until and during his visit to Italy.

Samson Agonistes might well have existed as it is without these seventeenth-century Italian productions. One could with justification trace its antecedents from the Greek poets and critics, through the sixteenth-century Renaissance from Trissino and Minturno to Tasso, then up through Vondel. Even the musical qualities of the work which certainly exist, and have been sensed by musicians who have written music for it, could be attributed directly to an interest in the Greek drama. Samson's monody "O dark, dark, dark . . . ," introduced with a change in verse form which in Italian musical drama indicated the entrance of a solo voice, is paralleled also in the ancient monody. The use of semichorus has actually no purpose beyond a musical one, yet its use could come from the Greek. But it is Milton himself who calls attention to the background of drama in Italy in his own century, a background that throws a light of peculiar interest upon Milton's mind.

Milton, then, was not original in his century in writing a classical drama with chorus in the Greek manner. Nor was Vondel "original and self-evolved." To give to Vondel, and through him to Milton, credit for grasping "the fact that the Hellenic drama had its origin in rhythmic song," is to isolate Milton from a great literary-musical movement from which he should not be, and would not have wished to be, isolated.

However, in stating his opinion that the Greeks used strophic form for their choral odes for the sake of the singing, and that singing is not essential, he disagreed with the humanists of earlier times. The entire aesthetic of musical drama was based on the necessity of song. He did, nonetheless, acknowledge his debt, as he took a last glance at the experiences of his youth: "thus much before-hand may be Epistl'd: that *Chorus* is here introduc'd after the Greek manner, not antient only but modern, and still in use among the *Italians.*"

The metaphysical ideas about music that were his heritage provided Milton with an essential poetic imagery, metaphorical on the whole, but useful, an imagery that expressed as no other could have done his faith in a universe infused with divine spirit. He deserted it only in his last works and in so doing was in rapport with his time. He turned from it, however, not as many men did, out of interest in new scientific experiment with sound, not even because of a puritanical bent that found music a distraction from the Word of God, but because he valued increasingly the significance of words and melody of poetry above the meaning and melody of notes —a view shared with the Italian poets and musicians who also subjected harmony to text.

He was surely not only aware of the new Italian music that resulted from this aesthetic, but deeply interested in it. The form and plot of *Comus* indicate knowledge of the *drammi per musica.* Even "Lycidas," although it is less obviously dramatic, although verse alone serves the purpose both of words and music, shows the influence of Italian productions. Organization and subject, the very subtitle, reveal common purpose, and it is tempting to suggest that the oratorical quality of "Lycidas" and its freedom of verse line may have been influenced by an imagined *stilo recitativo.*

When Milton wrote *Samson Agonistes,* neither the theory and practice of music nor speculation about music remained the same as when he was born. "Modes" had been replaced by "keys"; music and poetry existed as independent arts; rationalists had anatomized music and found it to be nothing but air, its purpose not to move but to entertain. The aims of the Camerata were all but forgotten. Milton himself disclaimed any need for music. But even here he revealed his feeling of kinship with the Italian humanists who, in their own way, had also depreciated old values of musical sound.

Notes

The references to the works of Shakespeare in this volume are to *The Complete Dramatic and Poetic Works of William Shakespeare*, ed. William Allan Neilson (Cambridge, Mass., 1906). References to the works of Milton are to *The Works of John Milton*, ed. F. A. Patterson (New York, 1931–1938).

PREFACE

1. Manfred F. Bukofzer, *Music in the Baroque Era* (New York, 1947), pp. 370–371, 390 ff.
2. *Ibid.*, pp. 392–393; Manfred F. Bukofzer, "Speculative Thinking in Medieval Music," *Speculum*, XVII, No. 2 (1942), 165–180.
3. Boethius, *De institutione musica*, Bk. I, secs. 1–2, in *Source Readings in Music History*, ed. Oliver Strunk (New York, 1950), pp. 84–85.
4. William Martyn, *Youths Instruction*, 2d ed. (London, 1612), p. 19 (misnumbered 11).
5. Christian Huygens, *The Celestial Worlds Discover'd* (London, 1698), p. 86.
6. Sir Thomas Browne, *Religio Medici*, Pt. II, sec. 9, *Works*, ed. Geoffrey Keynes (London, 1928), I, 88.

CHAPTER I

1. John Donne, "Preached at Lincolns Inne Upon Trinity-Sunday, 1620," *Sermons*, ed. George R. Potter and Evelyn Simpson (Berkeley, 1957), III, 148; Abraham Cowley, *Davideis*, Bk. I, sec. 37, *Poems*, ed. A. R. Waller (Cambridge, Eng., 1905), p. 254; Richard Crashaw, "A Hymn," lines 56–58, *The Poems*, ed. L. C. Martin (Oxford, 1927), p. 241.
2. *Richard II*, I.iii.161–162; *Du Bartas, his Divine weekes and workes*, tr. Josuah Sylvester (London, 1621), "The Sixt Day of the First Week," p. 128.
3. Donne, "A Lent-Sermon Preached at White-hall, February 12, 1618," *Sermons*, II, 170.
4. John Dee, *Propaedeumata Aphoristica* (London, 1618), Aphorism XI (here translated from the Latin).

5. Edward Benlowes, *Theophila* (London, 1652), Canto I, stanza lv.

6. William Drummond, Sonnet VIII, to his lute, *The Poems of William Drummond of Hawthornden*, ed. William C. Ward (London and New York, 1904), I, 115; Abraham Cowley, "The Garden," *Essays in Verse and Prose*, in *Essays, Plays and Sundry Verses*, ed. A. R. Waller (Cambridge, Eng., 1906), p. 424; Henry Hawkins ("H.A."), *Partheneia Sacra* (London, 1633), p. 140.

7. Background for these theories of harmony is given by Leo Spitzer, "Classical and Christian Ideas of World Harmony," *Traditio*, II (1944), 409–464, and III (1945), 307–364. See also James Hutton, "Some English Poems in Praise of Music," in *English Miscellany*, II, ed. Mario Praz (Rome, 1951), pp. 1–63. For the prevalence of the macrocosm-microcosm idea in Elizabethan England, see E. M. W. Tillyard, *The Elizabethan World Picture* (New York, 1944).

8. "Pythagoras, going about to make proportions of musick, as touching those celestiall orbes, found out an instrument called Heptachorde," wrote William Ingpen in *The Secrets of Numbers* (London, 1624), pp. 51–52. According to Giovanni Maria Lanfranco in *Scintille di musica* (Brescia, 1533), quoted by Gerald R. Hayes, *Musical Instruments and their Music, 1500–1750* (London, 1928–　　), II, 142, the sixteenth-century instrument, the *lyra da braccia*, had seven strings which were thought to represent the seven planets.

9. Plutarch, "On the Procreation of the Soul as discoursed in Timaeus," secs. 31–33, *Plutarch's Morals, translated from the Greek by Several Hands* (London, 1684–1694), corrected and revised by William W. Goodwin (Boston, 1870), II, 363 ff.

10. Philo, *De somniis*, 1.6.35, quoted by Hutton, "Some English Poems in Praise of Music," p. 14; Cicero, *De re publica*, VI.xviii.18–19, tr. C. W. Keyes, Loeb ed., pp. 271–273; Quintilian, *Institutio oratoria*, I.x.12, tr. H. E. Butler, Loeb ed., I, 165–167; Censorinus, *De die natale*, 13, tr. William Maude (New York, 1900), p. 10.

11. Plotinus, *Ennead* IV.4.8, *The Ethical Treatises*, tr. Stephen MacKenna (London, 1917), III, 56.

12. Cicero, *De re publica*, II.xlii.69, Loeb ed., pp. 181–183.

13. Plato, *Phaedo*, 85E–86C, tr. H. N. Fowler, Loeb ed., pp. 297–299.

14. Plotinus, *Ennead* IV.7.8D, *The Ethical Treatises*, III, 135. Cicero, in his *De oratore*, described man's whole frame and voice as a musical instrument, played upon by emotions (III.lvii.216, tr. H. Rackham, Loeb ed., II, 173): "The whole of a person's frame and every look on his face and utterance of his voice are like the strings of a harp, and sound according as they are struck by each successive emotion. For the tones of the voice are keyed up like the strings of an instrument, so as to answer to every touch."

15. Plutarch, "On the Procreation of the Soul as discoursed in Timaeus," sec. 33, *Plutarch's Morals*, II, 365.

16. St. Gregory of Nyssa, *In Psalmorum inscriptiones*, tract. I, cap. III, in *Patrologiae Cursus Completus. Series Graeca*, ed. J. P. Migne (Paris, 1856–1866), XLIV, 439 (here given in translation).

17. Clement of Alexandria, *The Exhortation to the Greeks*, I, tr. G. W. Butterworth, Loeb ed., pp. 3–15.

18. This was according to Origen. See Gustave Reese, *Music in the Middle Ages* (New York, 1940), p. 62.

19. Cassiodorus, *Institutiones*, sec. 5, in *Source Readings in Music History*, ed. Oliver Strunk (New York, 1950), p. 88. In the sixteenth century, Glareanus named a work *Dodecachordon* (*i.e.*, "instrument of twelve strings"), because it dealt with twelve ecclesiastical modes. The title of Milton's *Tetrachordon* is in the same tradition.

20. Clement of Alexandria, *The Instructor*, Bk. II, chap. IV, in *The Ante-Nicene Christian Library*, ed. Rev. Alexander Roberts and James Donaldson (Edinburgh, 1867), IV, 216.

21. See Henry George Farmer, "The Influence of Music: From Arabic Sources," The Musical Association, London, *Proceedings, 1925–1926* (1926), 89–124; and Eric Werner and Isaiah Sonne, "The Philosophy and Theory of Music in Judaeo-Arabic Literature," *Hebrew Union College Annual*, XVI (1941), 288 ff.

22. al-Makkarī, *Analectes*, in *The History of the Mohammedan Dynasties in Spain*, tr. Pasqual de Gayangos (London, 1840), II, 118–119.

23. Spitzer and Hutton both treat evidence of these theories in medieval and Neoplatonic writings. The fourteenth-century mystic, St. Catherine of Siena, compared "the forces of the mind with the major strings, and those of the senses with the minor," which when rightly used "Producono un suono simile a quello di un organo armonioso." Spitzer, "Classical and Christian Ideas of World Harmony," *Traditio*, II, 442.

24. *Three Books of Occult Philosophy, written by Henry Cornelius Agrippa, of Nettesheim, Translated out of the Latin into the English Tongue, by J.F.* (London, 1651), Bk. I, chap. VI, p. 14, and chap. XIV, p. 33; Bk. II, chaps. XXIV–XXVIII, pp. 255 ff. *Cf.* Gioseffo Zarlino, *Le istitutioni harmoniche* (Venice, 1558), *Prima parte*, cap. VII.

25. The ancients based their logic mainly on harp or cithara. The organ image appeared most commonly after 1600, following mechanical development of the organ in Germany and France, but it remained a cosmic symbol longer than did stringed instrument.

26. *Richard II*, II.i.149–150; *Henry VIII*, III.ii.104–106; *Richard III*, IV.iv.364–365.

27. *Pericles*, I.i.81–85; *King Lear*, IV.vii.14–17, and V.iii.216–217.

28. Richard Sibbes, "Angels' Acclamations," *Complete Works* (Edinburgh, 1862), VI, 331.

29. Francis Quarles, "The Invocation," *Emblemes* (London, 1635).

30. Sir John Davies, *Hymnes to Astraea*, "Hymn XIX," *The Complete Poems of Sir John Davies*, ed. Rev. Alexander B. Grosart (London, 1876), I, 147.

31. Davies, *Nosce teipsum*, in *ibid.*, I, 75, 35, 102. *Cf.* John Davies of Hereford, *Microcosmos* (1603), *The Complete Works*, ed. Rev. Alexander B. Grosart (Edinburgh, 1878), I, 30:

> And yet the body's but the Instrument
> Whereon the soule doth play what she doth please;
> But if the stringes thereof doe not concent,
> The harmony doth but the soule displease;
> Then tune the body Soule, or Playing cease.

32. *Du Bartas, his Divine weekes and workes*, "The Furies. The Third Part of the First Day of the II. Weeke," p. 203.

33. Donne, "A Lent-Sermon Preached at White-hall, February 12, 1618," *Sermons*, II, 170.

34. George Herbert, "Dooms-day," *The Poems of George Herbert* (London, 1958), p. 168.

35. Robert Fludd, *Utriusque cosmi . . . historia* (Oppenheim, 1617), tract. I, lib. III, cap. III, p. 90. *Cf.* Marin Mersenne, *Traité de l'harmonie universelle* (Paris, 1627), Livre II, theorem V, pp. 443 ff. He quarrels with Fludd's measurements and decides that his analogy is merely symbolic.

36. Drummond, "On the book ["Prefixed to Heptameron, the Seven Dayes, &c, by A. Symons, Saint Andrew's, 1621"], *Poems*, II, 106. Richard Crashaw described the spheres in terms of the familiar "chest" of viols and "sets" of instruments ("To the Name . . . of Jesus, A Hymn," lines 28–30, *The Poems*, p. 240):

> Goe & request
> Great Nature for the Key of her huge Chest
> Of Heavns, the self involving Sett of Sphears.

37. *Twelfth Night*, I.iv.33; *As You Like It*, II.vii.161–163.

38. Churchmen argued over which musical instruments might be designated as "organs," some claiming with St. Augustine that any instrument used to accompany singing was an organ (on Psalm LVI, quoted *N.E.D.*), others pointing out that Psalm CL distinguished between organs and stringed instruments, and thus designated two kinds of instrument. See Spitzer's discussion of the organ as a symbol of world music, in "Classical and Christian Ideas of World Harmony," *Traditio*, II, 443.

39. Sir John Beaumont, "To my Lord Viscount Purbeck," in *The Works of the English Poets*, ed. Alexander Chalmers (London, 1810), VI, 39.

40. Hawkins, *Partheneia Sacra*, p. 138.

41. *Du Bartas, his Divine weekes and workes*, "The Imposture. The II. Part of the First Day of the II. Week," p. 190.

42. *Coriolanus*, III.ii.112–114; *King John*, V.vii.21–24.

43. *Othello*, III.i.6–11.

44. *Hamlet*, III.ii.372–389; III.ii.73–76.

45. John Hoskins, *Directions for Speech and Style* (1599), ed. H. H. Hudson (Princeton, 1935), p. 8.

46. *Donne's Poetical Works*, ed. Herbert J. C. Grierson (London, 1953), I, 340, 348, 246, 271.

47. Fludd, *Utriusque cosmi . . . historia*, tract. I, lib. III, cap. VI, p. 94.

48. Andreas Ornithoparcus, *Musicae activae micrologus*, Bk. I, chap. I, tr. John Dowland (London, 1609), as *Andreas Ornithoparcus His Micrologus.*

49. *Du Bartas, his Divine weekes and workes*, "The Columnes. The IIII. Part of the Second Day of the II. Week," p. 301.

50. *The Tempest*, III.iii.98; Nathanael Culverwel, *An Elegant and Learned Discourse of the Light of Nature* (London, 1652), pp. 18–19. Two years previously, Athanasius Kircher, in his *Musurgia universalis* (Rome, 1650), presented this idea graphically. In Tom. II, lib. X, entitled *Decachordon naturae* (so called because the universe and all that is in it make up a ten-stringed instrument), the first chapter is headed, "Deus Opt. Max. Organaedo, Mundus organo comparatur" ("God compared to an organist, the world to an organ"). If the world is a temple of the gods, Kircher explains, it must have its organ, and here is pictured, superimposed on the universe, a great pipe organ. Even the least significant forms of life are instruments, too. A reed is segmented by frets. Nearby is a bird with wings outspread, the quills of the wing feathers small pipes mounted by keys, while from the long, pointed beak, strings stretch down to the keyboards that top the wings (pp. 366, 411, 416).

51. *Dryden's Poetical Works* (Cambridge, Mass., 1909), pp. 174, 252; *Essays of John Dryden*, ed. W. P. Ker (Oxford, 1926), I, 185.

52. *A Letter to a Friend in the Country, Concerning the Use of Instrumental Musick in the Worship of God* (London, 1698), p. 20.

53. S[ampson] Estwick, *The Usefulness of Church-Musick* (London, 1696), p. 2.

54. *A Letter to a Friend in the Country*, p. 2; Gabriel Towerson, *A Sermon Concerning Vocal and Instrumental Musick in the Church* (London, 1696), p. 6.

55. Alexander Pope, *Windsor Forest*, lines 279–280; *Essay on Man*, Epist. III, lines 290–296; Epist. I, lines 202, 33, *Pope's Complete Poems*, ed. Henry W. Boynton (Boston, [1903]).

56. *The Tatler*, No. 153, Saturday, April 1, 1710.

57. Jonathan Swift, *Gulliver's Travels*, "A Voyage to Laputa," chap. II, in *The Prose Works of Jonathan Swift*, ed. Herbert Davis (Oxford, 1959) XI, 161–162. Swift's satire is directed, as well, toward the more "scientific" musical mathematics of the late seventeenth and early eighteenth centuries. See Marjorie H. Nicolson, *Science and Imagination* (Ithaca, 1956), pp. 120–123.

CHAPTER II

1. Sir Thomas Browne, *Religio Medici*, Pt. 1, sec. 16, *Works*, ed. Geoffrey Keynes (London, 1928), I, 21.
2. Sir Walter Ralegh, *History of the World* (London, 1614), p. 2.
3. John Milton, *Paradise Regain'd*, IV.383–384; Robert Anton, *The Philosophers Satyrs* (London, 1616), sig. D. Sir Thomas Elyot, too, among others, saw in the bee visible representation of right government, "a perpetuall figure of a juste governaunce or rule." *The Governour* (1531), ed. H. H. S. Croft (London, 1883), I, 12.
4. *As You Like It*, II.i.1–18.
5. Abraham Cowley, *Davideis*, Bk. I, sec. 36, *Poems*, ed. A. R. Waller (Cambridge, Eng., 1905), p. 253.
6. Marin Mersenne, *Traité de l'harmonie universelle* (Paris, 1627), Livre I, theorem XIII, p. 24.
7. Browne, *Religio Medici*, Pt. II, sec. 9, *Works*, I, 88.
8. William Byrd, *Gradualia* (1605–07), dedication, in *Source Readings in Music History*, ed. Oliver Strunk (New York, 1950), p. 328.
9. *Parthenia or the Maydenhead of the first musicke that ever was printed for the Virginalls* (London, [1612/1613]), engraver's dedication.
10. William Perkins, "A Golden Chaine; or The description of Theologie," *The Workes of That Famous and Worthie Minister of Christ in the Universitie of Cambridge, Mr. William Perkins* (Cambridge, 1612), I, 38.
11. John Cotton, *Singing of Psalmes a Gospel-Ordinance* (London, 1647), p. 6.
12. Ludovick Bryskett, *A Discourse of Civill Life* (London, 1606), p. 147.
13. Mersenne, *Traité de l'harmonie universelle*, Livre II, pp. 305–306.
14. Henry Peacham, *Minerva Britanna or a Garden of Heroical Devises* (London, 1612), "To the Reader." See Rosemary Freeman, *English Emblem Books* (London, 1948).
15. Elias Ashmole, *Theatrum chemicum Britannicum* (London, 1652), "Prolegomena," sig. A2.
16. Samuel Daniel, *The Worthy tract of Paulus Jovius contayning a Discourse of rare inventions, both Militarie and Amorous called*

Imprese Whereunto is added a Preface contayning the Arte of composing them . . . by Samuell Daniell (London, 1585), prefatory letter to Daniel by "N.W."

17. Henry Reynolds, *Mythomystes* (1633), in *Critical Essays of the Seventeenth Century*, ed. J. E. Spingarn (Oxford, 1908), I, 156.

18. Geoffrey Whitney, *A Choice of Emblemes, and other Devices* (Leyden, 1586), "To the Reader."

19. *The Theater of Fine Devices . . . by Guillaume de la Perrière*, tr. Thomas Combe (London, 1614), "To the Reader."

20. Daniel, *The Worthy tract of Paulus Jovius*, prefatory letter by "N.W."

21. Andrew Marvell, "Upon Appleton House," stanza lxxiii, *The Poems & Letters of Andrew Marvell*, ed. H. M. Margoliouth (Oxford, 1927), I, 77.

22. George Puttenham, *The Arte of English Poesie*, Bk. II, chap. XII, in *Elizabethan Critical Essays*, ed. G. Gregory Smith (Oxford, 1950), II, 106.

23. Thomas Campion, *A New Way of Making Fowre Parts in Counter-point* (1617), preface, *Campion's Works*, ed. Percival Vivian (Oxford, 1909), p. 192.

24. Jean de Muris, *Ars novae musicae* (1319), in *Source Readings in Music History*, ed. Strunk, p. 175.

25. Thomas Ravenscroft, *A Briefe Discourse of the true (but neglected) use of Charact'ring the Degrees . . .* (London, 1614), p. 6.

26. John Farmer, *Divers & sundry waies of two parts in one, to the number of fortie, uppon one playnsong* ([London?], 1591), prefatory verses by Richard Wilkinson.

27. Marvell, "Musicks Empire," *Poems & Letters*, I, 47.

28. John Donne, "A Sermon preached upon Candlemas day," (1627?), *Sermons*, ed. George R. Potter and Evelyn Simpson (Berkeley, 1954), VII, 346.

29. Thomas Wright, *The Passions of the Minde* (London, 1604), p. 164.

30. Thomas Adams, "The Sinner's Passing-Bell," *The Works of Thomas Adams*, ed. Joseph Angus (Edinburgh, 1842), I, 337.

31. Fulke Greville, *The Life of the Renowned Sir Philip Sidney*, *The Workes in Verse and Prose of . . . Fulke Greville, Lord Brooke*, ed. Rev. Alexander B. Grosart (Edinburgh, 1870), IV, 139. *Cf.* Bovillus' designation of three orbs of contemplation—rational, angelic, and divine—discussed by E. F. Rice, Jr., *The Renaissance Idea of Wisdom* (Cambridge, Mass., 1958), p. 110.

32. John Milton, "At a solemn Musick."

33. Humphrey Sydenham, "The Wel-Tuned Cymball," *Sermons upon Solemne Occasions* (London, 1637), p. 23.

34. *Parthenia*, dedication.

35. George Wither, *A Preparation to the Psalter* (1619), Spenser Society reprint (Manchester, 1884), p. 85.

36. George Wither, *A Collection of Emblemes* (London, 1635), Bk. II, p. 82.

37. Plato, *Symposium*, 186E–187C, tr. W. R. M. Lamb, Loeb ed., p. 127, described this reconciliation of things at variance as an affair of love. The pseudo-Aristotelian *Problems*, XIX.38, tr. W. S. Hett, Loeb ed., I, 403, stated that "we enjoy harmony, because it is a mingling of opposites which bear a relation to each other." Cicero wrote in *De re publica*, II.xlii.69, tr. C. W. Keyes, Loeb ed., p. 183, "Perfect agreement and harmony is produced by the proportionate blending of unlike tones."

38. John Ferne, *Blazon of Gentrie* (London, 1586), Pt. II, p. 41. *Cf.* Whitney, *A Choice of Emblemes*, p. 194. The notion of "inveterate hatred" was attributed to Pliny.

39. John Guillim, *A Display of Heraldrie* (London, 1610), p. 200.

40. Pierre de la Primaudaye, *The French Academie . . . Newly translated into English by T.B.* (London, 1586), p. 19. *Cf.* John Norden, *Vicissitudo rerum* (1600) ([London], 1931), stanza lxxxvii:

> The Heavens have their moovings contrarie,
> But equally disposed, uphold the rest:
> Where, if they mov'd one way, their harmonie
> All of one straine, of discord dispossest,
> They soone would runne to ruine al opprest.

41. Henry Peacham, *The Compleat Gentleman* (London, 1622), chap. XI, p. 104.

42. Elyot, *The Governour*, Bk. I, chaps. I, VII, Croft ed., I, 3–4, 42–43.

43. *Troilus and Cressida*, I.iii.101–110.

44. Francesco Patrizi, *A Moral Methode of Civile Policie*, tr. R. Robinson (London, 1576), sigs. B^{v} and Dii^{r}.

45. Andrea Alciati's famous book of emblems, *Emblemata* (Paris, 1534), p. 26, pictures a blind man carrying a man with no legs. At his belt hangs a stringed instrument, possibly a symbol of mutual aid as well as of blindness.

46. John Case, *Apologia musices* (London, 1588), cap. VII, p. 50. Alciati, *Emblemata*, p. 6, used a stringed instrument to illustrate the truth that default of one prince in a treaty, like the breaking of one "string" in man's body, ruins the whole.

47. Samuel Rowley, *When you see me, You know me* (1605), London, 1931, facsimile ed.), sig. H2.

48. Ferne, *Blazon of Gentrie*, Pt. II, p. 41.

49. John Davies of Hereford, *Microcosmos* (1603), *The Complete Works*, ed. Rev. Alexander B. Grosart (Edinburgh, 1878), I, 46. *Cf.*

John Lyly's *Euphues*, in *The Complete Works*, ed. R. Warwick Bond (Oxford, 1902), II, 147: "Friends must be used, as Musitians tune their strings, who finding them in discorde, doe not breake them, but either by intention or remission, frame them to a pleasant consent."

50. John Donne, "Preached at Lincolns Inne Upon Trinity-Sunday, 1620," *Sermons*, III, 148.

51. It is impossible to give here a history of the use of numbers to explain world order or to disentangle the complex interrelationships of rational, metaphysical, and occult ideas that made up the number heritage of the Renaissance. It is necessary, however, to sketch some background of theory and criticism. Today, men feel oriented to the notion that music may be "angelic" or "divine" or that their minds are harmonious. They still use the image of a string out of tune to explain abstract discord. They are further removed, however, from Renaissance theories of number and proportion. It is a cliché today to say that music is akin to mathematics, but if, by that remark, anything at all specific is meant, it is in terms of a kind of measurement different from that intended by Charles Butler, when he referred, in the preface to his *Principles of Musik* (London, 1636), to the "secret Mysteries, which lye hid in this profound Mathematik." When one reads, in Stephen Batman's translation of Bartholomaeus (*Batman uppon Bartholome, his Book de Proprietatibus Rerum, newly corrected, enlarged and amended* [London, 1582], Bk. XIX, cap. CXXXIV), "for Musicke by the which concord & melodie is knowen in sound and in song, it is needfull to know the secret meaning of holy writ, for it is said, that the world is compounded & made in a certaine proportion of harmonie, as Isi[dore] saith," or in works on musical theory that "omnis Sonus est Quantus," that sound has length, breadth, and thickness, one feels little sense of familiarity. Yet these ideas, which go back to ancient times, were an essential part of Renaissance thought. *Cf.* Joannes Lippius, *Disputatio musica* (Witteberge, 1609–1610), Bk. II, and *Templum Musicum: or the Musical Synopsis, of the Learned and Famous Johannes-Henricus-Alstedius*, tr. John Birchensha (London, 1664), pp. 15–16.

52. Rudolph Wittkower, *Architectural Principles in the Age of Humanism* (London, 1949), pp. 90–91.

53. E. A. Burtt, *Metaphysical Foundations of Modern Physical Science* (London, 1925), chap. II.D, p. 50.

54. This passage appeared in the Vulgate, but was omitted from the Authorized Version (1611). The version quoted here is that of Miles Coverdale's Bible of 1535.

55. St. Augustine, *De musica*, tr. R. C. Taliaferro (Annapolis, 1939), p. 148; Leo Spitzer, "Classical and Christian Ideas of World Harmony," *Traditio*, II (1944), 432–433.

56. Boethius, *De institutione musica*, Bk. I, secs. 1–2, in *Source*

Readings in Music History, ed. Strunk, pp. 80–85. See Paul Henry Lang, *Music in Western Civilization* (New York, 1941), p. 60.

57. Isidore of Seville, *Etymologiarum sive originum libri xx*, Bk. III, sec. 23, in *Source Readings in Music History*, ed. Strunk, pp. 99–100; *Scholia enchiriadis*, in *ibid.*, pp. 134–135.

58. Roger Bacon, *Opus majus*, tr. R. B. Burke (Philadelphia, 1928), I, 198; *Opus tertium*, cap. LIX, *Opera*, ed. J. S. Brewer (London, 1859), I, 231–232. Arabian physicians, such as al-Kindi, worked out elaborate charts to clarify the intervallic relationship between cosmic and human elements and those in music. H. G. Farmer, "The Influence of Music: From Arabic Sources," The Musical Association, London, *Proceedings, 1925–1926* (1926), 99. Avicenna, who with Galen provided medical canon for many centuries, explained in detail the relationship of musical rhythm and pulse beat. Galen, he wrote, divided pulse meters into double time, 3:4 time, common time, 4:5, and 5:6 time, and he stated his own belief that, "for those who have sensitive touch and a keen sense of rhythm, with a training in the musical art, such minutiae of observation could be correlated in the mind." O. Cameron Gruner, *A Treatise on The Canon of Medicine of Avicenna* (London, 1930), sec. 532, pp. 292–293.

59. See Lynn Thorndike, *History of Magic and Experimental Science* (New York, 1934), III, 114. *Cf.* the verse from Thomas Norton's *Ordinall of alchimy* (1477), reprinted in Ashmole, *Theatrum chemicum Britannicum*, p. 60:

> Joyne your Elements Musically,
> .... Diapason,
> With Diapente, and with Diatesseron
> With their proporcions causen Harmony,
> Much like proportions be in Alkimy.

60. Manfred F. Bukofzer, "Speculative Thinking in Medieval Music," *Speculum*, XVII, No. 2 (1942).

61. *Three Books of Occult Philosophy, written by Henry Cornelius Agrippa, of Nettesheim, Translated out of the Latin into the English Tongue, by J.F.* (London, 1651), Bk. II, chap. II, p. 170, and chap. XXIV, pp. 255 ff.

62. Gioseffo Zarlino, *Le istitutioni harmoniche* (Venice, 1558), *Prima parte*, caps. I–VII.

63. *Ten Books on Architecture by Leone Battista Alberti. Translated into Italian by Cosimo Bartoli and into English by James Leoni, Venetian Architect* (1726), ed. Joseph Rykwert (London, 1955), Bk. IX, chap. V, p. 197. The authority here is Vitruvius, but he was less explicit than Renaissance architects in the application of musical proportions to the measurement of space. "Symmetry," he wrote, "is the appropriate harmony arising out of the details of the work itself." *De architectura*, I.c.ii, tr. Frank Granger, Loeb ed., I, 27. He regarded

knowledge of music as essential in the field of architectural acoustics in the adjusting of "*balistae, catapultae* and *scorpiones.*" *Ibid.*, I.c.i., Loeb ed., I, 13. Disciples of the Neoplatonic love philosophy usually denied the existence of beauty in the auditory image. Beauty, they wrote, is more than proportion. Inspiration, not mathematics, should be the guide to creation.

64. Morrison Comegys Boyd, *Elizabethan Music and Musical Criticism* (Philadelphia, 1940), p. 173n.

65. *Batman uppon Bartholome*, addition to Bk. XIX, fol. 425v.

66. Ferne, *Blazon of Gentrie*, Pt. I, p. 50.

67. William Ingpen, *The Secrets of Numbers; According to Theologicall, Arithmeticall, Geometricall and Harmonicall Computation* (London, 1624), p. 48.

68. Butler, *Principles of Musik*, pp. 12–13.

69. John Dee, *The Elements of Geometrie of the Most auncient Philosopher Euclide of Megara . . . Translated by H. Billingsley* (London, [1570]), sig. Bii .

70. Ingpen, *Secrets of Numbers*, pp. 85–86, 94.

71. Burtt, *Metaphysical Foundations of Modern Physical Science*, chap. II. D, pp. 50, 52.

72. Mersenne, *Traité de l'harmonie universelle*, Livre II, theorem VI, p. 354.

73. *A Tracte Containing the Artes of curious painting . . . by J. Paul Lomatius . . . Englished by R[ichard] H[aydock]* (Oxford, 1598), p. 33: "Now the first part from the toppe of the heade to the nose, answereth to the space betwixt that, and the chinne, in a triple proportion, which maketh a Diapente and a Diapason. That betweene the chinne in a double proportion, which makes a diapason: whereunto the head answereth in the same proportion. The three faces betweene the throat pit and the privities answere to the second, betwixt them & the knee in a sesquialter proportion; whence ariseth a Diapente: but with the legge they are Unisones, for it hath the same proportion with the thigh." *The Painting of the Ancients, in Three Books . . . Written first in Latine by Franciscus Junius, F.F. And now by Him Englished, with some additions and Alterations* (London, 1638), p. 258: "Wee see therefore, that not onely Musicians from Painters, but also contrariwise Painters from Musicians have borrowed termes of Art: and that for no other cause, but onely to shew that in both those Arts the same respect of that manifold proportion, which consisteth in numbers, is had."

74. See D. J. Gordon, "Poet and Architect: The Intellectual Setting of the Quarrel between Ben Johnson and Inigo Jones," *Journal of the Warburg and Courtauld Institutes*, XII (1948–1949), 152 ff.

75. *Ben Jonson*, ed. C. H. Herford, Percy and Evelyn Simpson (Oxford, 1925–1952), VII, 809–810.

76. Sir Henry Wotton, *The Elements of Architecture* (1624) (London, 1904), pp. 42–43. Pythagorean influence on Sir Christopher Wren is touched upon by Eduard F. Sekler in *Wren and his Place in European Architecture* (London, 1956), p. 35.

77. Edmund Bolton, *The Elements of Armories* (London, 1610), pp. 169–189.

78. Edward Benlowes, *Theophila* (London, 1652), Canto III, stanza lii; *Hamlet*, III.iv.140–141.

79. Marin Mersenne, *Harmonie universelle* (Paris, 1636), Livre VIII ("Livre de l'utilité de l'harmonie"), pp. 1–2; Athanasius Kircher, *Musurgia universalis* (Rome, 1650), p. 415.

80. Thomas Campion, *A Booke of Ayres* (1601), No. XXI, *Campion's Works*, p. 17; *A New Way of Making Fowre Parts in Counter-Point*, *ibid.*, p. 195; *ibid.*, dedication, p. 191.

81. See Charles W. Hughes, "Rhythm and Health," in *Music and Medicine*, ed. Dorothy M. Schullian and Max Schoen (New York, 1948), pp. 158 ff.

82. Puttenham, *The Arte of English Poesie*, in *Elizabethan Critical Essays*, II, 88, 67.

83. Thomas Campion, "Observations in the Art of English Poesie," *ibid.*, 328–329, 334–335.

84. Samuel Daniel, "A Defence of Rhyme," (1603?), *ibid.*, 360.

85. Peacham, *The Compleat Gentleman*, p. 98.

86. "We see," wrote Francis Bacon, "that tunes and airs, even in their own nature, have in themselves some affinity with the affections: as there be merry tunes, doleful tunes, solemn tunes; tunes inclining men's minds to pity; warlike tunes, &c." *Sylva Sylvarum*, Century II, sec. 114, *The Works of Francis Bacon*, ed. James Spedding, Robert L. Ellis, and Douglas D. Heath (London, 1857), II, 389. Because "affections" were revealed in musical inflection, music had been, since Cicero and Quintilian, a model for the orator. According to Cicero, "The tones of the voice are keyed up like the strings of an instrument, so as to answer to every touch. . . . For one kind of tone must be taken by anger . . . Another belongs to fear." *De oratore*, III.lvii.216, lviii.217–218, tr. H. Rackham, Loeb ed., II, 173 ff. Quintilian was even more explicit about "the advantages which our future orator may reasonably expect to derive from the study of Music." *Institutio oratoria*, I.x.22 ff., tr. H. E. Butler, Loeb ed., I, 171 ff. *Cf.* Roger Ascham, *Toxophilus* (1545) *English Works*, ed. William Aldis Wright (Cambridge, Eng., 1904), p. 15.

87. Rowley, *When you see me, You know me*, sigs. H–H2.

88. *Richard II*, II.i.12–14.

89. *Ibid.*, II.i.195–199; V.v.42–50.

90. Ingpen, *The Secrets of Numbers*, p. 8.

91. Francis Bacon, *Advancement of Learning*, Bk. I, *Works*, III, 266; *De augmentis scientiarum*, Bk. III, chap. I, *Works*, IV, 337–339.

92. Peacham, *Minerva Britanna*, p. 204.

93. Wither, *A Collection of Emblemes*, Bk. II, p. 82. John Lyly used the same image in his *Euphues*, *Works*, II, 151: "In Musicke there are many discords, before there can be framed a Diapason, and in contracting of good will, many jarres before there be established a friendship, but by these meanes, the Musicke is more sweet, and the amitie more sound."

94. William Byrd, *Psalmes, Songs, and Sonnets* (London, 1611), "To all true lovers of Musicke."

95. Henry Hawkins ("H.A."), *Partheneia Sacra* (London, 1633), pp. 140–141.

96. *The Nature of Man. A learned and usefull Tract written in Greek by Nemesius . . . Englished . . . by Geo: Wither* (London, 1636), p. 126.

97. Peacham, *Minerva Britanna*, p. 45. (A verse in Thomas Jenner's book of emblems, *The Soules Solace* [London, 1631], p. 27, describes man tuned by God's minister, and concludes with the moral: "As Instruments, unless in tune, are slighted: / So men, except new made, ne're God delighted.") *Donne's Poetical Works*, ed. Herbert J. C. Grierson (London, 1953), I, 368.

98. Whitney, *A Choice of Emblemes*, p. 92. The same proof that industry corrects nature appears in the emblems of Joannes Sambucus (1564), *Les Emblemes de Signeur Jehan Sambucus* (Antwerp, 1567), p. 61.

99. John Davies of Hereford, "Inough's as good as a feast," *Wittes Pilgrimage*, *Works*, II, 53.

100. John Donne, "Epithalamion made at Lincolnes Inne," lines 63–66, *Donne's Poetical Works*, ed. Grierson, I, 143.

101. *Timon of Athens*, I.ii.100 ff.

102. Fulke Greville, "Treatie of Humane Learning," stanza 112, *Workes*, II, 48.

103. Henry Vaughan, "The World." In emblem books Hercules was portrayed choosing between Virtue, holding a book, and Vice, with mask and lute. A lady balanced precariously on a ball, reaching for scepter and fiddle bow, represented one caught by trivialities. See Gabriel Rollenhagen, *Nucleus emblematum* (Utrecht, 1611), pp. 7, 14. Wither used Rollenhagen's plates and drew similar morals.

104. John Lyly, *Campaspe*, V.i, *Works*, II, 350; William Austin, prefatory verse to Ravenscroft, *A Briefe Discourse*.

105. Joseph Glanvill, *Scepsis Scientifica; or, Confest Ignorance, the way to Science . . .* (London, 1665), prefatory address.

106. Elyot, *The Governour*, ed. Croft, I, 3.

CHAPTER III

1. Phineas Fletcher, "To Mr. Jo. Tomkins," *Poetical Works of Giles and Phineas Fletcher*, ed. Frederick S. Boas (Cambridge, Eng., 1909), II, 234; Humphrey Sydenham, "The Wel-Tuned Cymball," *Sermons upon Solemne Occasions* (London, 1637), pp. 22–23.

2. See, for example, Sir Walter Ralegh, *A Treatise of the Soule*, in *Works* (Oxford, 1829), II.

3. *Cf.* John Donne, "To the Countesse of Bedford. Honour is so sublime," lines 34–35, *Donne's Poetical Works*, ed. Herbert J. C. Grierson (London, 1953), I, 219: ". . . our Soules of growth and Soules of sence/Have birthright of our reasons Soule. . . ."

4. Plato, *Phaedo*, 66E–67A, tr. H. N. Fowler, Loeb ed., pp. 231–233; Plotinus, *Ennead* VI.9.11, *The Ethical Treatises*, tr. Stephen MacKenna (London, 1917), V, 251–252.

5. St. Thomas Aquinas, *Summa contra Gentiles*, I.iii, cap. XLVII, tr. Joseph Rickaby, quoted in Evelyn Underhill, *Mysticism* (New York, 1955), p. 361.

6. Underhill, *Mysticism*, pp. 369, 361.

7. Paul Oskar Kristeller, *The Philosophy of Marsilio Ficino* (New York, 1943), p. 216; *ibid.*, pp. 388 ff., and *Marsilio Ficino's Commentary on Plato's Symposium*, tr. Sears Reynolds Jayne (Columbia, Mo., 1944), Third Speech, chap. I, p. 148.

8. Godfrey Goodman, *The Fall of Man* (London, 1616), p. 42.

9. Joseph Glanvill, *Some Philosophical Considerations touching the Being of Witches and Witchcraft* (London, 1667), p. 15.

10. John Milton, *The Christian Doctrine*, I.vii.

11. Plato, *Symposium*, 215C, tr. W. R. M. Lamb, Loeb ed., p. 219.

12. Aristotle, *Politics*, VIII.v, 1340a, tr. H. Rackham, Loeb ed., p. 657.

13. Cicero, *De divinatione*, I.xviii.34, and I.l.114, tr. W. A. Falconer, Loeb ed., pp. 263, 347.

14. *A Treatise Concerning the Lawfulness of Instrumental Musick in Holy Offices, by Henry Dodwell, M.A. To which is prefixed, a Preface in Vindication of Mr. Newte's Sermon, concerning the Lawfulness and Use of Organs in the Christian Church, &c. From the Exceptions of an Anonymous Letter to a Friend in the Country, concerning the Use of Instrumental Musicke in the Worship of God, &c.*, 2d ed. (London, 1700), p. 35.

15. *Du Bartas, his Divine weekes and workes*, tr. Josuah Sylvester (London, 1621), "The Tropheis. The l. Book of the Fourth Day of the Second Week," p. 421. Charles Butler, also, in his *Principles of Musik* (London, 1636), p. 114, credited music with this "Extraordinari" power which could not only drive the evil spirit out of Saul, but which was made use of "by the Prophets thereby (as it seemeth)

to excite a Special Enthusiasm, or divine Rapture for soom present Oracle."

16. Plato, *The Republic*, III.398E ff., tr. Paul Shorey, Loeb ed., I, 247 ff.; Aristotle, *Politics*, VIII.v.1340^{a-b}, Loeb ed., p. 659.

17. Richard Hooker, *Of the Laws of Ecclesiastical Polity,* Bk. V, sec. xxxviii, ed. Ronald Bayne (London and New York, 1925), II, 146.

18. Plato, *Phaedo*, 85E–86C, Loeb ed., pp. 297–299; Plato, *Timaeus*, 33–37, 47C–D, tr. Rev. R. G. Bury, Loeb ed., pp. 63–73, 109.

19. Cicero, *De re publica*, VI.xviii.18, tr. C. W. Keyes, Loeb ed., p. 273.

20. *Macrobius' Commentary on the Dream of Scipio*, Bk. II, chaps. I, II, III, tr. William Harris Stahl (New York, 1952), pp. 185–197. *Cf. Iamblichus on the Mysteries of the Egyptians, Chaldeans, and Assyrians*, tr. Thomas Taylor (Chiswick, 1821), p. 133: "The soul before she gave herself to body, was an auditor of divine harmony; and . . . hence, when she proceeded into body, and heard melodies of such a kind as especially preserve the divine vestigie of harmony, she embraced these, from them recollected divine harmony, and tends and is allied to it, and as much as possible participates of it."

21. John Case, *Praise of Musicke* (London, 1586), p. 40.

22. Plato, *Phaedrus*, 249B–D, tr. H. N. Fowler, Loeb ed., pp. 481–483. *Cf. Symposium*, 210–211, Loeb ed., pp. 203 ff.

23. Richard Crashaw, "To the Name . . . of Jesus, A Hymn," lines 64–65, *The Poems*, ed. L. C. Martin (Oxford, 1927), p. 240; George Herbert, "Church Musick," *The Poems of George Herbert* (London, 1958), pp. 57–58.

24. Plotinus, *Ennead* I.3.1; I.6.3; I.6.5; I.6.7; I.6.6., *The Ethical Treatises*, I, 51–86. *Cf.* Proclus, *The Philosophical and Mathematical Commentaries*, tr. Thomas Taylor (London, 1788–1789), I, 62.

25. Cicero, *De finibus*, I.xxi.72, tr. H. Rackham, Loeb ed., p. 75.

26. Quoted by Théodore Gérold, *Les Pères de l'église et la musique* (Paris, 1931), pp. 56–57.

27. Sextus Empiricus, *Against the Professors*, VI.37, tr. the Rev. R. G. Bury, Loeb ed., IV, 389–391. *Cf.* Lactantius, *The Divine Institutes*, Bk. VI, chap. XXI, tr. William Fletcher, in *The Ante-Nicene Christian Library*, ed. Rev. Alexander Roberts and James Donaldson (Edinburgh, 1867), XXI, 409–410.

28. *Quaestiones et responsiones ad orthodoxos*, Resp. to Quest. CVII, in *Patrologiae Cursus Completus. Series Graeca*, ed. J. P. Migne (Paris, 1856–1866), VI, 1354.

29. Clement of Alexandria, *The Instructor*, Bk. II, chap. IV, in *The Ante-Nicene Christian Library*, IV, 215–216.

30. St. Basil, *Homilia in Psalmum Primum*, in *Patrologiae Cursus Completus. Series Graeca*, XXIX, 210 ff.

31. St. Chrysostom, *In Psalmum XLI*, in *ibid.*, LV, 156–157.

32. *Quaestiones et responsiones ad orthodoxos*, Resp. to Quest. CVII in *ibid.*, VI, 1354; St. Jerome, Commentary on Eph., III.5.19, quoted in Gérold, *Les Pères de l'église et la musique*, p. 111.

33. Clement of Alexandria, *Exhortation to the Greeks*, I, tr. G. W. Butterworth, Loeb ed., pp. 11–13.

34. St. Gregory of Nyssa, *In Psalmorum inscriptiones*, tract. I, cap. III, in *Patrologiae Cursus Completus, Series Graeca*, XLIV, 438 ff. The Christian could draw upon Hebrew belief as well as Greek, for God had demanded of Job (Job 38:4, 6, 7): "Where wast thou when I laid the foundations of the earth? . . . Whereupon are the foundations thereof fastened? or who laid the corner stone thereof; When the morning stars sang together, and all the sons of God shouted for joy?"

35. St. Chrysostom, *In Psalmum XLI*, in *Patrologiae Cursus Completus. Series Graeca*, LV, 156.

36. St. Augustine, *Confessions*, X.xxxiii, tr. William Watts, Loeb ed., II, 165–169.

37. St. Augustine, *De musica*, tr. R. C. Taliaferro (Annapolis, 1939), p. 148.

38. Hugh of St. Victor, "Didascalicon de studio legendi," quoted in Underhill, *Mysticism*, p. 77.

39. Underhill, *Mysticism*, p. 77. See Richard Rolle, *The Fire of Love or Melody of Love*, tr. Richard Misyn, done into modern English by Frances M. M. Comper (London, 1920).

40. Johan Huizinga, *The Waning of the Middle Ages* (New York, 1954), p. 267.

41. See especially Pontus de Tyard, *Solitaire Second, ou prose de la musique* (Lyons, 1555). See also Francis A. Yates, *The French Academies in the Sixteenth Century* (London, 1947).

42. One cannot say that Puritans (using the term now loosely to mean all groups who urgently desired further reform of the Church) were unmusical or that they generally disapproved of music. There was frequent admonition against letting any recreation, music included, absorb time better devoted to more spiritual works. But this point of view was by no means exclusively Puritan. The evidence is that Puritans loved and practiced music as other people did. The difference in their attitude is marked chiefly in their evaluation of musical sound and of its effect on the soul.

43. Thomas Cartwright, *A replye to an Answere*, quoted in notes to Hooker's *Of the Laws of Ecclesiastical Polity*, II, 147. The Puritan objected to all "curious" or antiphonal singing, but over-intricacy was decried by all conscientious churchmen.

44. John Whitgift, *The Defence of the Answer to the Admonition, against the Reply of T.C.* (1574), tract. XV, chap. III, Ans. to Ad. 13,

in *The Works of John Whitgift*, ed. for the Parker Society by the Rev. John Ayre (Cambridge, 1851–1853), III, 106.

45. Henry Ainsworth, *Counterpoyson. Considerations touching the points in difference between the Godly Ministers & people of the Church of England, and the seduced brethren of the Separation* ([London] 1642), p. 139. First edition, 1608.

46. Joseph Brookbank, *The Well-Tuned Organ, or an Exercitation; wherein, This Question is fully and largely discussed, Whether or no Instrumental, and Organical Musick be lawful in Holy Publick Assemblies?* (London, 1660), p. 4.

47. Cartwright, *A replye to an Answere*, quoted in notes to Hooker, *Of the Laws of Ecclesiastical Polity*, II, 147.

48. John Cotton, *Singing of Psalmes a Gospel-Ordinance* (London, 1647), pp. 5–6.

49. Cotton Mather, *Magnalia Christi Americana* (London, 1702), Bk. V, p. 55.

50. Thomas Wright, *The Passions of the Minde* (London, 1604), pp. 168–169.

51. Because of this law of nature, emblematically imaged in musical instruments, lovers and friends responded to each other's moods. Not only two lutes, but the *viole d'amour*, demonstrated this loving sympathy, since the second set of strings beneath the fingerboard sounded in response to the higher ones which were bowed.

52. References cited above, notes 43, 44.

53. Case, *Praise of Musicke*, pp. 41, 151–152.

54. East Apthorp ("missionary at Cambridge, Boston"), "Of Sacred Poetry and Music. A Discourse at Christ-Church, Cambridge, at the opening of the Organ, on Tuesday XXI, August 1764."

55. Hooker, *Of the Laws of Ecclesiastical Polity*, II, 146–147.

56. George Wither, *A Preparation to the Psalter* (Manchester, 1884), pp. 83, 81. After Wither became a Puritan, he apparently changed his mind on the subject of Elisha's prophecies. In his last published work, "Nil Ultra," in *Three Private Meditations* (1666), Publications of the Spenser Society, No. 18 (Manchester, 1875), p. 40, he wrote:

> Things may result sometimes perchance,
> Ev'n from a trifling circumstance,
> Which will be helpful to advance
> Th'effecting of a Grand Design,
> Once e're Elisha would begin
> To speak, a Fidler was call'd in;
> Of use, that seem'd then to have been
> For his Work. . . .

57. Butler, *The Principles of Musik*, pp. 5, 1, 6.

58. Sydenham, "The Wel-tuned Cymball," *Sermons upon Solemne*

Occasions, pp. 17, 19–23. *Cf.* Wright, *The Passions of the Minde*, pp. 159 ff.

59. Brookbank, *The Well-tuned Organ*, p. 44.

60. Charles Hickman, *Dr. Hickman's Sermon on St. Caecilia's Day 1695. A Sermon preached at St. Bride's Church on St. Caecilia's Day, Nov. 22, 1695; Being the Anniversary Feast of the Lovers of Musick* (London, 1696), pp. 16–17.

61. William Perkins, *A Golden Chaine; or, The Description of Theologie, etc.* in *The Workes of that Famous and Worthie Minister of Christ in the Universitie of Cambridge, Mr. William Perkins* (Cambridge, 1612), I, 38.

62. *The Holy Harmony: Or, A Plea for the abolishing of Organs and other Musicke out of Protestant Churches of Great Britain* (London, 1643), sig. A2.

63. Cotton, *Singing of Psalmes a Gospel-Ordinance*, pp. 4–6.

64. Matthew Poole, *A Reverse to Mr. Oliver's Sermon of Spiritual Worship. A Sermon on the same Subject. Preached before the Lord Mayor, at St. Paul's Church, August 26th, 1660* (London, 1698), "To the Ingenuous Reader," and pp. 20, 14.

65. James Peirce, *A Vindication of the Dissenters* (London, Latin ed., 1710; 2d ed. in English, 1718), p. 386.

66. John Newte, *The Lawfulness and Use of Organs in the Christian Church, Asserted in A Sermon Preach'd at Tiverton in the County of Devon Upon the 13th of September, 1696. On Occasion of an Organ's being Erected in that Parish-Church*, 2d ed. (London, 1701), pp. 16, 30, 12–13.

67. *A Letter to a Friend in the Country, Concerning the Use of Instrumental Musick in the Worship of God; in Answer to Mr. Newte's Sermon Preach'd at Tiverton in Devon, on the Occasion of an Organ being Erected in that Parish-Church* (London, 1698), pp. 16–17, 53, 49–50, 54.

68. Dodwell, *A Treatise Concerning the Lawfulness of Instrumental Musick in Holy Offices*, Preface, pp. 2, 45, 49, 61–62.

69. *Ibid.*, pp. 48, 35.

CHAPTER IV

1. George Chapman, *Ovids Banquet of Sence*, stanza xxii, *Poems*, ed. Phyllis Brooks Bartlett (New York and London, 1941), p. 58; James Howell, "To My Noble Lady, the Lady M. A. from Westminster 1 April 1637," in *Epistolae Ho-Elianae: The Familiar Letters of James Howell* (Boston and New York, 1907), III, 106. Howell's letters were first published in London in 1645.

2. George Wither, *A Collection of Emblemes* (London, 1635), Bk. II, p. 82.

3. From the time of Plato it had often been said that music created amity and harmoniousness between people. The Arcadians were supposed to have fallen into civil war when they forsook music, for music, wrote Henry Peacham in *The Compleat Gentleman* (London, 1622), p. 164, "preserveth people in concord and amitie." It brought health to the body and quiet to the mind—each a kind of concord or love. That music effected friendship between people was admitted even by the Puritan, for according to John Cotton, in *Singing of Psalmes a Gospel-Ordinance* (London, 1647), p. 4, "it helpeth to aswage enmity, and to restore friendship and favour as in Saul to David."

4. Thomas Campion, *A Booke of Ayres* (1601), No. VII, *Campion's Works*, ed. Percival Vivian (Oxford, 1909), p. 23.

5. Leo Hebraeus, *The Philosophy of Love* (*Dialoghi d'amore*, 1501?), tr. F. Friedeberg-Seeley and Jean H. Barnes (London, 1937), Dialogue II, p. 88.

6. Stephen Gosson, *The Schoole of Abuse* (1579), ed. Edward Arber, English Reprints (London, 1868), p. 26; *Othello*, II.i.202.

7. See Thomas Dekker, *The Honest Whore*, Pt. I, V.ii.260–270, *The Dramatic Works*, ed. Fredson Bowers (Cambridge, Eng., 1955), II, 101; *The Taming of the Shrew*, III.i.64–68; *Much Ado About Nothing*, I.i.162–164. See Eric H. Partridge, *Shakespeare's Bawdy* (London, 1947).

8. Richard Rolle, *The Fire of Love or Melody of Love*, tr. Richard Misyn, done into modern English by Frances M. M. Comper (London, 1920), Introduction, xix, xxii; Dante, "Paradiso," XXIII.97–111, *The Divine Comedy of Dante Alighieri*, tr. Charles Eliot Norton (Cambridge, Mass., 1920), p. 84.

9. George Herbert, "Easter," lines 11–14, *The Poems of George Herbert* (London, 1958), p. 36; Richard Crashaw, "To the Name . . . of Jesus, A Hymn," lines 74, 91, *The Poems*, ed. L. C. Martin (Oxford, 1927), p. 241; Ben Jonson, *Loves Triumph*, lines 78–81, *Ben Jonson*, ed. C. H. Herford, Percy and Evelyn Simpson (Oxford, 1925–1952), VII, 738.

10. Plato, *Timaeus*, 36E–37A, tr. Rev. R. G. Bury, Loeb ed., pp. 73–109; Phineas Fletcher, *The Purple Island* (1633), V.47, *Poetical Works of Giles and Phineas Fletcher*, ed. Frederick S. Boas (Cambridge, 1909), II, 63.

11. John Donne, "Loves growth," *Donne's Poetical Works*, ed. Herbert J. C. Grierson (London, 1953), I, 34. *Cf.* Robert Herrick's definition in *Poetical Works*, ed. F. W. Moorman (London, 1921), p. 13:

> Love is a circle that doth restlesse move
> In the same sweet eternity of love.

Love's circle, formed by giving, receiving, and returning of love, was imaged in the allegory of the three Graces, the three figures interlocked in an unbroken ring. See Edgar Wind, *Pagan Mysteries in the Renaissance* (London, 1958), pp. 31 ff. The significance of the circle image is the subject of Marjorie H. Nicolson, *The Breaking of the Circle* (Evanson, Ill., 1950).

12. Sir John Davies, *Orchestra*, stanza xcvi, *The Complete Poems of Sir John Davies*, ed. Rev. Alexander B. Grosart (London, 1876), I, 197–198; Chapman, *Ovids Banquet of Sence*, stanzas xx, xcviii, xcix, *Poems*, pp. 58, 77–78.

13. See chapter II, pp. 32–40.

14. The animistic philosophy of the Greeks imagined a universe, each part of which had intelligence and therefore awareness of its motions. See Aristotle, *Metaphysics*, I.iii.16–iv.1, tr. Hugh Tredennick, Loeb ed., I, 25.

15. Tommaso Buoni, *Problemes of Beautie and all humane affections. Written in Italian by Tho. Buoni . . . Translated into English by S. L. Gent.* (London, 1606), pp. 85, 87 (page misnumbered). Milton, in his prolusion "On the Music of the Spheres," referred to "the very loving and affectionate relations of the orbs."

16. Thomas Stanley, "The Magnet," in *Minor Poets of the Caroline Period*, ed. George Saintsbury (Oxford, 1921), III, 104; Donne, "*A nocturnall upon S. Lucies day*," lines 33–34, *Donne's Poetical Works*, I, 45.

17. *Marsilio Ficino's Commentary on Plato's Symposium*, tr. Sears Reynolds Jayne (Columbia, Mo., 1944), Third Speech, chap. III, p. 151.

18. Thomas Morley, *A Plaine and Easie Introduction to Practicall Musicke* (London, 1597), Annotations, "To the Reader." *Cf.* Plato, *Symposium*, 187C, tr. W. R. M. Lamb, Loeb ed., p. 129.

19. Andrew Marvell, "Musick's Empire," *The Poems & Letters of Andrew Marvell*, ed. H. M. Margoliouth (Oxford, 1927), I, 47.

20. "The Passionate Pilgrim," Sonnet VIII.

21. *Marsilio Ficino's Commentary on Plato's Symposium*, Third Speech, chap.III, p. 150.

22. Maurice Valency, *In Praise of Love* (New York, 1958), p. 235. An excellent study of this aspect of Renaissance aesthetics may be found in Anthony Blunt, *Artistic Theory in Italy, 1450–1600* (Oxford, 1940).

23. The proverb has its background in Plato's *Symposium*, 196D–E, Loeb ed., p. 157, where it is attributed to Euripides. Plutarch elaborates on it in his *Symposiaques* (*Morals*, tr. Philemon Holland, London, 1603, pp. 653–654). It provided a motto for Gabriel Rollenhagen in his *Nucleus emblematum* (Utrecht, 1611), used also by George Wither, *A Collection of Emblemes*, Bk. II, No. XX, p. 82.

24. Jonson, *Loves Triumph*, lines 159–160, *Ben Jonson*, VII, 740.

25. Aristotle, *Poetics*, VII.8–9, tr. W. H. Fyfe, Loeb ed., p. 31;

Plotinus, *Ennead* I.6.1, *The Ethical Treatises,* tr. Stephen MacKenna (London, 1917), I, 77 ff. *Cf.* Aristotle, *Metaphysics,* XIII.iii.11, Loeb ed., II, 193: "The main species of beauty are orderly arrangement, proportion, and definiteness; and these are especially manifested by the mathematical sciences."

26. Plotinus, *Ennead* I.6.1, *The Ethical Treatises,* I, 77 ff.

27. Avicenna, *Traité sur l'amour,* ed. M. A. F. Mehren (Leyden, 1894), p. 8.

28. Plato, *Symposium,* 211C, Loeb ed., p. 207 and *passim.*

29. *Marsilio Ficino's Commentary on Plato's Symposium,* Third Speech, chap. I, and First Speech, chap III, pp. 148, 128. Ficino's *Commentarium in Convivium Platonis de amore* first appeared in his translation of the works of Plato, the first edition of which was probably printed in Florence in 1484. Jayne's translation is based on the 1561 edition of Ficino's works published in Basel.

30. *Ibid.,* First Speech, chap IV, Fifth Speech, chaps. II and VI, pp. 130, 167, 175.

31. *Ibid.,* Sixth Speech, chap. II, pp. 183–184.

32. *Ibid.,* Chap. VI, p. 189.

33. Valency, *In Praise of Love,* p. 150.

34. *Marsilio Ficino's Commentary on Plato's Symposium,* Seventh Speech, chaps. V–XII and XIV, pp. 224–231.

35. *Ibid.,* Sixth Speech, chap. VIII, p. 193.

36. Marsilio Ficino, "De divino furore," in *Opera omnia* (Basel, 1561), pp. 612 ff. Translated by the present author.

37. *Ibid.,* pp. 651, 1453, as translated by D. P. Walker, *Spiritual and Demonic Magic from Ficino to Campanella* (London, 1958), pp. 6, 9.

38. Andreas Capellanus, *The Art of Courtly Love,* tr. John Jay Perry (New York, 1941); Robert Burton, *The Anatomy of Melancholy,* Pt. III, sec. 2, mem. 2, subs. 2 (London and New York, 1932), III, 87.

39. *Du Bartas, his Divine weekes and workes,* tr. Josuah Sylvester (London, 1621), "Babylon. The Second Part of the Second Daye of the II Weeke," p. 258.

40. *Love's Labour's Lost,* IV.iii.312–313.

41. Pico della Mirandola, *A Platonick Discourse upon Love,* tr. Thomas Stanley, appended to his *Poems* (London, 1651), Bk. II, sec. 6, p. 230; Bk. III, secs. 6, 7, 8, p. 256; Bk. II, sec. 11, p. 234, and sec. 20, p. 241.

42. Lorenzo de' Medici, *Commento sopra alcuni de' suoi sonetti, Opera* (Bari, 1913), I, 1–141; Benedetto Varchi, *Due lezioni* (Florence, 1549); Flaminio Nobili, *Trattato dell' amore humano* (Lucca, 1567); Torquato Tasso, *I dialoghi amorosi* (1570) (Lanciano, 1914); Symphorien Champier, *La nef des dames* (Paris, 1515); Mario Equicola, *Libro di natura d'amore* (Venice, 1536). I am indebted to the biblio-

graphy given by John Charles Nelson, *Renaissance Theory of Love* (New York, 1958).

43. Marjorie Hope Nicolson points out in her *Mountain Gloom and Mountain Glory* (Ithaca, New York, 1959), p. 69, that the idea that beauty depends on color and proportion is as old as Cicero and Augustine.

44. Annibale Romei, *The Courtiers Academie: . . . Originally written in Italian by Count Haniball Romei . . . translated into English by I.K.* (London, [1585]), pp. 19–25. The conflict between nature and art is obviously too vast a subject to be treated here.

45. Buoni, *Problemes of Beauty*, p. 7.

46. Edmund Spenser, "An Hymne in Honour of Beautie," lines 19, 58, 65–66, *The Complete Poetical Works* (Cambridge, Mass., 1908), pp. 746–747.

47. Donne, *An Anatomie of the World*, "The first Anniversary," lines 250, 306, 339–340; *Epithalamion*, VII.179, *Donne's Poetical Works*, I, 239–241, 138.

48. Sir Philip Sidney, *Astrophel and Stella*, "Other Sonnets of Variable Verse," Sixth Sonnet, stanzas i and vi, *Works*, ed. Albert Feuillerat (Cambridge, Eng., 1912), II, 292–293.

49. John Davies of Hereford, "An ode in Commendation of Musick," *Wittes Pilgrimage, The Complete Works*, ed. Rev. Alexander B. Grosart (Edinburgh, 1878), II, 52; *Microcosmos, ibid.*, I, 63.

50. "Wonder" was defined by Descartes in his *Passions of the Soul*, art. LXX, in *Philosophical Works*, ed. E. S. Haldane and G. R. T. Ross (Cambridge, Eng., 1911–1912), I, 362, as "a sudden surprise of the soul which causes it to consider with attention the objects which seem rare and extraordinary." Wonder, in Neoplatonic philosophy, was preliminary to love.

51. As Chapman translated "A Hymne to Hermes," Hermes, by his playing, "tooke Apollo prisoner to his love." *The Works of George Chapman*, ed. R. H. Shepherd (London, 1875), II, 298; Ovid, *Art of Love*, III.315–316, tr. J. H. Mozley, Loeb ed., p. 141.

52. Abraham Cowley, *Davideis*, Bk. III, section 56, *Poems*, ed. A. R. Waller (Cambridge, Eng., 1905), p. 342.

53. Leo Hebraeus, *The Philosophy of Love*, Dialogue III, p. 266.

54. Pietro Bembo, *Gli Asolani* (Venice, 1503), Bk. III, pp. 107 ff.; Giuseppe Betussi, *Il Raverta* (Venice, 1562), pp. 21, 30; Jonson, *Love's Welcome, Ben Jonson*, VII, 807. Beauty is born of proportion, wrote Bembo. It may be perceived both by sight and by hearing. His remarks are qualified, however, by the fact that he wrote, not about music alone, but about music sung by his lady. Betussi named three qualities of beauty—in souls, bodies, and sounds.

55. *Midsummer Night's Dream*, III.l.141–144. In *Cymbeline*, II.iii.12–17, Shakespeare combined (with bawdy implications) the

idea referred to by Buoni, that lovers "delight in morning Musicke," with Ficino's suggestion of music's power to penetrate, in the description of Cloten's attempt to win Imogen by music: "I am advised to give her music o' mornings; they say it will penetrate . . . if you can penetrate her with your fingering, so; we'll try with tongue too. If none will do, let her remain." Deterioration of the Neoplatonic ideas of beauty is obvious in Robert Burton's *Anatomy of Melancholy* (Pt. III, sec. 2, mem. 2, subs. 2, p. 66), where beauty is named as a cause of love: " 'Tis beauty in all things which pleaseth and allureth us, a fair hawk, a fine garment, a goodly building, a fair house, etc."

56. Marin Mersenne, *Harmonie universelle* (Paris, 1636), Livre VIII, p. 47; *Twelfth Night*, II.iv.21–22.

57. Johan Huizinga, *The Waning of the Middle Ages* (New York, 1954), p. 204. See also E. A. Burtt, *Metaphysical Foundations of Modern Physical Science* (London, 1925), p. 5. Thomas Hobbes attacked the scholastic belief in "substantial forms" and "real essences" in chap. XLVI of his *Leviathan* (London, 1651): ". . . they say that the figure, and colour, and taste of a piece of bread has a being there where they say there is no bread. And upon the same ground they say that faith, and wisdom, and other virtues, are sometimes 'poured' into a man, sometimes 'blown' into him from heaven. . . ." Quoted and discussed by Basil Willey, *The Seventeenth Century Background* (London, 1942), pp. 103–104. Sidney, *Astrophel and Stella*, "Other Sonnets of Variable Verse," Third Sonnet, *Works*, II, 288. For a discussion of the identity of love and harmony in music, see Guido Casoni, *Della magia d'amore* (Venice, 1596), fol. 31v ff.

58. Thomas Watson, *Passionate Centurie of Love* [*c.* 1581], Sonnet XIIII [XIV], Publications of the Spenser Society, No. 6 ([Manchester], 1869), p. 28; Phineas Fletcher, *Sicelides*, final chorus to Act III, *Poetical Works of Giles and Phineas Fletcher*, I, 234; Thomas Carew, *Poems*, ed. Rhodes Dunlap (Oxford, 1957), p. 39.

59. The epithets "sweet" and "soothing" (*dolce* and *suave*), as applied to music, had aesthetic implications in the Renaissance, and before, that cannot be discussed here. Giovanni de' Bardi, the late sixteenth-century musical humanist, devoted a long section of his *Discourse on Ancient Music* to the necessity of sweetness (*dolcezza*) in music. Translated in *Source Readings in Music History*, ed. Oliver Strunk (New York, 1950), p. 300. For Renaissance meanings, see Alfred Einstein, *The Italian Madrigal*, tr. Alexander H. Krappe, Roger H. Sessions, and Oliver Strunk (Princeton, 1949), I, 216.

60. *The Book of the Courtier from the Italian of Count Baldassare Castiglione: done into English by Sir Thomas Hoby anno 1561* (London, 1900), Bk. I, pp. 75–90; Bk. IV, 343–353.

61. *Antony and Cleopatra*, II.v.1–2; *Twelfth Night*, I.i.1–3.

62. Phineas Fletcher, *Piscatorie Ecloges*, III.16, *Poetical Works of*

Giles and Phineas Fletcher, II, 190; Sidney, *Astrophel and Stella*, Sonnet XXXVI, *Works*, II, 257; Campion, song from the *Lord's Maske*, *Campion's Works*, p. 96. Many a moralist thought, as did Philip Stubbes in *The Anatomie of Abuses* (London, 1583), p. 128, that the sweetness of music (compared to honey) leads to licentiousness. For other references to sweetness in music, see pp. 41–42. Sir Francis Kynaston in a poem "To Cynthia/On Sugar and her Sweetness," wrote that sugar has "a quality provocative," because Venus "Is said to have a sovereign domination" over its "propogation." *Minor Poets of the Caroline Period*, II, 167.

63. See G. F. Sensabaugh, "Platonic Love and the Puritan Rebellion," *Studies in Philology*, XXXVII (1940), 475 ff.

64. *The Book of the Courtier*, Bk. IV, pp. 353–361. Castiglione "transmitted this concept pretty much as it was formulated in the *trecento*," according to Valency, *In Praise of Love*, p. 221.

65. Christopher Marlowe, *The Tragical History of Doctor Faustus*, V.iii.89, ed. Havelock Ellis (London, n.d.), p. 223; Donne, "The Expiration" and "The Extasie," *Donne's Poetical Works*, I, 68, 51–53; William Cartwright, "Ariadne Deserted by Theseus," in *The Plays and Poems*, ed. G. Blakemore Evans (Madison, Wis., 1951), p. 489. *Cf.* Jonson's "To Celia": "Drink to me only with thine eyes,/And I will pledge with mine."

66. *Du Bartas, his Divine weekes and workes*, "The second day of the first Week," p. 25.

67. Crashaw, "Musicks Duell," lines 145–150, *The Poems*, p. 153. Famianus Strada's story of the poet and the nightingale is in his *Prolusiones Academicae*, Lib. II, prolus. 6, acad. 2.

68. *Twelfth Night*, II.iii.59–61; *Merchant of Venice*, V.i.67–68.

69. William Cartwright, *A Royal Slave*, II.iii, *The Plays and Poems*, p. 212. Later in the century, the famous Dr. Thomas Willis, in "Of the Soul of Brutes," *The Remaining Medical Works* (London, 1681), p. 50, explained in medical terms this drawing out of soul. If love of a sensible object be very strong, he wrote, "the whole Sensitive Soule, or the whole Syntasis of the Spirits is inclined towards the beloved thing, lifts up to it the whole Nervous System, and together with the solid parts, draws, and leads the Humours: so when we are indulged with a fair Aspect or Melody, the whole Soul seems to go out at the Eye or the Ear."

70. *Love in its Exstasie*, a "Royall Pastorall written long since, by a Gentleman Student at *Aeton*" (London, 1649), III.4; William Strode, "On Alma's Voice," *Poetical Works*, ed. Bertram Dobell (London, 1907), p. 132; *Much Ado About Nothing*, II.iii.60–63. The image of soul being drawn through the ear appears also in love poetry in France. See, for example, Pierre de Ronsard, "A Madame Marguerite,"

Le Cinquiesme livre des odes, Oeuvres complètes, ed. Paul Laumonier (Paris, 1914–1919), II, 379:

> Avecque ta voix nompareille
> Leur tires l'ame par l'oreille
> D'un vertueux enchantement;

and Du Bellay, "Ode au Prince de Melphe," Pause X, *Poésies françaises et latines de Joachim du Bellay*, ed. E. Courbet (Paris, 1919), II, 95:

> Là d'une Musique fournie
> Nous orrons la doulce harmonie,
> Dont les discords melodieux
> De mile douceurs nompareilles
> Tirent l'ame par les oreilles,
> Nous ferons compaignons des dieux.

71. Chapman, *Ovids Banquet of Sence*, stanzas xvii, xviii, xxii, *Poems*, pp. 57–59.

72. John Norris, "A wish," stanza ii, *A Collection of Miscellanies* (Oxford, 1687), p. 89.

73. Joseph Brookbank, *The Well-tuned Organ, or an Exercitation; wherein, This Question is fully and largely discussed, Whether or no Instrumental, and Organical Musick be lawful in Holy Publick Assemblies?* (London, 1660), p. 44.

74. John Newte, *The Lawfulness and Use of Organs in the Christian Church, Asserted in A Sermon Preach'd at Tiverton in the County of Devon Upon the 13th of September, 1696. On Occasion of an Organ's being Erected in that Parish-Church*, 2d ed. (London, 1701), pp. 29–30.

75. John Norris, *The Theory and Regulation of Love* (Oxford, 1688), pp. 43–44; *A Collection of Miscellanies*, "To the Reader"; *An Idea of Happiness* (Oxford, 1687), pp. 424–425.

CHAPTER V

1. Clement of Alexandria, *The Exhortation to the Greeks*, I, tr. G. W. Butterworth, Loeb ed., p. 9.

2. Robert Burton, *Anatomy of Melancholy*, Pt. I, sec. 1, mem. 2, subs. 3 (London and New York, 1932), I, 148. See also Ruth Leila Anderson, *Elizabethan Psychology and Shakespeare's Plays* (Iowa City, 1917), pp. 10–12.

3. F. Sherwood Taylor, *The Alchemists* (New York, 1949), p. 7.

4. Aristotle, *Meteorologica*, III.vi.378a, tr. H. D. P. Lee, Loeb ed., pp. 287–289.

5. John Donne, "Elegie on Mris Boulstred," line 48, *Donne's Poetical Works*, ed. Herbert J. C. Grierson (London, 1953), I, 283.

6. Joseph Glanvill, *Some Philosophical Considerations Touching the Being of Witches and Witchcraft* (London, 1667), p. 41.

7. John Milton, *Paradise Lost,* V.469–490.

8. George Hakewill, *An Apologie of the Power and Providence of God in the Government of the World* (Oxford, 1627), p. 39.

9. Taylor, *The Alchemists,* pp. 117–121.

10. D. P. Walker, *Spiritual and Demonic Magic from Ficino to Campanella* (London, 1958), chap. I. The present study is greatly indebted to this book for translations of Ficino and for sixteenth-century Italian background.

11. Marsilio Ficino, *De vita,* III.iii, III.xxi, *Opera omnia,* pp. 535, 563, tr. Walker, *Spiritual and Demonic Magic from Ficino to Campanella,* pp. 13, 16.

12. *Du Bartas, his Divine weekes and workes,* tr. Josuah Sylvester (London, 1621 ed.), "The Columnes. The IIII. Part of the Second Day of the II. Week," p. 301.

13. *Marsilio Ficino's Commentary on Plato's Symposium,* tr. Sears Reynolds Jayne (Columbia, Mo., 1944), Sixth Speech, chap. III, pp. 184–185.

14. John Milton, "Il Penseroso," lines 93–96, 151–154; *The Tempest,* V.i.57–58.

15. Ficino, *De vita,* III.xxi, *Opera omnia,* p. 563, tr. Walker, *Spiritual and Demonic Magic from Ficino to Campanella,* p. 10; *Three Books of Occult Philosophy, written by Henry Cornelius Agrippa, of Nettesheim, Translated out of the Latin into the English Tongue, by J.F.* (London, 1651), p. 257.

16. *Templum Musicum: or the Musical Synopsis, of the Learned and Famous Johannes-Henricus-Alstedius,* tr. John Birchensha (London, 1664), p. 16. The treatise was first published in Frankfort in 1611, as part of Alstedt's *Elementale Mathematicum.*

17. Walker, *Spiritual and Demonic Magic from Ficino to Campanella,* pp. 16–18. This description of planetary music was common lore.

18. *Julius Caesar,* I.ii.140–141; *King Lear,* I.ii.127–131; Hakewill, *An Apologie of the Power and Providence of God in the Government of the World,* p. 99.

19. Milton, *Paradise Lost,* IV.667–673.

20. Edmund Spenser, *The Faerie Queene,* III.vi.7–8, *Complete Poems* (Cambridge, Mass., 1908), pp. 366–367. See John E. Hankins, "Hamlet's 'god kissing carrion,'" *PMLA,* LXIV, No. 3, Pt. I (1949), 507–516; *Hamlet,* II.ii.181–185 (the Neilson edition reads, "good kissing carrion").

21. Ficino, *De vita,* III, as summarized by Walker, *Spiritual and Demonic Magic from Ficino to Campanella,* p. 41.

22. Walker, *Spiritual and Demonic Magic from Ficino to Campanella*, pp. 17, 19–24. Ficino gives rules for this music: "Find out what powers and effects any particular star has in itself, what positions and aspects. . . . And insert these into the meaning of the text. . . . Consider which star chiefly rules which place and man. Then observe what modes . . . and songs these regions and persons generally use, so that you may apply similar ones. . . . The daily positions and aspects of the stars are to be noticed; then investigate to what speech, songs, movements, dances, moral behaviour and actions, most men are usually incited under these aspects. . . ."

23. *Du Bartas, his Divine weekes and workes*, "The Columnes," p. 302.

34. *A Briefe and Short Instruction of the Art of Musicke* (London, 1631), prefatory verses.

25. Sir Philip Sidney, *Astrophel and Stella*, Sonnet XXXVI, and "Other Sonnets of Variable Verse," Third Sonnet, in *Works*, ed. Albert Feuillerat (Cambridge, Eng., 1912), II, 257, 288.

26. Walker, *Spiritual and Demonic Magic from Ficino to Campanella*, pp. 40–41.

27. Levinus Lemnius, *The Touchstone of Complexions . . . Englished by T. Newton* (London, 1576), fols. 22–24; *Templum Musicum: or the Musical Synopsis, of the Learned and Famous Johannes-Henricus-Alstedius*, p. 4.

28. Pico della Mirandola, *Conclusiones Orphicae*, in Walker, *Spiritual and Demonic Magic from Ficino to Campanella*, p. 22; Henry Reynolds, *Mythomystes*, in J. E. Spingarn, *Critical Essays of the Seventeenth Century* (Oxford, 1908), I, 166, 153. See Avery Dulles, *Princeps Concordia: Pico della Mirandola and the Scholastic Tradition* (Cambridge, Mass., 1941).

29. Walker, *Spiritual and Demonic Magic from Ficino to Campanella*, pp. 70–71.

30. *Three Books of Occult Philosophy, written by Henry Cornelius Agrippa*, Bk. I, chap. XIV, pp. 32 ff., and chap. XXXVIII, p. 75.

31. Walker, *Spiritual and Demonic Magic from Ficino to Campanella*, pp. 107–144, 211.

32. William Ingpen, *The Secrets of Numbers; According to Theologicall, Arithmeticall, Geometricall and Harmonicall Computation* (London, 1624), p. 94.

33. John Heydon, *The Harmony of the World, being a Discourse of God, Heaven, Angels, Stars, Planets, Earth; the Miraculous Descentions and Ascentions of Spirits . . . etc.* (London, 1662), pp. 75–77.

34. Robert Fludd, *Utriusque cosmi . . . historia* (Oppenheim, 1617), tract. I, lib. III, p. 90.

35. John Norton, *The Ordinall of alchimy* (1477), in Elias Ashmole, *Theatrum chemicum Britannicum* (London, 1652), p. 60.

36. See Johann Daniel Mylius, *Philosophia reformata* (Frankfort, 1622), and the *Musaeum Hermeticum* (Frankfort, 1625).

37. Heinrich Khunrath, *Amphitheatrum sapientiae aeternae* (1609), plate reproduced in Taylor, *The Alchemists*, at p. 150.

38. See John Read, *Through Alchemy to Chemistry* (London, 1957), pp. 64 ff.

39. Ashmole, *Theatrum chemicum Britannicum*, p. 464. This frontispiece appears in the Huntington Library copy, not in the copies at the British Museum and the Bodleian.

40. *The Complete Works in Prose and Verse of Francis Quarles*, ed. Alexander B. Grosart (Edinburgh, 1881), III, 16.

41. Edward Benlowes, "A Poetic Descant upon a Private Musick-Meeting," stanzas xvii, xxiii, in *Minor Poets of the Caroline Period*, ed. George Saintsbury (Oxford, 1921), I, 483.

42. Ben Jonson, *Newes from the New World Discover'd in the Moone*, lines 97–98, 193–210, in *Ben Jonson*, ed. C. H. Herford, Percy and Evelyn Simpson (Oxford, 1925–1952), VII, 516, 519.

43. Jonson, *Mercurie Vindicated from the Alchemists at Court*, lines 94–114, *ibid.*, 412.

44. Abraham Cowley, note to *Davideis*, in *Poems*, ed. A. R. Waller (Cambridge, Eng., 1905), p. 275.

45. Thomas Carew, "Celia singing," in *Poems*, ed. Rhodes Dunlap (Oxford, 1957), p. 38.

46. Ben Jonson, *Cynthia's Revels*, IV.iii.236–238, *Ben Jonson*, IV, 115.

47. *The Winter's Tale*, V.iii.98–111; *Pericles*, III.ii.82–93. Neilson prints "vial" for "viol" in line 84 of the *Pericles* passage, but the latter seems to me (as to many editors) better suited to the context.

48. Milton, "Il Penseroso," lines 85–88; *Comus*, lines 817 ff., 554–561.

49. John Donne, "The First Anniversary," lines 13, 49, 221, 391–398, *Donne's Poetical Works*, I, 231 ff.

50. John of Salisbury, *Frivolities of Courtiers*, from *Policraticus*, Bk. I, chap. VI, tr. Joseph B. Pike (Minneapolis, 1938), p. 30.

51. Aristotle, *De anima*, II.viii,420a–420b, tr. W. S. Hett, Loeb ed., pp. 113–119.

52. See pp. 86–87.

53. *Three Books of Occult Philosophy, written by Henry Cornelius Agrippa*, pp. 257–258.

54. *The Mirror of Alchimy, composed by the thrice-famous and learned Fryer, Roger Bachon . . . and also a most excellent discourse of the admirable force and efficacie of Art and Nature . . .* (London, 1597), p. 62.

55. Francis Bacon, *Advancement of Learning*, Bk. II, *The Works*

of Francis Bacon, ed. James Spedding, Robert L. Ellis, and Douglas D. Heath (London, 1857), III, 381.

56. *Macbeth*, I.v.26–31; Milton, *Paradise Lost*, IV.804–805. As late as 1677, John Webster, "Practitioner in Physick," in *The Displaying of supposed Witchcraft* (London, 1677), p. 341, quoted "that most learned Physician," Thomas Bartholinus, to argue that "air is altered by the various prolation of words, as well that air, which doth enter into the little pores of the vessels ending in the skin by transpiration, as that which is carried into the Ears, Nostrils, and Lungs." "The breath," he continued, quoting Bartholinus, "is heated by the various prolation of words," either words alone or words "bound up in the Rhythme," and so "various effects may be produced, without Cacodemons, or vain superstition."

57. Ben Jonson, *Poetaster*, IV.iii.79–82, in *Ben Jonson*, IV, 268; *Twelfth Night*, II.iii.54–58.

58. George Chapman, *Ovids Banquet of Sence*, stanza xxiii, *Poems*, ed. Phyllis Brooks Bartlett (New York and London, 1941), p. 59. *Cf.* Milton's "At a Vacation Exercise," beginning "Hail native Language":

> I have some naked thoughts that rove about
> And loudly knock to have their passage out;
> And wearie of their place do only stay
> Till thou hast deck't them in thy best aray
> That so they may without suspect or fears
> Fly swiftly to this fair Assembly's ears. (23–28)

59. Richard Crashaw, "Musicks Duell," lines 66–67, 90–91, 102–103, *The Poems*, ed. L. C. Martin (Oxford, 1927), pp. 150–152.

60. "To a lady who did sing excellently," *The Poems of Edward Lord Herbert of Cherbury*, ed. G. D. Moore Smith (Oxford, 1923), pp. 44–45.

61. William Cartwright, *The Plays and Poems*, ed. G. Blakemore Evans (Madison, Wis., 1951), p. 462.

62. Chapman, *Ovids Banquet of Sence*, stanzas xviii, xxiv, xi, *Poems*, pp. 56–60.

63. Maurice Valency, *In Praise of Love* (New York, 1958), p. 233.

64. Sidney, *Astrophel and Stella*, "Other Sonnets of Variable Verse," Seventh Sonnet, *Works*, II, 294.

65. Thomas Stanley, "Celia Singing," in *Minor Poets of the Caroline Period*, III, 117.

66. Philip Ayers, "Cynthia, singing a Recitative Piece of Music," in *ibid.*, II, 281–282.

CHAPTER VI

1. Giulio Caccini, *Le nuove musiche*, "Foreword," in *Source Readings in Music History*, ed. Oliver Strunk (New York, 1950), p. 392.

The translation is based upon that in John Playford's *A Brief Introduction to the Skill of Music* (London, 1667, and later editions).

2. See Paul Henry Lang, *Music in Western Civilization* (New York, 1941), pp. 198, 295; D. P. Walker, "Musical Humanism in the 16th and Early 17th Centuries," in *The Music Review*, II (1941), 1–13, 111–121, 220–227, 288–308, and III (1942), 55–71; Francis A. Yates, *The French Academies of the Sixteenth Century* (London, 1947), pp. 38, 45, 86, etc. For a summary of the long conflict between words and notes, see Alfred Einstein, *The Italian Madrigal*, tr. Alexander H. Krappe, Roger H. Sessions, and Oliver Strunk (Princeton, 1949), I, 167 ff.

3. Plato, *The Republic*, III.398D, tr. Paul Shorey, Loeb ed., I, 245.

4. Giovanni Bardi, *Discourse on Ancient Music*, in *Source Readings in Music History*, ed. Strunk, p. 292.

5. Caccini, *Le nuove musiche*, in *ibid.*, p. 378.

6. Bardi, *Discourse on Ancient Music*, in *ibid.*, p. 295.

7. Vincenzo Galilei attacked his teacher, Zarlino, on these issues in his *Diologo della musica antica e della moderna* (1581), in *ibid.*

8. See Claude V. Palisca, "Vincenzo Galilei's Counterpoint Treatise," *Journal of the American Musicological Society*, IX, No. 2 (1956), p. 85.

9. Galilei, *Dialogo della musica antica e della moderna*, in *Source Readings in Music History*, ed. Strunk, pp. 317–319. *Cf.* Cicero, *De oratore*, II.xlv,189 ff., tr. H. Rackham, Loeb ed., I, 333–335.

10. Galilei, *Dialogo della musica antica e della moderna*, in *Source Readings in Music History*, ed. Strunk, p. 313.

11. Giulio Caccini, dedication to *Euridice*, in *ibid.*, p. 371; Jacopo Peri, foreword to *Euridice*, *ibid.*, p. 374; Marco da Gagliano, preface to his setting of Ottavio Rinuccini's *Dafne*, in *Le origini del melodramma*, ed. *Angelo Solerti* (Turin, 1903), p. 81. Armen Carapetyan, in "The Concept of *Imitazione della Natura* in the Sixteenth Century," *Journal of Renaissance and Baroque Music*, I, No. 1 (1946), 66, relates imitation of speech in music to the whole imitation of nature movement—as he does also (p. 60), the parallels commonly drawn between four-voice writing and the four elements.

12. G. C. Monteverdi, printed with foreword to Claudio Monteverdi, *Il quinto libro de' madrigali* (1605), in *Source Readings in Music History*, ed. Strunk, p. 407. Cf. Pietro della Valle, "Della musica dell'età nostra," in *Le origini del melodramma*, ed. Solerti, p. 151.

13. See Manfred F. Bukofzer, *Music in the Baroque Era* (New York, 1947), pp. 60 ff., and Donald Jay Grout, *A Short History of Opera* (New York, 1947), pp. 61–68.

14. Claudio Monteverdi, foreword to *Madrigali guerrieri ed amorosi*, in *Source Readings in Music History*, ed. Strunk, p. 414.

15. William Prynne, *Histrio-mastix* (London, 1633), pp. 276, 283, 284.

16. Caccini, foreword to *Le nuove musiche*, in *Source Readings in Music History*, ed. Strunk, p. 378; John Cotton, *Singing of Psalmes a Gospel-Ordinance* (London, 1647), p. 5; Galilei, *Dialogo della musica antica e della moderna*, in *Source Readings in Music History*, ed. Strunk, p. 313. (D. P. Walker, in "Musical Humanism in the 16th and Early 17th Centuries," *The Music Review*, III, 63, writes :"The chief exponent of musical puritanism is Galileo.") John Wesley wrote, many years later: "I was much surprised in reading an 'Essay on Music,' . . . to find that the music of the ancients was as simple as that of the Methodists." *John Wesley's Journal*, ed. Nehemiah Curnock (London, [1910]), I, 290. The entry is for "Sat. 22 Oct. 1768."

17. See George Wither, *A Preparation to the Psalter* (Manchester, 1884), p. 79.

18. Thomas Campion, *Observations in the Art of English Poesie*, chap I, in *Elizabethan Critical Essays*, ed. G. Gregory Smith (Oxford, 1950), II, 329. *Cf.* William Webbe, *A Discourse of Englishe Poetrie*, *ibid.*, I, 230, and "E.K."'s gloss to Edmund Spenser, "December," *Shepheardes Calender, The Complete Poetical Works* (Cambridge, Mass., 1908), p. 55.

19. Webbe, *A Discourse of Englishe Poetrie*, *Elizabethan Critical Essays*, I, 231.

20. Thomas Campion, "Come let us sound," *Campion's Works*, ed. Percival Vivian (Oxford, 1909), p. 17, discussed by Catherine Ing, *Elizabethan Lyrics* (London, 1951), p. 117.

21. Gustave Reese, *Music in the Renaissance* (New York, 1954), p. 835. For the use of the word "ayre," see below, chap. VII, note 30.

22. Thomas Morley, *A Plaine and Easie Introduction to Practicall Musicke* (London, 1597), p. 179.

23. Thomas Ravenscroft, *A Briefe Discourse of the true (but neglected) use of Charact'ring the Degrees* . . . (London, 1614), "Apologie" and "Preface," sec. 5.

24. McD. Emslie, "Nicholas Lanier's Innovations in English Song," in *Music and Letters*, XLI, No. 1 (Jan. 1960), 13–27. Emslie points out that the notation in Jonson's *Lovers Made Men* (1617), indicating that it was sung in *stilo recitativo*, was not included in the 1617 text. It appeared first in 1640.

25. Lang, *Music in Western Civilization*, pp. 414, 410.

26. See, for example, Ing, *Elizabethan Lyrics*.

27. Ben Jonson, *Loves Triumph*, lines 155–162, *Ben Jonson*, ed. C. H. Herford, Percy and Evelyn Simpson (Oxford, 1925–1952), VII, 740.

28. Thomas Carew, *Poems*, ed. Rhodes Dunlap (Oxford, 1957). pp. 62, 184.

CHAPTER VII

1. See above, chapter IV.

2. *Three Books of Occult Philosophy, written by Henry Cornelius Agrippa, of Nettesheim, Translated out of the Latin into the English Tongue by J. F.* (London, 1651), Bk. I, chap. VI, p. 14. *Cf. Batman uppon Bartholome, his Book de Proprietatibus Rerum, newly corrected, enlarged and amended* (London, 1582), Bk. XI, chap. VI, fol. 167r.

3. Robert Fludd, *Mosaicall Philosophy* (London, 1659), p. 147. The Latin edition was published in 1638.

4. *Macbeth,* I.vi.3–6; John Milton, *Samson Agonistes,* 10.

5. See *Three Books of Occult Philosophy, written by Henry Cornelius Agrippa,* Bk. I, chap. VI, p. 14.

6. Francis Bacon, *Sylva Sylvarum,* Century III, sec. 274, *The Works of Francis Bacon,* ed. James Spedding, Robert L. Ellis, and Douglas D. Heath (London, 1857), II, 432.

7. E. A. Burtt, *Metaphysical Foundations of Modern Physical Science* (London, 1925), chap. III, C, p. 74.

8. Marsilio Ficino, "De sono," ed. Paul Oskar Kristeller, in "The Scholastic Background of Marsilio Ficino, With an Edition of Unpublished Texts," *Traditio,* II (1944), 299–306.

9. Diogenes Laertius, *Lives and Opinions of Eminent Philosophers,* Bk. X, par. 52 ff., tr. R. D. Hicks, Loeb ed., II, 583. *Cf.* Lucretius, *De rerum natura,* IV.524 ff., tr. W. H. D. Rouse, Loeb ed., pp. 285 ff.

10. Aristotle, *De anima,* II.vii, 419a; II.viii, 420a–420b; II.xii, 424a, tr. W. S. Hett, Loeb ed., pp. 109, 115–117, 137.

11. See especially al-Fārābī, *Grand traité de la musique,* in Rodolphe von Erlanger, *La Musique arabe* (Paris, 1930–   ), I. The history of these ideas, as of many others in this chapter, deserves fuller treatment than can be undertaken in this study, which will include only those details pertinent or necessary for tracing one particular current of thought—the idea that music, by motion of air, moves the spirits of the listener and may alter thus either body or soul.

12. Aristotle, *De anima,* II.viii.420a, Loeb ed., p. 113.

13. *Ibid.,* II.xii.424b, Loeb ed., p. 139. The effects of thunder and "great ordnance," wrote Francis Bacon, *Sylva Sylvarum,* Century II, par. 126, *Works,* II, 395, "are from the local motion of the air which is a concomitant of the sound . . . and not from the sound." One argument against there being a music of the spheres was that the impact of resulting motion would be devastating. Aristotle, *On the Heavens,* II.ix.291a, tr. W. K. C. Guthrie, Loeb ed. pp. 195–197; Alessandro Piccolomini, *Instrumento della filosofia naturale* (Venice, 1576), Lib. IV, cap. XII, pp. 104 ff. Aristotle's argument against sounding of the spheres was not based on absence of air in the stellar regions (the

aether that filled the uppermost regions could presumably carry sound), but on his belief that stars are not self-propelled, that they are carried passively, as a ship drifts down stream.

14. Aristotle, *Generation of Animals*, II.vi.744[a]; V.ii.781[a], tr. A. L. Peck, Loeb ed., pp. 225–227, 507.

15. Aristotle, *De anima*, II.xi.423[b], p. 133.

16. *Ibid.*, II.xii.424[a], p. 137.

17. Aristotle, *Movement of Animals*, VII, 701[b], tr. E. S. Forster, Loeb ed., pp. 463–465, and notes to *Generation of Animals*, Loeb ed., pp. 592–593.

18. Aristotle, *De anima*, II.xii.424[a], Loeb ed., p. 137.

19. D. P. Walker, *Spiritual and Demonic Magic from Ficino to Campanella* (London, 1958), pp. 6–7.

20. Gregor Reisch, *Margarita philosophica* (Basel, 1503), Bk. V, chap. I; *Three Books of Occult Philosophy, written by Henry Cornelius Agrippa, of Nettesheim*, p. 257; Robert Fludd, *Utriusque cosmi . . . historia* (Oppenheim, 1617), tract. II, pt. II, lib. I, cap. III, p. 166.

21. Interpolation by Thomas Lodge in his translation of Simon Goulart's summary of Du Bartas, *A Learned Summary upon the famous Poeme of William of Saluste Lord of Bartas . . . Translated out of the French by T. L.* (London, 1621), p. 264.

22. Helkiah Crooke, *A Description of the Body of Man* (London, 1615), pp. 607–609, 692–697.

23. John Davies of Hereford, *Mirum in Modum* (1603), *The Complete Works*, ed. Rev. Alexander B. Grosart (Edinburgh, 1878), I, 7–9; *Microcosmos*, *ibid.*, 30.

24. Thomas Wright, *The Passions of the Minde* (London, 1604), pp. 45, 60. *Cf.* Davies of Hereford, *Microcosmos*, *Works*, I, 33–40. For a study of Elizabethan psychology, see Ruth Leila Anderson, *Elizabethan Psychology and Shakespeare's Plays* (Iowa City, 1927).

25. Wright, *The Passions of the Minde*, p. 65.

26. Crooke, *A Description of the Body of Man*, p. 402; Timothy Bright, *A Treatise of Melancholie* (London, 1586), p. 63.

27. This tale of the Danish king was often repeated, as it was by George Wither, *Preparation to the Psalter* (Manchester, 1884), p. 79. For reference to Le Jeune, see Francis Yates, *The French Academies of the Sixteenth Century* (London, 1947), p. 59.

28. J. C. Scaliger, *Exotericarum exercitationum liber XV de subtilitate, ad Hieronymum Cardanum* (Frankfurt, 1582), p. 901. The first edition was published in 1557.

29. John Case, *Apologia musices* (London, 1588), chap. IV, pp. 21–22.

30. Sir John Davies, *Orchestra*, stanza xliv, *The Complete Poems of Sir John Davies*, ed. Rev. Alexander B. Grosart (London, 1876), I, 177; George Chapman, *Hero and Leander*, "Fift Sestyad," lines 42–44,

and *Ovids Banquet of Sence*, stanza xxii, in *Poems*, ed. Phyllis Brooks Bartlett (New York and London, 1941), pp. 153, 58. References to music as air are not necessarily the result of this materialistic trend. Hearing had, from ancient times, been associated with air, as seeing with light. The strings of an instrument and the vocal parts of a song had long been compared to the four elements. Play on words was further enriched by the musical usage (which had first appeared in England in 1590, according to *N.E.D.*) of "ayre" to designate a melodic song. Why these songs were called "ayres" (*aria* in Italian, *air* in French) is not known. The word "air" (hence "ayre") carried the connotation of manner or outward appearance of character, a meaning that Thomas Campion suggested when he wrote in the preface to his *Two Bookes of Ayres* in 1613 (*Campion's Works*, ed. Percival Vivian [Oxford, 1909], pp. 114–115) that every country has its "proper Ayres, which the people thereof naturally usurpe in their Musicke." Thomas Morley, in *A Plaine and Easie Introduction to Practicall Musicke* (London, 1597), p. 147, suggested this meaning when he equated "airs" with "modes." Roger North, writing *c.* 1710, reflected a changed meaning of the term "ayre," but he made the following historical comment: "First as for the word *Ayre*, it was taken into the language of Harmony from a conceipted analogy with the flow of a gentle and well tempered air abroad, as if that yielded the sound." *Roger North on Music*, ed. John Wilson (London, 1959), p. 73. See editor's comments, p. 67.

31. Wright, *Passions of the Minde*, Bk. V, pp. 159 ff., 168, 170.

32. René Descartes, *Musicae compendium* (first printed 1650), tr. Lord Brouncker as *Renatus DesCartes Excellent Compendium of Musicke* (London, 1653), pp. 1, 6.

33. Robert Burton, *The Anatomy of Melancholy*, Pt. II, sec. 2, mem. 6, subs. 3 (London and New York, 1932), II, 116. John Hollander, *The Untuning of the Sky* (Princeton, 1961), p. 173, quotes a passage from George Sandys, *Ovid's Metamorphoses Englished* (1632), that repeats Scaliger's idea.

34. Owen Felltham, *Resolves: A Duple Century* (London, 1628), "A Second Centurie," chap. LXXXVIII, p. 254.

35. *Ibid.*, chap XCVIII, pp. 286–287; LXXXVIII, p. 254.

36. Marin Mersenne, *Questions harmoniques* (Paris, 1634), pp. 4, 56.

37. Galileo Galilei, *Dialogues Concerning Two New Sciences* (Leyden, 1638), "First Day," p. 144, tr. Henry Crew and Alfonso de Salvio (New York, 1914, republished Dover edition), p. 101. The translation indicates pagination of the Leyden edition. See A. Wolf, *A History of Science, Technology, and Philosophy in the 16th & 17th Centuries* (London, 1950), p. 52.

38. Galileo Galilei, *Opera* (Florence, 1842), IV, 336 ff., quoted in

Burtt, *Metaphysical Foundations of Modern Physical Science*, p. 88. Mersenne's *Harmonicorum libri* (Paris, 1636) also gives an account of acoustical vibration.

39. Sir Kenelm Digby, *Two Treatises: in the one of which, The Nature of Bodies; in the other, The Nature of Mans Soule is looked into* (London, 1665), pp. 305, 5.

40. Galileo Galilei, *Dialogues Concerning Two New Sciences*, ed. cit, pp. 98–99.

41. *Ibid.*, pp. 102–108.

42. René Descartes, *Principles of Philosophy* (1644), Pt. IV, principle CLXXXIX; and *The Passions of the Soul* (1645–1646), art. XXXI, in *Philosophical Works*, ed. E. S. Haldane and G. R. T. Ross (Cambridge, Eng., 1911–1912), I, 289, 345–346.

43. Descartes, *The Passions of the Soul*, arts. XIII, XVI, *Philosophical Works*, I, 337–340.

44. *Ibid.*, art. XXVII, *Philosophical Works*, I, 344.

45. *Ibid.*, arts. XXXVI, XXXVII, *Philosophical Works*, I, 348.

46. Thomas Willis, "The Anatomy of the Brain," in *The Remaining Medical Works* (London, 1681), pp. 111, 119.

47. Anthony Le Grand, *An Entire Body of Philosophy, According to the Principles of the Famous Renate Des Cartes* (London, 1694), Pt. II, chap. VII, pp. 39–40.

48. Robert Boyle, *The Usefulnesse of Experimental Philosophy* and *Observations upon the Effects of Languid and Unregarded Motions*, in *The Philosophical Works of . . . Robert Boyle*, ed. Peter Shaw (London, 1725), I, 91–94, 480–487. For a review of Guericke's and Boyle's experiments with air, see Wolf, *A History of Science, Technology, and Philosophy in the 16th & 17th Centuries*, pp. 99 ff.

49. Giorgio Baglivi, "A Dissertation of the Anatomy, Bitings, and other Effects of the venemous Spider, call'd Tarantula," preface dated 1695, published with Baglivi's *The Practice of Physick* (London, 1723), pp. 370–373.

50. Richard Mead, *A Mechanical Account of Poisons* (London, 1702), pp. 71 ff.; John Quincy, *Lexicon Physico-Medicum* (London, 1717), under "Music." A study of the use of music in medicine is in progress.

51. Thomas Mace, *Musick's Monument* (London, 1676), preface and p. 3.

52. William Wotton, *Reflections upon Ancient and Modern Learning* (London, 1694; 1697 edition used here), pp. 329, 333. The first edition does not include the phrase "if ever they were had."

53. John Wallis, "Concerning the strange effects reported of Music in former Times, beyond what is to be found in later Ages," Royal Society, *Philosophical Transactions*, abridged edition (London, 1809),

Vol. IV (1694–1702), p. 305; Alexander Malcolm, *A Treatise of Musick* (Edinburgh, 1721), p. 292.

54. *A Letter to a Friend in the Country, Concerning the Use of Instrumental Musick in the Worship of God; in Answer to Mr. Newte's Sermon Preach'd at Tiverton in Devon, on the Occasion of an Organ being Erected in that Parish-Church* (London, 1698), p. 5.

CHAPTER VIII

1. John Milton, *On the Morning of Christ's Nativity*, "The Hymn," stanza xiii; "Il Penseroso," line 126; "Lycidas," lines 28, 124. Denis Saurat, *Milton: Man and Thinker* (New York, 1925), pp. 301 ff.

2. For drafts of Milton's early poems, see *The Cambridge Manuscript of John Milton*, ed. F. A. Patterson (New York, 1933).

3. "Musical" has a somewhat different meaning, although still abstract, in the lines:

> How charming is divine Philosophy!
> Not harsh, and crabbed as dull fools suppose,
> But musical as is *Apollo's* lute, (*Comus*, 475–477)

where it signifies a satisfying intellectual pleasure.

4. *Marsilio Ficino's Commentary on Plato's Symposium*, tr. Sears Reynolds Jane (Columbia, Mo., 1944), pp. 130, 193, 189. See discussion of these passages above, at pp. 84–86.

5. G. F. Sensabaugh, "The Milieu of *Comus*," *Studies in Philology*, XLI (1944), 238–249.

6. Verses by Edmund Waller and Francis Sambrooke. Waller's lines were sent to Lawes, "who had . . . set a Song of Mine in the Year 1635." Sambrooke's appeared, with Milton's sonnet, in the 1648 volume of *Choice Psalmes put into Musick . . . by Henry and William Lawes*. Both verses are reprinted in Willa McClung Evans, *Henry Lawes* (New York and London, 1941), pp. 110–111, 182–183.

7. The tractate "Of Education," written at about this time, reflects genuine appreciation of instrumental as well as vocal music, but both are recommended chiefly for after-dinner relaxation. The music that has "great power over dispositions" was probably (to judge from the usual interpretation of Plato's definition of music) that in which harmony is servant to the word: Milton recommended "the Lute, or soft Organ stop *waiting on elegant Voices* [italics added] either to Religious, martial, or civil Ditties; which if wise men and Prophets be not extreamly out, have a great power over dispositions and manners." Music is also useful, Milton continued, as an aid to digestion.

8. Aristotle, *Meteorologica*, III.vi.378[a], tr. H. D. P. Lee, Loeb ed., pp. 287–289. See above, p. 103. There are echoes in Milton's passage of the musical proportions of architecture defended by his friend, Sir

Henry Wotton, in his *The Elements of Architecture* (1624) (London, 1904). See above, pp. 37–38.

9. See E. A. Burtt, *Metaphysical Foundations of Modern Physical Science* (London, 1925), chap. VII. D. 3, pp. 236–237.

CHAPTER IX

1. See Willa McClung Evans, *Henry Lawes* (New York and London, 1941). For musical activities of Milton's father, see Ernest Brennecke, Jr., *John Milton and His Music* (Columbia University Press, 1938).

2. *Ben Jonson*, ed. C. H. Herford and Percy and Evelyn Simpson (Oxford, 1925–1952), II, 308–309.

3. W. W. Greg, *Pastoral Poetry and Pastoral Drama* (London, 1906), p. 396.

4. G. F. Sensabaugh, "The Milieu of *Comus*," *Studies in Philology*, XLI (1944), 238–249.

5. It was preceded by *La morte d'Orfeo* (1619) by Stefano Landi and *L'Aretusa* (1620) by Filippo Vitali.

6. "Questa Favola descritta nel Poema del Cavalier Marino à voi s'appresenta sparsa di pensiere, e ripiena d'affetti; alterato però con inventioni dal Signor Ottavio Tronsarelli e ristretta nel termine d'un giro di Sole tra lo spatio di brevissimi giorni composta, e con non minore velocità di tempo d'alcune machine abbellita, e mirabilmente rappresentata nel Palazzo dell'Illustrissimo Sig. Marchese Evandro Conti, non riempita da importuna lunghezza di vani Intermedij, che alienando le menti de gli uditori, non adornano, ma adombrano le Attioni, ordinata con singolare accortezza dal Sig. Francesco de Cuppis, dalle note esquisite del Signor Domenico Mazzocchi raddolcita, e da rare voci di famosissimi Cantori sommamente honorata. Testimonio d'ogni pio detto sono i Principi, e le Principesse di Roma, che con lo splendore della loro presenza illustrarono il Theatro di quella nobil Favola, ove comparve l'Invidia, & al favorevol suono dell'amico Plauso (?) se cadde, e tacque." *La catena d'Adone posta in musica de Domenico Mazzocchi* (Venice, 1626), preface.

7. Janus Nicius Erythraeus [Giovanni Vittorio Rossi], *Pinacotheca* (Cologne, 1642), quoted in Alessandro Ademollo, *I teatri di Roma* (Rome, 1888), p. 9.

8. The libretto was published as *La catena d'Adone, favola boschereccia di Ottavio Tronsarelli.* It was published twice in Rome in 1626, in Venice in 1627, and in Bologna in 1648. See *Le origini del melodramma*, ed. Angelo Solerti (Turin, 1903), p. 244. Between 1625 and 1634 numerous other works of Tronsarelli were performed and published: two sacred musical works were performed in Rome in 1625 and 1631 (*Erminia sul Giordano* and *Martirio de' Santi Abundio*);

in 1632 was published an entire volume of dramas for music—*Drammi musicali* (Rome, 1632); and in 1634 a volume of poems, *L'Apollo*, appeared in Rome.

9. This is according to Erythraeus. See Ademollo, *I teatri di Roma*, p. 9. Tronsarelli drew upon Cantos XII and XIII of the work (Giambattista Marino, *L'Adone* [Venice, 1623]): "La fuga" and "La prigione."

10. The quotations in this chapter are taken from the libretto of *La catena d'Adone* published in Rome in 1626.

11. F. T. Prince, *The Italian Element in Milton's Verse* (Oxford, 1954), p. 69.

12. The allegory of *L'Adone*, although it was appended to the work by Don Lorenzo Scoto, was always printed with the poem and is here treated as a part of it.

13. It is significant, too, that Carew often found "source and model" in the lyrics of Marino, whom he possibly knew in Paris (see introduction to Thomas Carew, *Poems*, ed. Rhodes Dunlap [Oxford, 1957], p. xxxii).

CHAPTER X

1. Sir Herbert J. C. Grierson, *Milton & Wordsworth* (Cambridge, Eng., 1937), p. 9.

2. See Maurice Valency, *In Praise of Love* (New York, 1958), pp. 130 ff. Milton's debt to the *canzone* is discussed by F. T. Prince, *The Italian Element in Milton's Verse* (Oxford, 1954).

3. John Crowe Ransom, "A Poem Nearly Anonymous," in *American Review*, I (1933), 179–203, 444–467. J. Milton French, in "The Digressions in Milton's 'Lycidas,'" *Studies in Philology*, L (1953), 485–490, disagrees with the "'digression' philosophy of criticism" for "Lycidas," and argues, as does the present writer, for a three-part form, each part paralleling the others.

4. Samuel Johnson, *The Lives of the Poets* (London, 1805), I, 134–135; E. M. W. Tillyard, *Milton* (London, 1930), pp. 80 ff.

5. Prince, *The Italian Element in Milton's Verse*, p. 71.

6. James Holly Hanford, *A Milton Handbook*, 4th ed. (New York, 1946), p. 169, and "The Pastoral Elegy and Milton's *Lycidas*," *PMLA*, XXV (1910), 403–447; George Saintsbury, *A History of English Prosody* (London, 1908), II, 221.

7. Laurence Binyon, "Note on Milton's Imagery and Rhythm," *Seventeenth Century Studies Presented to Sir Herbert Grierson* (Oxford, 1938), p. 185.

8. Allen Tate, *Reactionary Essays on Poetry and Ideas* (New York, 1936), Preface.

9. By "choral," the author does not mean "madrigalesque." "Lycidas" in no way suggests the madrigal with its contrapuntal complications which necessitated a repetition of phrase and a superimposing of line which would have made the condensed thought and balanced construction of Milton's poetry unintelligible. A chorus singing any part of "Lycidas" would have to chant or sing it in the manner of the Greek chorus, designated by Doni as "chorodia" (G. B. Doni, *Compendio del trattato de' generi e de' modi della musica* [Rome, 1635]). "That Milton had the actual choruses of Greek tragedy in his mind," wrote Saintsbury, "there can be no doubt." *A History of English Prosody*, II, 221.

10. See Manfred F. Bukofzer, *Music in the Baroque Era* (New York, 1947), p. 44. He emphasizes the influence of dance forms on vocal music, pp. 38 ff.

11. David Masson, *The Poetical Works of John Milton* (London, 1874), II, 269.

12. The cantata, in so far as it is related to music drama, is also related to "Lycidas," but its shortness at this date and its almost fragmentary character preclude it as a source for Milton's longer and more pretentious work. It developed later into a form closely resembling oratorio.

13. See Bukofzer, *Music in the Baroque Era*, pp. 48 ff.

14. W[illiam] S[latyer], *The Psalmes of David* (London, 1643), "To the Reader."

15. Ottavio Rinuccini, *Euridice*: libretto published 1600, and with the poems of Rinuccini in 1622; score in 1601, 1615, etc. Alessandro Striggio, *La favola d'Orfeo*: libretto 1607; score in 1609 and 1615. At the first performance each spectator was given a printed copy of the libretto. See Henry Prunières, *Monteverdi, His Life and Work*, tr. Marie D. Mackie (London and Toronto, 1926), p. 57. Gabriello Chiabrera, *Il pianto d'Orfeo*: published with Chiabrera's *Favolette de rappresentarsi cantando* in 1615 and again in 1622; as *Orfeo dolente, musica di Domenico Belli* in 1616. Stefano Landi, *La morte d'Orfeo*: in score 1619 and 1639. There is no record of a performance of *La morte d'Orfeo*. See Donald Jay Grout, *A Short History of Opera* (New York, 1947), p. 69n. See for bibliographical data Alfred Loewenberg, *Annals of Opera*, 1597–1940 (Cambridge, Eng., 1943). A ballet, *Orpheus und Euridice*, by the German composer Heinrich Schütz (1638), is lost.

16. The first edition of the libretto and also the variants of words in the score are reprinted in Angelo Solerti, *Gli albori del melodramma* (Milan, 1904), III, 241 ff. The quotations are from this edition. The musical setting described here is Monteverdi's, as it appears in Francesco Malipiero's edition of Monteverdi's complete works, *Tutte le opere di Claudio Monteverdi* (Asolo, 1926–1942), II.

17. Solerti, *Gli albori del melodramma,* III, 272.

18. *Ibid.*

19. References are to the libretto as reprinted in *ibid.*, 293 ff., from the musical score published in Venice in 1619.

20. *Templum Musicum: or the Musical Synopsis, of the Learned and Famous Johannes-Henricus-Alstedius,* tr. John Birchensha (London, 1664), p. 60.

21. The essay is reprinted by Angelo Solerti in *Le origini del melodramma* (Turin, 1903), pp. 148 ff.

22. In Doni, *Compendio del trattato de' generi e de' modi della musica,* pp. 112 ff.

23. See Hanford, *A Milton Handbook,* p. 408.

24. See Vincenzo Giustiniani, *Discorso sopra la musica de' suoi tempi* (1628), reprinted in Solerti, *Le origini del melodramma,* pp. 98 ff.

CHAPTER XI

1. Even in the *Aminta,* the chorus takes no part at all within Acts I and II, the choral passages coming at the ends of the acts. Tasso's *Il Re Torrismondo* is dated 1587, and in the use of chorus is more Senecan than Greek. The chorus is used only sparingly within the acts, not at all in Acts I and III. Similarities have been justly noted between *Samson Agonistes* and the early seventeenth-century *sacra rappresentazione, L'Adamo,* by Giovanni Andreini (Milan, 1613), but the chorus there is silent during great parts of the action.

2. Jodelle composed at least one play, *Cléopâtre* (1552), in which the use of chorus is striking. Choral parts are primarily lyrical, but the chorus takes definite part in the action. In Garnier's *Les Juifves* (1583) the chorus is also a vital part of the action, and its fate depends on the outcome of the play. The kinship of *Les Juifves* and *Samson Agonistes* has been noted by Charles Sears Baldwin, *Renaissance Literary Theory and Practice* (New York, 1939), p. 144; Baldwin writes of the former that "its literary type is still clear in the nobler *Samson Agonistes* of Milton." Even in Garnier's *Porcie* (1568), which is much more Senecan, the chorus takes up quite as much space as it does in the *Aminta.* By 1600, however, the Senecan influence had asserted itself in France and almost eliminated the Greek.

3. Samuel Johnson, *Lives of the English Poets* (London, 1805), I, 157.

4. George Edmundson, *Milton and Vondel* (London, 1885), p. 168. Edmundson urges the indebtedness of *Samson Agonistes* to Joost van den Vondel's *Samson* (1660).

5. Denis Saurat, *Milton: Man and Thinker* (New York, 1925), p. 221.

6. W. R. Parker, *Milton's Debt to Greek Tragedy in Samson Agonistes* (Baltimore, 1937).

7. Pierre Corneille, *Discours de l'utilité et des parties du poëme dramatique* (1660), *Oeuvres* (Paris, 1862), I, 40. This view was prevalent in France at a much earlier date. Pierre de Laudun d'Aigaliers wrote in *L'Art poétique français* (1597), Bk. V, chap. VII, ed. Joseph Dedieu (Toulouse, 1909), p. 163: "Les personnages [des choeurs] . . . disent après chacun acte, de peur que le theatre ne demeurast vuide et que le peuple fust distraict." He criticized Garnier (p. 164) because he used chorus within the act. François Ogier, in his preface to Jean de Schelandre's *Tyr et Sidon, Tragédie* (Paris, 1628), condemned all choruses as unpleasant. Jean Desmarets de Saint-Sorlin in the preface to his *Scipion* (Paris, 1639) said that the public would not tolerate a chorus. Corneille used chorus in *Andromède*, but this production "is rather an elaborate masque interspersed with regular dramatic scenes than a tragedy" (George Saintsbury, *A Short History of French Literature* [Oxford, 1917], p. 270).

8. Lady Pembroke's group—Sir William Alexander, Fulke Greville, Samuel Daniel, among others—was strongly influenced by Robert Garnier and did use chorus, but these writers were not interested in writing for the public stage. Moreover, they tended to imitate Garnier's Senecan qualities, rather than the Greek, or—and this is especially true of Fulke Greville—to exaggerate the lyrical element and to write amazingly long and philosophical choral odes which stand independent of the play as political or moral debates. Even in this group, the use of chorus declined. See Alexander Maclaren Witherspoon, *The Influence of Robert Garnier on Elizabethan Drama* (New Haven, 1924). Ben Jonson used a chorus in his tragedy, *Catiline*, which was not a popular success, but "in the popular drama it never struck root, and the occasional introduction of a 'Chorus' illustrates only the Elizabethan ingenuity in adapting alien material to the radically different conditions of their own stage" (*Ben Jonson*, ed. C. H. Herford, Percy and Evelyn Simpson [Oxford, 1925–1952], II, 115).

9. John Webster, *Complete Works*, ed. F. L. Lucas (London, 1927), I, 107.

10. William Davenant, *Works* (London, 1673), pp. 341 ff.; John Dryden, *Oedipus: a Tragedy* (London, 1679).

11. Joseph S. Kennard, *The Italian Theatre* (New York, 1932), I, 200.

12. When chorus is introduced, it is used scarcely at all except at the ends of acts, as in Filippo Cappello's *Arcindo* (Vicenza, 1617) or Ansaldo Cebà's *Alcippo, Spartana* (Genoa, 1623). Horatio Persio

apologized for the use of chorus (almost entirely eliminated in the printed version) in his *Maria Stuarda* (Naples, 1603), as did Valerio Mattiazzo in the preface to *L'Irene* (Vicenza, 1615).

13. *Le rivoluzioni del teatro musicale italiano dalla sua origine fine al presente ... opera di Stefano Arteaga* (Venice, 1785), I, 261–262. The criticism is of Giovanni Mario Crescimbeni, *Connentarj alla volgar poesia* (Rome, 1702–1722), I, Bk. IV, chap. X. Crescimbeni's *L'Istoria della volga poesia* was published in Rome in 1698. *L'Euridice* and *La Dafne*, by Ottavio Rinuccini, were published in Florence in 1600, his *Arianna* in Mantua, 1608; Gabriello Chiabrera's *Il rapimento di Cefalo* in Florence, 1600; Andrea Salvadori's *La Flora* and *La Regina Sant' Orsola* in Florence, 1625 and 1628. (There seems to be no record of *La Medusa*. The name could be a misprint for *L'Aretusa* by Filippo Vitali, published in Rome, 1620.) All of these appeared in numerous editions of the authors' collected works, and most of them in musical score. With the exception of Salvadori's productions, they are reprinted by Angelo Solerti, *Gli albori del melodramma* (Milan, 1904).

14. Giovanni Trissino, for instance, wrote in his *De la Poetica*, Pt. V, *Opere*, ed. Marquis S. Maffei (Verona, 1729), II, 112: "Vero è, che sì come gli antiqui Poeti ne li loro Cori poneano ditirambi, et anapesti, i quali si cantavano, a me è paruto in vece di quelli usare ne la lingua nostra Canzoni, e Rime, che sono cose attissime a cantarsi." The choruses of Sperone Speroni's *Canace* (Padua, 1543) were sung. Lodovico Dolce wrote of his *Marianna* (Venice, 1565) that it was done "col canto." See Antonio Capri, *Il melodramma dalle origini ai nostri giorni* (Modena, 1938), p. 21. The music of Andrea Gabrieli exists for the final choruses of *Oedipus Rex* performed at Vicenza in 1585. In France, the interest of the Pléiade in the union of poetry and music makes it most probable that Jodelle and Garnier intended to use music.

15. Corneille, *Discours de l'utilité et des parties du poëme dramatique, Oeuvres*, I, 40.

16. Alessandro Striggio, *La favola d'Orfeo* (Mantua, 1607); Ridolfo Campeggi, *Andromeda* (Bologna, 1610); Gabriello Chiabrera, *Angelica in Ebuda* (Florence, 1625). All are reprinted by Solerti, *Gli albori del melodramma*. Dati's comment is in the first volume of *Prose fiorentine* (Florence, 1661). Arteaga, *Le rivoluzioni del teatro musicale italiano*, chap. I, distinguished between opera and tragedy on fairly superficial grounds, one difference being that of style (p. 18): "Questo nella tragedia debbe essere puramente drammatico, nel dramma musicale debbe essere drammatico lirico." Their aim, however, is the same, he concluded (p. 46): "Il fine ultimo della tragedia, e dell'Opera è dunque lo stesso. . . ."

17. *Cf. A Commentary upon the Divine Revelation of the Apostle*

and Evangelist John by David Pareus, tr. Elias Arnold (Amsterdam, 1644), preface, p. 20.

18. For a description of choral movement in musical drama, see Marco da Gagliano's preface to his setting of Rinuccini's *Dafne* (Florence, 1608, in Solerti, *Gli albori del melodramma*, II, 71): "... il coro canti la canzone in lode d'Apollo, movendosi in sèguito a destra, a sinistra, e a dietro; fuggendo però tuttavia l'affettazione del ballo. E questo sì fatto modo potrà servire in tutti i cori." Ovid, who sings the prologue, is also directed (p. 70) to move in dance step, "ma con gravità." Rinuccini revealed a conscious attempt to follow the form of Greek drama when he excused the changes of scene in *L'Euridice* by claiming precedence in the *Ajax* of Sophocles (dedication to first edition, Solerti, *Gli albori del melodramma*, II, 107).

19. In *Dafne*, the chorus is assigned 164 lines out of 445, about 37 per cent of the whole, almost all in the form of choral ode. In *Euridice*, the chorus has almost a third of the total of 790 lines, and only slightly more of the choral part is in the form of dialogue.

20. *Favolette di Gabriello Chiabrera da rappresentarsi cantando* (Florence, 1615). The works are reprinted by Solerti, *Gli albori del melodramma*.

21. Parker, *Milton's Debt to Greek Tragedy in Samson Agonistes*, pp. 140–141.

22. Even in this hybrid sort of performance, however, the chorus was associated with ancient drama. Claude François Menestrier, for instance, in *Des ballets anciens et modernes* (Paris, 1682), p. 293, considered it necessary to differentiate between ballet and tragedy, and he claimed that the Italians kept alive the use of the ancient chorus in their interludes: "Les Italiens pour retenir la maniere des anciens Choeurs ont des intermedes dans leurs Tragedies & leurs Comedies où l'on danse des entrées de Ballet au son des voix & des instrumens."

23. Salvadori, *La Regina Sant'Orsola*, "Argomento." His *La Flora* is still further from the classical model and resembles the masque much more.

24. See Romain Rolland, *Histoire de l'opéra en Europe avant Lully et Scarlatti* (Paris, 1895). For a history of the Barberini Palace, see Anthony Blunt, "The Palazzo Barberini: The Contributions of Maderno, Bernini, and Pietro da Cortona," *Journal of the Warburg and Courtauld Institutes*, XXI, Nos. 3 and 4 (1958), 256–287.

25. Manuscript copies of both libretto and score of *Chi soffre, speri* are in the Vatican Library. A copy of the *Argomento et Allegoria* (Rome, 1639) is in the Library of Congress. Hugo Goldschmidt outlines the plot in *Studien zur Geschichte der italienischen Oper im 17. Jahrhundert* (Leipzig, 1901), I, 90 ff.

26. Alessandro Ademollo, *I teatri di Doma nel secolo decimosettimo* (Rome, 1888), pp. 25 ff.

27. A bibliography of Doni's works on music is given by Angelo Solerti, *Le origini del melodramma* (Turin, 1903), pp. 186 ff. He reprints excerpts from them, as well as from Pietro della Valle's *Discorso della musica dell'età nostra* (1640).

28. Henry Prunières, *L'Opera italien en France avant Lulli* (Paris, 1913), p. 43. Mazarin was an intimate friend of Leonora Baroni.

29. See Girolamo Tiraboschi, *Vita del Conte Fulvio Testi* (Modena, 1780), p. 152: "Ivi ancor vedesi, *L'Isola d'Alcina*, Tragedia, un Componimento Drammatico per Musica nel di natalizio della Duchessa di Modena."

30. Leone Alacci, in his *Drammaturgia* (Rome, 1666; brought to date Venice, 1755), records an *Il Sansone . . . dialogo per musica* by Pietro dell'Isola, printed in Palermo in 1638. Scipione Maffei wrote an oratorio, *Il Sansone*, a short piece for three solo voices, performed in 1699, but composed earlier. It was published in *Poesie del Sig. Marchese Scipione Maffei* (Verona, 1752), II, 297–306. Of special interest is *Il Sansone* by Benedetto Ferrari, to be discussed later.

31. Manfred F. Bukofzer, *Music in the Baroque Era* (New York, 1947), pp. 123–124.

32. See Domenico Alaleona, *Studi su la storia del'oratorio musicale in Italia* (Turin, 1908). As evidence of the seventeenth-century classification of oratorio as drama one may point out the comments of so able a judge as Arcangelo Spagna. In his *Oratorii overo melodrammi sacri* (Rome, 1706; reprinted in part by Alaleona, *Studi su la storia del'oratorio musicale in Italia*, pp. 382–395) he laments the use of the narrator in oratorio because it prevents the oratorio from being what he calls a perfect spiritual *melodramma*. He pleads for the observance of Aristotelian unity of time and of dramatic form—in itself an indication that he regarded oratorio as a dramatic production. Girolamo Tiraboschi, *Storia della letteratura italiana* (Modena, 1786–1794), VIII, 493, classifies oratorio thus: "Al genere Drammatico ridur si possono gli Oratorii per Musica." Even in England, Francis Peck, in the preface to his poem, *Herod the Great*, which he published in his *New Memoirs of Milton* (London, 1740), associated oratorio and tragedy (and incidentally gave Milton sharp criticism): "Writers of poetical genius do wrong to go off from profane history to Scripture for subjects of their tragedies and oratorios."

33. Preface to Giovani Francesco Anerio, *Teatro armonico spirituale* (Rome, 1619). Reprinted by Alaleona, *Studi su la storia del'oratorio musicale in Italia*, pp. 345–349.

34. Reprinted in *ibid.*, p. 70.

35. Janus Nicius Erythraeus [Giovanni Vittorio Rossi], *Pinacotheca*

(Cologne, 1642), Bk. II, chap. LXIII. See Prunières, *L'Opera italien en France avant Lulli*, p. 15.

36. *La Fede*, printed in *Le rime del signor Francesco Balducci* (Venice, 1662).

37. André Maugars, *Responce faite à un curieux sur le sentiment de la musique d'Italie* (Paris, 1865), pp. 29–30. Reprinted by Alaleona, *Studi su la storia del'oratorio musicale in Italia*, pp. 250–251. The oratorios at San Marcello were in Latin, and their roots differ from those of the oratorio in Italian which developed at Vallicella. They followed the Biblical text more closely, but they reflected the same influences from the secular drama.

38. See Alaleona, *Studi su la storia del'oratorio musicale in Italia*, p. 255.

39. The manuscript of the musical score is in the Biblioteca Estense in Modena. The oratorio is summarized by Arnold Schering, *Geschichte des Oratoriums* (Leipzig, 1911), pp. 104–106.

40. For the occasion, Ferrari wrote the text of *Andromeda* (Venice, 1637), for which Manelli composed the music. In 1638 Ferrari wrote the text for *La maga fulminata* (Venice, 1638), given also at San Cassiano and dedicated to Feilding. In 1639 he wrote both text and music for *L'Armida* (Venice, 1639), presented at the theater of SS. Giovanni e Paolo, where in the same year there appeared *L'Adone* by Monteverdi. Both these works were probably given in the fall and winter of 1639, not in the spring, when Milton was in Venice.

41. Feilding returned to England in May, 1639, however, and Milton may possibly have missed him. Note the case argued for the acquaintanceship of Feilding and Milton by Feilding's descendant, Cecilia, Countess of Denbigh, in her biography of Feilding, *Royalist Father and Roundhead Son* (London, 1915).

INDEX

Numbers in parenthesis refer to note numbers, either to the note itself at the end of the volume, or—when the note is not sufficiently informative—to the quotation or the segment of text to which the note number is attached.